S0-BZK-862

Songbirds in Your Garden

The Audubon Book of True Nature Stories
The Wonders I See
Discovery: Great Moments in the Lives of Outstanding
    Naturalists
How to Attract Birds the Year 'Round
Flashing Wings: The Drama of Bird Flight
The Walking Adventures of a Naturalist *(Winner of the
    John Burroughs Medal; originally titled* From Laurel
    Hill to Siler's Bog)
Living World Books *(editor and contributor)*
The Audubon Nature Encyclopedia *(editor in chief and
    contributor)*
The Audubon Society Encyclopedia of North
    American Birds *(Winner of a silver medal and citation
    at the Leipzig Book Fair and the Merit Award of the Art
    Directors Club of New York)*
How Birds Fly: Under the Water and Through the Air

SONGBIRDS IN YOUR GARDEN

JOHN K. TERRES

Foreword by Roger Tory Peterson
Introduction by Edwin Way Teale
Illustrated by Matthew Kalmenoff

PERENNIAL LIBRARY

Harper & Row Publishers, New York
Cambridge, Philadelphia, San Francisco, Washington
London, Mexico City, São Paulo, Singapore, Sydney

TO MARION
(1904–1977)

Who made our garden
Tall, with love
For all
God's creatures,
Great and Small

A hardcover edition of this book was originally published in 1953 by Thomas Y. Crowell Company.

SONGBIRDS IN YOUR GARDEN. Copyright 1953, © 1968, 1977 by John K. Terres. Foreword copyright © 1987 by Harper & Row, Publishers, Inc. All rights reserved. Printed in the United States of America. No part of this book may be used or reproduced in any manner whatsoever without written permission except in the case of brief quotations embodied in critical articles and reviews. For information address Harper & Row, Publishers, Inc., 10 East 53rd Street, New York, N.Y. 10022. Published simultaneously in Canada by Fitzhenry & Whiteside Limited, Toronto.

First PERENNIAL LIBRARY edition published 1987.

Library of Congress Cataloging-in-Publication Data

Terres, John K.
    Songbirds in your garden.

    1. Birds, Attracting of.   2. Birds—United States.
I. Title.
[QL676.5.T4   1987   639.9'782973   86-45701
ISBN 0-06-091377-0 (pbk.)

87 88 89 90 91 HC 10 9 8 7 6 5 4 3 2 1

Contents

Foreword

by Roger Tory Peterson

FEEDING BIRDS has been a passion of mine since I was a teenager in high school, well over sixty years ago. In the hills around Jamestown, in western New York State, where I lived, January and February could be *very* cold; temperatures of 40 below were not unknown. But bitter weather did not keep me from replenishing my feeders thrice a week in the woods north of town, including the very woodlot where a new building will soon house the Institute for the Study of Natural History that has been established in my name.

Setting out on my skis with a knapsack full of seed and suet, it took me about two hours to cover the route from my home to Moon Brook and back. The chickadees and tree sparrows always seemed to be waiting for me. The brash chickadees would actually feed from my hand; the timid tree sparrows would not.

The birds' favorite seed, I recall, was "hemp"—known today as *cannabis* (or marijuana). Sometimes as I made the rounds I would pop a few of the round kernels into my mouth and chew them. They tasted better than the flat sunflower seeds and didn't require shelling. The birds seemed to be wild about hemp; they preferred it to millet or cracked corn. Reflecting on this, I suspect that those mouthfuls of hemp may have accounted for some of my aberrant behavior.

In Connecticut, where I now live, we have about seventy acres, hardly a suburban garden, nor would I call it an estate; that would be too pretentious. It is basically a rocky ridge covered with oaks, mostly second growth. But from the house and the nearby studio, which are connected by a path through the hemlocks and cedars, I can look from any window and enjoy the birds at the feeders or in the gardens. Lacking water, except on the far side of our property, we had a pump-filled pond excavated outside the studio. Occasionally a kingfisher comes in.

Over a period of thirty years I have spotted about 150 species of birds on our land, nearly 60 of which have nested at some time or other.

The gardens around the house and alongside the studio are planted with shrubs attractive to certain species, and edged with trees which have given haven to robins, wood thrushes, tanagers, orioles, rose-breasted grosbeaks, and several kinds of warblers. Bird houses, hung from the lower limbs, are quickly taken over by wrens, chickadees, and titmice. But we are too wooded for bluebirds or tree swallows. By leaving the garage door open we have induced phoebes to nest, but in recent years they have refused our invitation, probably because the trees have been closing in. These plain, endearing little flycatchers prefer the semi-open terrain of nearby farms where horses or cattle are their intimates.

We cannot have everything; plant succession dictates what species will live on our property. But we have noticed that during the thirty years of our residence we have gained more birds than we have lost. Because of our program of feeding, gardening, and the erection of nest boxes, several species are much more commonly seen today than they were when we moved in. Cardinals, for example. They were just beginning to penetrate the Connecticut Valley back in the 1950s. Nor were there any tufted titmice. These little gray birds with the jaunty top knots were seldom seen east of the Hudson when I first explored Connecticut. The largesse of sunflower seeds at countless feeders has insured the winter survival of these two southerners with the result that they have now invaded most of New England. So has the mockingbird, but for a different reason. *Multiflora* rose, an introduced plant considered by some to be a pest, is a winter staple. The juicy red "hips" are small enough for a mocker to swallow. In New England, mockingbirds seem to favor shopping centers, railroad stations, and motels; probably because of the berry-bearing shrubs that are invariably planted to dress up the premises.

Over the years a number of books have been written about attracting birds, going back to the old classic by Gilbert Trafton published in 1910. I have written introductions or forewords to two or three of them. None of these books has proven more practical or popular than this one by Dr. John Terres, which, in its various editions, has sold more than 500,000 copies since its initial publication in 1953. I suspect that one of the reasons for its wide popularity is its friendly, informal style, spiced with lots of firsthand anecdotes by the author, who has tried out most of the things he describes. It is not a bare bones how-to-do-it book.

Attracting birds, like birding itself, is becoming ever more sophisticated. More people are doing it, and every now and then someone comes up with a novel idea. In this much updated version of his classic, John Terres passes on some of these new ideas for us to try.

Birdwatching, birding, or whatever we call it, has become one of the fastest growing outdoor hobbies. It can be a science, an art, a recreation, a sport, or whatever we choose to make it. It can even be a religious experience as one of my clerical friends insists. And there are many levels, from the watcher at the window to the hardcore elitist who makes lists or who might even travel to the ends of the earth to see new species.

Just how many birdwatchers there are is much debated. Estimates range from two million (conservative) to forty million (undoubtedly an exaggeration). The largest category is made up of what might be called the "white-breasted nuthatch type of birdwatcher"—the person who feeds birds at the windowsill or in the garden. It has been estimated that in the United States these good people spend at least half a billion dollars a year on bird seed. I suspect the figure is closer to a billion. Everyone up and down our road feeds birds. Some of my neighbors also plant for birds and put out bird boxes. A few have installed bird baths fed with the garden hose.

This book by Dr. Terres takes us step by step from the window into the garden, be it a suburban backyard, a farm, or an estate in the country. With a little encouragement—let's call it enticement—the local bird population will increase. It might even double or triple.

Preface

FIFTEEN YEARS PASSED between the first edition of this book (1953) and the second edition of 1968; another nine years to the third edition. In the third (1977) edition I made many small but necessary changes to introduce new information and to help bring the book up to date. I have done the same for this reprinting (1987), including an up-to-date list of references and an addition to the Appendix: The Phonetics of Songs of Some American Birds. In answer to a frequent question from many readers, I have written a detailed account of the method (or methods) whereby I, and others before me, have gotten various kinds of birds to come to our hands for food (see Hand-feeding, or Hand-taming in the appendix at the back of the book) and a completely revised list of books that will offer readers a reasonably up-to-date reference library of selected titles (see "Recommended References"). In the appendix I have also revised the table entitled Potential Life Span of Some Birds to show that some of our garden birds, as shown by more recent banding returns, live in the wild for an astonishingly long time. I have also expanded considerably the Nesting Records for Some Birds of City and Country Gardens to include birds across the United States and in Canada, with new descriptions added of their nests. I have also included an account of a new peanut butter mixture for birds that has brought astonishing results and discussions of whether birds taste their food, how often birds eat, their storing of food, and so on.

This revision also gives me the opportunity to give special thanks to people who have been particularly helpful with the earlier editions —W. L. McAtee, former Chief of the Division of Food Habits Research of the U.S. Biological Survey (now the Fish and Wildlife Service), who critically read the manuscript of the first edition; to Dr. Arthur A. Allen of Cornell University for advice on the care and feeding of young birds; to Frank F. Gander in California who sent me notes from his long experience in attracting birds in that state; to John V. Dennis of Leesburg, Virginia, who sent me lists of birds attracted to feeders throughout the West; to T. E. Musselman of Quincy, Illinois, to Bill Duncan and Dick Irwin of Kentucky, William Highhouse of Pennsylvania, and Stiles Thomas of New Jersey, who sent me reports of their work with bluebird trails; to Ruth Thomas of Morrilton, Arkansas, who sent me some results of her experiments with feeding birds in the garden; to Dr. Douglas A. Lancaster and members of his staff of the Cornell Laboratory of Ornithology at Ithaca, New York, and to Dr. Oliver L. Austin, Jr., and his wife, Elizabeth S. Austin, both of the Florida State Museum, for helpful recommendations through the years and for critically reading my "Recommended References" for this present edition.

I owe special thanks to Nancy Turel, Librarian of the National Audubon Society, and to her assistant Sema Gurun, for making available long serial lists of ornithological publications that I do not have in my library; to National Audubon's Andrew Bihun, Jr., for many favors and for his useful suggestions about the care and feeding of young birds drawn from his considerable experience with them; and to Rich Sintchak for California birds that ate Marvel-Meal.

Although their names are too numerous to include, I offer my heartfelt thanks to all those readers of *Songbirds in Your Garden*, and they know who they are, who have written me through the years, relating experiences of their own in bird-attracting and offering suggestions for some changes and for proposing, from time to time, new material for inclusion.

To my two editors at Thomas Y. Crowell Company, Ed Doremus and Hugh Rawson, my thanks for their skillful editing and kindly advice.

My thanks also to Hugh Van Dusen, Stephanie Gunning, and Janet Goldstein, my editors at Harper & Row.

And most of all my gratitude to my late wife, Marion, whose keen observations of all living things in our garden and her special love for its flowers, trees, and birds inspired me first of all to write this book. I think she knew how much I appreciated her always valued advice and practical criticisms. I have tried to show what our garden meant to her in my dedication of this edition.

Introduction

by Edwin Way Teale

A FRIEND OF MINE, now a noted ornithologist, once told me that when he was a small boy he used to climb into treetops during each warbler migration and lie motionless for hours among the upper branches to see the colorful little birds alight on nearby limbs. Field glasses bring distant birds to us in magnified details. But there is a special thrill in watching their activity only a few feet away. To enjoy this treat, people all over America are setting up feeding trays and suet holders and birdhouses and birdbaths in their yards. They are planting bushes with berries and seeds especially attractive to songbirds. An interest in birds for themselves, a desire to protect them and let them live their own natural lives, is increasingly characteristic of present-day civilization. It is a long step ahead from songbirds served on the table or songbirds imprisoned in cages.

A hundred years ago, when Henry Thoreau scattered crumbs and corn on the snow outside his hut at Walden Pond, he was enjoying the sport of bird-feeding which is now familiar from one end of the United States to the other. As the pressure of population increasingly regiments us and crowds us closer together, an association with the wild, winged freedom of the birds will fill an ever growing need in our lives. It is not only the beauty of birds and their value as insect and weed destroyers that draw us to them. The desire to be closely associated with wild birds is a human characteristic of long standing. Early travelers found hollow gourds hung around Indian villages to provide nesting sites for purple martins. Thus, even before Christopher Columbus reached the New World, American birds were living in birdhouses.

More of them today live in such homes than at any time in the past. An interest in attracting birds to gardens and yards is now at its highest point. Landscape gardeners recommend bird-attracting bushes. Nurseries feature special combinations designed to bring more songbirds to your back yard. Whole factories are devoted to the manufacture of feeders, houses, baths, and other equipment catering to the modern interest in drawing wild birds close to home. Trolly feeders, windvane feeders, glass-enclosed feeders, automatic-supply feeders—feeders of infinite variety are available. Becoming acquainted with individual birds, with free, unrestrained, unafraid birds day after day just outside the window is a sport that has assumed the proportions of a major American pastime.

And few things bring greater returns in enduring enjoyment. Much of the fun of this hobby is communicated by John Terres in *Songbirds in Your Garden*. It is a book filled with contagious enthusiasm as well as with helpful hints and facts. You can enjoy it for its good bird stories and at the same time profit from its explicit directions. It is the kind of book that will start a good many people along the road of one of the most rewarding avocations of a lifetime. For as John Burroughs observed in his first nature book, written three-quarters of a century ago, when you take the first step in bird-watching, "you are ticketed for the whole voyage."

1

Some Beginnings

ALTHOUGH MY MOTHER fed birds in winter when I was a child, I did not attempt it until many years later. I have a vivid memory of her in a heavy shawl and long skirts that touched the snow, sweeping away a place under a south-facing window of our home and scattering bread crumbs and chicken feed there for the juncos. These were the winter "snowbirds" for which she had a great affection and of which she spoke pityingly when the snows and bitter winds of December came. That was early in this century—the winters were colder then—and, to her, these were "the birds, God's poor, who cannot wait." Later my mother told me that her bird-feeding must have begun about 1910 or 1912, sometime after my father moved us from Philadelphia to Mantua, the country village in southern New Jersey where I grew up.

Some of our earliest Americans fed birds as my mother did. Thoreau, at his cabin by Walden Pond, during the winter of 1845–46, threw out on the hard crusted snow half a bushel of ears of sweet corn that had not ripened. Blue jays came to eat, and flocks of chickadees to pick up the bits of corn left by a feeding red squirrel. A small group of chickadees came to glean their dinner out of Thoreau's woodpile and the bread crumbs he spread at his door, uttering, "faint, flitting, lisping notes like the tinkling of icicles in the grass." They were so tame one alighted on an armful of wood that Thoreau was carrying in and, without fear, pecked at the sticks piled near his face.

In the winter of 1876–77, Edward Howe Forbush, who became a distinguished Massachusetts ornithologist, began a program of feeding birds about his country home. He hung suet at his windows and built a rough feeding board, near a windowsill on which he scattered crumbs and grain.* From inside a few feet away, the eighteen-year-old naturalist could watch and study the behavior of *living* birds, as he did for most of his long life.

Later, Forbush and a distinguished colleague, William Brewster of Cambridge, Massachusetts, developed and experimented with types of birdhouses which Forbush set about his home, even attaching some of them to the outside window frames of his house. Forbush's purpose was not only the close study of birds and to provide for them in winter when natural foods might be locked under snow and ice, but to hold some of them the year around. He knew of their usefulness in eating insects harmful to his woodland, his fruit trees, and his garden crops.**

In 1899, Detrich Lange, professor and instructor of nature study in the public schools of St. Paul, Minnesota, published *Our Native Birds: How to Protect Them and Attract Them to Our Homes*. It was apparently the first book in America devoted almost wholly to attracting birds. The chapter on bird-feeding was written by a guest author, Mrs. Elizabeth B. Davenport of Brattleboro, Vermont, who,

* See Forbush, Edward Howe, "How to Attract Birds About Our Homes," *Bird-Lore*, Sept.-Oct. 1905.

** Forbush, besides being the author of the three-volume *Birds of Massachusetts and Other New England States*, his greatest work, wrote one of the earliest books on economic ornithology, *Useful Birds and Their Protection*, published in 1908. As an encyclopedic reference on what birds eat, it offers an account of the services of birds in eating insects and rodents destructive to farm crops, includes a full chapter on attracting birds, illustrated with Forbush's own excellent photographs and line drawings, and is still a useful source of information. It is available in some libraries.

in the winter of 1895–96, began methods of feeding birds in her garden such as we use today. She attracted twenty-one species of birds, some of which continued to come for the food she provided and to remain with her the following summer. Of her pioneering efforts, Mrs. Davenport wrote: "I began this work from love of, and companionship of, these feathered friends . . . I know of no other pursuit that brings richer rewards."

In 1910 appeared a book, *Methods of Attracting Birds*, by Gilbert H. Trafton, supervisor of nature study at Passaic, New Jersey. The book was sponsored by the National Association of Audubon Societies (now the National Audubon Society) and was the most complete book on the subject up to that time. Besides chapters on building birdhouses, birdbaths, and winter feeding and planting for birds, it included chapters on bird protection in schools and on bird photography.

One of the most interestingly written bird books of the time, with an introduction by Theodore Roosevelt, former president of the United States, was Ernest Harold Baynes's *Wild Bird Guests* published in 1915. It not only demonstrated Baynes's love for birds and his devotion to them and to their protection but was filled with the enthusiasm and charm of the writer. Baynes was a former newspaper man, a photographer, a highly popular lecturer, a naturalist, and organizer of some two hundred bird clubs throughout the country. He called his hometown of Meriden, New Hampshire, "The Bird Village." There most of the town's residents attracted birds throughout the year; a town where the birds had been so tamed by the residents that they allowed themselves to be picked up.

"There is no mystery about it," wrote Baynes. "It is simply a matter of being quiet and gentle with your guests and of using a little thought and ingenuity for their welfare." Pine grosbeaks, white-winged crossbills, redpolls, pine siskins, nuthatches, and chickadees were among the wild birds tamed at Meriden.

One severe winter, when pine grosbeaks came down from the north, they were so fearless that Baynes and his wife and other bird-attractors in Meriden could sit down in the middle of a flock and have the birds come to their laps to feed. The grosbeaks even alighted on the heads of children who were watching them and sometimes allowed Baynes to pick them up, one in each hand.

During some snowy winters, when the redpolls and pine siskins came in flocks of hundreds to Meriden, the streets were alive with the birds. They swarmed over the open square of the town and into the yards of the residents. If a person stood still, holding millet or crumbled doughnuts in the extended open hand, palm up, siskins and redpolls alighted there to feed. Baynes found the black-capped chickadee the tamest of all. This is the tiny bird (weighing about one third of an ounce) that Ralph Waldo Emerson called "a scrap of valor" for its fearlessness and its ability to withstand bitter winter cold.

In the early morning, before Baynes and his wife were up, their chickadees came to the bedroom windowsill, sat there in a row, and hammered on the glass with their small bills to let the Bayneses know they wanted to be fed. When Baynes opened the window, in came the chickadees to eat the crumbled black walnut kernels Baynes had spread for them on the dressing table.

One morning, Baynes invited the chickadees in for breakfast. He and his wife set their breakfast table close to the open window and sprinkled bits of walnut kernels on the tablecloth. While the Bayneses were eating, in came the chickadees. They looked up at their hosts, then picked up the nuts and flew off with them into the garden.

One day, while Baynes was living in Stoneham, Massachusetts, he saw a flock of black-capped chickadees in a tree. He held out a handful of broken walnut kernels in his open palm and whistled the "phoebe" call of this bird. Instantly one of them flew down to his hand, picked up a piece of nut, and flew off. On its return trip, Baynes tested its tameness further. He held a piece of walnut between his lips and extended the forefinger of his right hand just in front of his chin as a perch. The chickadee alighted on his finger, leaned forward, and with its bill took the kernel from Baynes's mouth. One winter day, Mrs. Baynes, at their home in Meriden, went out into the yard and in her open palm held up broken kernels of English walnuts. Instantly five of the flock of chickadees that wintered in their garden flew down and alighted on her head, shoulders, and extended hand.

Even when Baynes was in the winter woods some distance from his home, sitting in the snow eating his lunch, chickadees flocked about him, alighting on his cap, shoulders, and snowshoes. When he held a sandwich in his mouth, one of the chickadees alighted on the other end and with small bites helped him eat it. One spring day, after being away on a lecture tour of several months, Baynes was delighted on coming home to be met in his lane, half a mile from his house, by a band of his chickadees. While they flew along escorting him home, they alternately flew to him and alighted on his head and shoulders.

If you follow the instructions in this book, you will have opportunities to live as closely with birds as did Baynes and many others. In time, you may have many delightful experiences with individually friendly and tamable birds. But unless you live in winter in snow-covered parts of the northern United States and Canada, you may not have the remarkable experiences that Baynes had with large, fearless flocks of pine grosbeaks, pine siskins, and redpolls. About every two to six years these birds, year-round residents from Canada and Alaska, move southward in fall and winter in great flocks into Maine, Massachusetts, Pennsylvania, and beyond. They are driven south, not by severe winters but from occasional shortages of their natural foods—crop failures of seeds and wild fruits in the forests of the north. Even if you live to the south of these periodic invasions by northern finches, you will have those constant day-to-day bird visitors to your garden that will learn to come to your hands for food. But first, you must start with a winter feeding program.

In our garden at Little Neck, New York, my wife and I

had the unending delight and thrill of small, bright-eyed wild birds alighting on our hands for food—black-capped chickadees, white-breasted nuthatches, downy woodpeckers, and, in summer, a catbird, a house wren, and a pair of nesting rose-breasted grosbeaks; during nine years of bird-attracting in North Carolina, a red-bellied woodpecker, a pine warbler, a ruby-crowned kinglet, and pine siskins. This is not unusual. Some of my friends and correspondents in the northern United States and Canada have hand-fed chestnut-backed chickadees, purple finches, flickers, hairy woodpeckers, the very tame gray jays, evening grosbeaks, hoary redpolls, Bohemian waxwings, starlings, and others. In Florida, I knew of a man who got mockingbirds, a Carolina wren, and tufted titmice on his estate to alight on his hands and feed, and even to get a mated pair of tall, wild, sandhill cranes to come walking each day to meet him and take food from his hands.

Such are the friendships and intimacies with wild birds that are possible for one who feeds and protects them. And as your garden birds become an increasing part of your life, you will experience a new happiness, a deepening interest, and an enrichment of your daily living beyond your expectations.

It is more than fifty years since I first began to attract birds. In all that time, living with birds in my backyard or garden wherever I have been, I have never known a dull moment. This is the highest recommendation I can offer you for a hobby and an enduring daily occupation that has given me some of the happiest, most absorbing, and contented times of my life.

2

Feeding Birds to Attract Them

SOMETIMES IT IS purely chance that gives us a new interest
which may last a lifetime. Many, many years ago, when I
was a government field biologist in upstate New York, I
worked with a soil conservation program that helped vastly
to increase wildlife on farmlands, but I did not attract songbirds to my own backyard. I had studied birds for many
years and I had gone to the woods and the marshes and the
open fields to find them. At that time I had not learned that
I could bring many of the birds to me, instead of traveling
long distances by automobile or afoot to see them.

One day someone told me of a farmer nearby who fed
chickadees, nuthatches, tree sparrows, and other native
birds. Much interested in the success I heard this man had
in taming wild birds, I visited him one cold January morning. I was unprepared for the reception I was to get.

I had walked only part way up his snow-choked driveway when I heard a flutter of wings. Before I realized
what was happening, a chickadee, a mite of a bird dressed
in black and gray feathers, alighted on my shoulder!

Filled with wonder at this experience, I stood still, not
daring to move. The tiny bird looked up into my face, a
question clearly showing in its beady black eyes. Suddenly
a man spoke.

"Take some of these peanuts. Blacky wants to be fed."

I moved slightly and the chickadee flew from my shoulder to the woolen cap of the ruddy-faced farmer who stood by some shrubbery near his house a few yards away.

"Here!" The man tossed me some shelled peanuts. "Put half a kernel on your lower lip and don't move."

I did as I was told and Blacky the chickadee came flying directly for my face. As the little bird neared me it swooped downward, then up. I felt a slight tickling of my face as the bird's feet touched my chin, the momentary clasp of its claws as it gently pecked the peanut from my lips, and then the light flutter of its wings as it flew up to the branch of a tree to eat its prize.

The farmer's grin told me how astonished I must have looked. It was the first time that I had ever had a wild bird come to me with no more fear than if I were a tree or a bush. I have never forgotten the thrill of that experience and what it taught me about the trust that we can instill in a wild creature by showing it patience, kindness, and understanding.

Since that day I have had many chickadees and other kinds of songbirds come to my hands to feed. Everyone who feeds birds should make it his goal so to gain the trust of at least one wild bird at his feeder, or feeders, that it will come to him, to his children, and to his guests for food. An experience of this kind will win the hearts of more people than all the pleading for bird conservation made in all the bird books ever written.

When Should You Start Feeding Birds?

Many people begin putting out food for birds in autumn. They usually stop feeding late in spring when they are sure that the winter is over and there will be no more snowstorms to cover insects, wild fruits, and other natural foods of birds. The first winter that I attracted birds I made a serious mistake that I vowed never to repeat. I lived in upstate New York and the winter had been cold with lots of snow. I had gotten many birds in the habit of coming to my feeders until they depended upon me for their regular food supply. Late in March of that year I thought that spring had come. For two weeks we had warm sunny days and during that time, with the grass greening and tree buds starting to open, I stopped feeding the birds. Those that I had been feeding apparently left my yard and the area around me, and returned to natural feeding areas some distance away.

Then, on the night of April 10, a big snowstorm struck. In the morning my feeders were filled with snow. Quickly I swept them clean and refilled them with food for the birds. Some birds came to my feeders but for a long time afterward I wondered how many whose natural feeding area was now covered with snow might have gone hungry that day or perhaps died in the cold and stormy week that followed.

That experience taught me, as it should you, not to stop feeding birds early in the spring. I no longer risk their lives by finishing my feeding too early. Ever since that regrettable spring I feed the birds all the year round.

You may not wish to feed birds in the summer, but once you have started during cold weather, *don't stop feeding until you are sure that the winter is over*. In the New York city region it is safe to end your winter feeding program about April 20; in the South, about two weeks earlier. Find out the average date of the last snowfall of the winter in your area, then feed for at least a week or two after that. In the fall, if you are not sure that you can keep up your feeding program all winter, it is better for the sake of the birds not to start.

If you start to feed birds in any month of the year, you will probably succeed in attracting them. The best time to begin is in the fall before birds have settled down in their chosen wintering territories and have fixed their habits of searching for food over about the same courses each day. If you set up your feeder early and keep it filled with food you will attract many wintering birds that will become accustomed to visiting it before cold weather begins. Within the past sixteen years I have lived in three different places, all within three hundred to four hundred miles of New York city. At each new locality I began feeding birds about October 1.

Your First Step—Putting Up the Bird-Feeder If you want your bird guests to be comfortable while eating, and safe from dogs and cats, you will want a table for them. Set it about 4½ feet above the ground on a 2×4 or 4×4 (4×4-inch-square) post, which should be set in the ground about 24 to 30 inches deep.

Before you set up your feeding station post, or support, be sure that it will be in place on the open lawn or at the edge of the lawn where you and your family can see it from one of your windows. Be sure that you do not put it directly under the low-spreading limbs of a tree or bush from which squirrels can jump down upon it. We feed the squirrels but we don't allow them on our feeders where they keep birds from feeding for dangerously long periods in cold and snowy weather. Be certain, also, that your location for the feeder is in a place somewhat protected from cold winter winds, perhaps on the south side of your house, and within 10 to 20 feet of a clump of evergreens or other shrubbery into which small birds can fly to escape from hawks and other creatures that occasionally feed on songbirds.

After you have decided on the location of your feeder, you may want to make your own feeding tray, or "table" that you will set for your bird guests.

My first feeding station, built many years ago, was a simple open tray. Out of boards ⅞ inch thick I made a shallow rectangular box 18 inches long by 12 inches wide, and about 2 inches deep. In the bottom of it I bored half a dozen holes 1 inch in diameter to allow rain water or melting snow to drain out of the feeder. Although the holes would also permit some of the seeds or grain to drop to the ground, I didn't worry about their going to waste. The sharp-eyed birds would find the seeds quickly and would enjoy eating them just as much on the ground or in the lawn grass as in the feeder.

The tray I nailed to the top of a post, which, after I had

set it a couple of feet deep in the ground, supported the feeding tray at a height of about 4½ feet above the lawn.

One of the first birds to come to our plain, unpretentious feeder was an English sparrow.* Before long, other birds —juncos, tree sparrows, and white-throated sparrows— joined the house sparrows where all of these birds fed peaceably, side by side. In all the years of bird-attracting that I have experienced since then, I can always be sure that when we put a feeding station in a new location, house sparrows will lead the other birds to it. Even if house sparrows did not eat Japanese beetles and other insects in my garden, I think I would still welcome them to the feeders for their "guide services" to other birds.

We have been using our open feeder for many years and it has been very satisfactory to the birds. The only change or improvement I made was to build it larger—it is now 36 inches long and 24 inches wide and it accommodates more birds feeding in it at the same time. Many birds, excepting starlings, English sparrows, red-winged blackbirds, and certain others that flock together, do not like to be crowded closely with others, either of their own kind, or other species, while they are feeding. The larger the feeding tray, the more space they will have in which to feed without fighting among themselves.

Advantages of the Open Feeder

Although the open feeder has the disadvantage of exposing the food in it to rain and snow, it is so easily made and so attractive to birds that I recommend it highly to every beginner. Later you may want to put a roof over it, or replace it with one of those handsome "roofed over" bird-feeders that look like neat little model homes. You can buy these from dealers in bird-feeders and bird nesting boxes, but I suggest that you use the open feeder *at first until the birds get the habit of coming to it.* In my experience, the birds see the food more easily in the open tray and will learn sooner to come to your feeding station than if it were covered with a roof. This is a very important point to observe because many people have telephoned me

* Now called house sparrow.

or written to say, "Why is it that birds won't come to my feeding station? I keep it supplied with food and yet the birds never come near it."

Usually I find that these beginners fail to attract birds because they use a roofed feeder at the *start*, instead of an open one. Birds either do not see the fine seeds within it or may be too cautious and timid in the beginning to venture under the roof of the feeder. Later, when they become accustomed to coming to your open feeding station, many of them will not object to the roofed feeder and will be quite at home in it. Every year a small flock of white-throated sparrows, a bird that in the eastern states nests from New England and the Adirondack Mountains northward, spends the winter in our back yard in suburban New York city. One of these white-throated sparrows (I think it was the same one) during the winter of 1951-1952 spent a lot of time in a roofed weather vane feeder I had set up

THE WEATHER VANE FEEDER. Use boards ¾ inch or ⅞ inch thick. Make feeder 24 inches wide across the front and back (width) and about 20 inches deep, front to back. Make 10 inches high at the front, about 8 inches high at the back. Cut vanes or "arms" of feeder to extend at least 20 inches in front of feeder and slope sides of feeder about 2 inches downward, from front to back, on which to nail roof. These vanes turn feeder away from the wind. Top of dowel in feeder (see sketch at center and at left) rotates in a round hole slightly larger than the dowel. Also make hole through bottom of feeder a little larger than dowel so rotating feeder does not bind against dowel. Attach wooden strip about 1½ inches high across front of feeder (where bird is sitting) to prevent seeds from being blown out on ground.

just outside my living room window. Two of the sides of this feeder are made of wood, the third is glass, and the fourth side is open. Often this sparrow, after having eaten his fill of the small seeds that he always found there, sat in the open side of it for fifteen minutes or more, gazing drowsily around and sometimes closing his eyes to sleep for a few moments. If others of his kind flew into the feeder they would rudely shoulder him aside despite his opened beak and protests at being disturbed.

Although bread does not have a high nutritional value for birds, many of them like it, perhaps for the salt it contains. I find the greatest value of bread is its conspicuousness in the feeders. Birds see it from a long way off, particularly white bread, and it attracts their attention when finer seeds might not. Blue jays are fond of bread and one of them with a twisted, crippled leg came to our feeders for it all one winter. Blue jays feed very early in the morning, before most other birds. Our crippled jay grew so tame that if I had not put bread in the feeders the night before, early the next morning he would fly to the top of our grape arbor near our back door and watch for me. If I did not come out when he seemed to think I should, he called sharply to attract my attention.

What Kinds of Bird Food Should You Use?

Robins, grackles, red-winged blackbirds, tree sparrows, juncos, cardinals, chickadees, and many other birds like bread. When I put the bread in the feeders, or scatter it on the ground, I break it up into pieces about the size of my finger tips so the birds can eat it easily.

After you start feeding birds, you will undoubtedly have some of those big, black-and-purple grackles coming to your feeder for bread. You will be amused as we always are at their wisdom. If the bread we put out becomes too dry and hard for them to swallow, they will fly with the pieces, one at a time, to our birdbath and dunk them until the bread is soft. Then they will bolt the pieces down and look around at us with what we imagine is a look of great self-satisfaction.

Robins are especially fond of toast. We have found that

our robins prefer their toast ground up, and so we humor them by running it through a meat grinder before serving it to them.

Although I believe it is best to attract birds largely with seeds, fruits, nuts, and other foods that they are used to eating in the wild, they sometimes develop surprising tastes for certain foods that we humans like. When I was a boy I raised an orphaned robin that had a mania for ice cream! At night we kept him in a canary cage and he never failed to awaken when one of us came home from the store with ice cream. Even though I had covered his cage with a cloth to keep drafts off him while he slept, he chirruped excitedly when he heard the scraping of our spoons in the dishes. After I had teased him by making him beg, I fed him some of my ice cream out of my own dish. With each mouthful this lusty young robin closed his eyes and shivered, but he always opened his mouth and yelled for more as long as I would offer it to him.

I do not recommend that you try to attract birds with ice cream. There are other kinds of foods that are cheaper and that birds will like better.

The Best Bird Seed Mixture

I believe that the *best* seed mixture is the one that you let the birds in your own garden decide upon for themselves. I built a rectangular frame of wood, the same size as the inside of our open feeder. It had eight compartments and looked like one of those frames that separate the ice cubes in your electric refrigerator. After I had dropped the frame into our open feeder, I filled each compartment with a different kind of seed. For months we kept a record of the seeds that were most eaten and in that way *let the birds tell us* what kind of a small-seed mixture they liked best. Now, instead of buying a ready-made bird seed mixture, we buy our seeds separately and mix them ourselves. You may not wish to do this, but it repaid us, and was a fascinating experiment besides. The birds in our garden now get the seeds they like and there is little waste because we do not offer them seeds that they won't eat. If an experiment of this kind seems like too much trouble, you can always buy the ready-prepared wild bird seed mixtures, sold by many of the local supermarkets and dealers in bird-attracting supplies.[1] These will attract lots of birds to your garden.

EXPERIMENTAL BIRD CAFETERIA. This will help you to determine which seeds are most popular with the birds.

Until you have discovered what seed mixture is the best one for your back yard birds, you can attract them by putting baby chick feed and scratch grain in your feeder. A seed formula my wife and I use in our suburban New York city garden attracts juncos, white-throated sparrows, fox sparrows, song sparrows, tree sparrows, red-winged blackbirds, grackles, cowbirds, and other seed-eating birds. Our mixture contains about equal parts of hemp seeds, the small and the large-seeded millets, white millet, buckwheat, and finely cracked corn. If we want chickadees and nuthatches to come to our open feeder, we add sunflower seeds, but we prefer to put our sunflower seeds in a special feeder where the small chickadees and nuthatches can feed undisturbed by the larger birds.

Early in my experience in attracting birds, I heard a story that I have never forgotten. A woman who had spent many happy hours watching birds in her village garden developed a heart ailment that put her to bed in an upstairs

The Trolley Feeding Station

[1] See a list of dealers in bird-attracting supplies in the Appendix.

room for a long rest. Far more worrisome to her than confinement, she fretted over not being able to see her garden birds.

Her son, anxious to help her, talked with a man in a nearby town who attracted birds regularly to his back yard. Between them they built a feeding shelf for the birds which they attached to the sill just outside the ill woman's window. For a week they kept it well-supplied with food, but no birds came to it because the food was apparently too high above the ground for them to see it.

Then the two men built a trolley feeder by first stringing a "running wire," or a lightweight cable from the base of a large tree in the garden to the sill of the convalescent's window. Next, they built an open feeder, and to the top of it, they fastened two small pulleys. The two pulley wheels fitted nicely over the wire so that the feeder now had a track to run on. To the feeder they fastened a long wire which they ran to the bedroom window from which the feeder could now be drawn along the running wire. All was ready now for their experiment.

THE TROLLEY FEEDER. Build about 12 inches high, from feeding shelf floor to peak of roof; about 18 inches long; and about 12 inches wide. Cut end pieces so that roof slopes about 2 inches downward. Fasten metal trolleys to roof, or to uprights at ends of the feeder if feeder is to be open. Use longer trolley on uphill side to level feeder. The suet cake holder and the wire suet cage are attached to the wooden uprights. Put nailing strip about 1½ inches high along edges of tray to keep seeds from blowing away.

After they had filled the feeding tray with bread, sunflower seeds, and a bird seed mixture, they left the feeder suspended about four feet above an open area in the center of the garden. After a small group of birds were coming to it regularly, they drew the feeder along the ascending wire, a few feet each day. The birds followed it because it was never far from the place where they had been feeding in it the day before. Within a short time the birds had accompanied the feeder in its upward progress all the way to the upstairs window. There the birds came every day to bring happiness to the woman who had been starved for the sight of them.

I know a few people who have not had to use a trolley feeder to get birds to come to their window shelf feeders, but most of us need it for this purpose. The best way to discover whether or not you need the trolley feeder is first to try feeding the birds at your window sill. If they don't come there after a week or ten days, you probably need it to do the trick. After using the trolley feeder to get the birds in the habit of coming to your window, you can set the trolley feeder up on a post in your garden and use it as a fixed feeding station, or you can keep it at the window to serve as your window shelf feeder.

Window feeders are very desirable for several reasons. They bring the birds so close to you that you won't need binoculars or field glasses to see them, and the children and all of the family can enjoy the birds in comfort while indoors on many a cold winter day. If you are interested in sketching or photographing birds, they will give you plenty of opportunities for close-up portraits of them. If you are intrigued by the behavior of birds, as you surely will be, you will learn a lot more about the way some birds bully or dominate others, their colors, the details of their feathers, how they feed, and other interesting things that might escape you if the birds were much farther away.

Through feeding them at my window, I discovered that birds shiver from winter cold just as we do. At my window shelf I have watched fox sparrows, song sparrows, juncos,

Discoveries
You Will Make
About Birds at
Your Window

and chickadees tremble violently early on frigid mornings in winter. When I lived in upstate New York, at 30 degrees below zero I saw small birds at my window feeder hold up their feet alternately in their body feathers to keep their feet warm. During these bitterly cold days, I sometimes found the bodies of small birds lying frozen on the snow under trees in woodlands where they had roosted the night before. I knew that they had died of the extreme cold, but I also knew that the cold weather wouldn't have killed them if they had been able to find sufficient food during the day to carry them through the long winter night.

After an experience of this kind, I would hurry home and fill my feeders to their fullest, determined that this should not happen to the birds that were wintering in and around my yard.

How Much Cold Can Your Birds Endure?

How can the tiny chickadees and juncos wintering in your garden live through nights when the wind roars through the trees and sweeps through your shrubbery with the cold, cutting edge of a knife? That many of them can is to me, one of the most astonishing facts in all the out-of-doors. How do they do it?

Within the small feathered body of a chickadee, weighing less than an ounce, a small furnace with its tiny heart for a pump and a maze of blood vessels to carry heat keeps its body aglow with a warmth that will keep the bird alive at 30 and 40 degrees below zero. But this tiny furnace, like that of your own body, or the furnace down in your cellar, needs fuel; and fuel to a bird, or to any living creature, is food.

In Ohio a few years ago, a scientist became interested in this problem. How long could small birds survive cold weather without food?

First, he experimented with house sparrows. In our northern states, where we usually have the coldest winters, the nights are 14 to 15 hours long. House sparrows could live, exposed to the cold through a night this long, *if the temperature went no lower than 5 degrees above zero.* At 20 degrees *below* zero they could live only 10 hours, or about two-thirds of the night; at 30 degrees *below* zero, they lived only 7 hours, or about half the night.

How then can chickadees, juncos, and tree sparrows, which he discovered will live through slightly colder weather than house sparrows—how can they live through a night when the temperature drops to 30 or 40 below zero?

The answer is—food and shelter. *If* they have eaten well late in the day, or just before going to bed, and *if* they are able to find an evergreen thicket, or other sheltered nook in which to sleep, then their own body heat carries them through the cold winter night.

One of the most popular (with the birds) window feeders I ever saw was a homemade shelf about 12 inches wide and about 36 inches long—the same length as the window sill. The feeding shelf had a strip of wood about 1½ inches high tacked all around its three outer sides to keep the bird seed mixture from blowing away and was set tight against the window sill and level with it. Beneath the shelf the owner had nailed two wooden braces, one at each end, which were slanted at a 45-degree angle from the outer edge of the shelf down to the side of the house where nails held them in place.

The Window Shelf Feeder

THE WINDOW SHELF FEEDER. A simple, easy-to-make type can be built from boards about ⅞ inch thick. Build an upright about 12 inches high at each end. To these attach a small feed hopper (left) and suet cake holder (right).

The day that I visited the owner of this window feeder, I saw purple finches, evening grosbeaks, chickadees, and nuthatches take their turns feeding outside the window within two feet of us while we watched them from the inside through a lace curtain. The curtain permitted us to see the birds, but prevented them from seeing us.

Each end of this window feeding tray had a small feeder hopper, the kind that poultry raisers use in chicken houses, which had been nailed on the feeding shelf. These feeder hoppers, about 18 inches high and the width of the shelf, held several quarts of bird seed which trickled out of the bottom of the hoppers as the birds fed upon it. The owner explained that if he wanted to go away for a few days in winter, he filled the hoppers which assured him that the birds would have enough to eat until he returned.

Suet to Take the Place of Insects for Birds

Up to now you may have gotten the impression that bread, toast, and seeds are the only foods that attract birds to the feeders. The downy woodpecker and the slightly larger hairy woodpecker that come to our yard will eat nothing except the beef suet we put out for them, or perhaps the peanut butter that I smear into the bark of the oak tree in our back yard. We put out peanut butter especially for chickadees and the brown creeper, a little bird that usually visits us briefly in fall and spring, but the woodpeckers are more than welcome to it, too. *Add corn meal or suet to peanut butter to prevent the birds from choking.*

Apparently suet, which chickadees, nuthatches, blue jays, starlings, and other birds also will eat, is a quick source of heat and energy for birds, which makes it particularly valuable to them in winter. It also is a good substitute for the insects that birds usually feed upon but may not find so plentiful in cold weather.

In a small town where I lived a number of years ago, I had several fine apple trees in my back yard. When I first moved there, I immediately set up my feeders to start attracting birds, which I knew would help protect my apple trees from insects that feed upon them. One of my neighbors, a good man and a "practical" one by reputation, came one day to see what kind of nonsense I had introduced into his community.

At first he looked suspiciously at my neat, brown-painted feeders and questioned me about the cost of the bird seed mixture that he saw in them. Then he noticed a pair of downy woodpeckers methodically pecking over each branch of the apple trees and hitching up and down their trunks. I assured him that the little birds were digging out the white grubs of insect borers, which are destructive to apple and other fruit trees. I did not need to tell him of the hundreds of stomach contents of these birds that had been examined by scientists. Nor did I need to say that the results of these bird-food-habit studies had been published in government bulletins to tell people like himself of the kinds of insects that birds feed upon. He had heard about the good that birds do and he nodded his approval of the woodpeckers that were tapping away at my apple trees. "Now that," he agreed emphatically, "*is* a great service to your trees!"

He was surprised when he learned that my woodpeckers were not attracted to my bird seed mixture, but came for beef suet. I showed him the three little wire suet containers, bought from a dealer in bird-attracting equipment, which I had nailed about 5 feet from the ground to the sides of several trees in my back yard. These can be made from hardware cloth or an old wire soap dish.

While we watched, the woodpeckers ceased their hunt for the borer grubs momentarily to visit one of our suet feeders. A white-breasted nuthatch fed at another, a chickadee at the third one. Clinging to the sides of the tree trunks, above or below the small wire cages, they pecked through the ½-inch wire mesh openings at the firm, white beef suet, picking it out in small pieces. I explained to my neighbor that I put the suet in wire cages to keep European starlings, blue jays, grackles, and other of the larger birds that like it from flying away with big chunks of it and leaving the smaller birds without a supply.

At that moment a starling flew down to the most distant suet feeder, alighted on top of the wire cage, and frightened off the little nuthatch that was feeding there. The starling pecked eagerly down through the wire but could bring out only small pieces of the suet. The nuthatch, which it had frightened away, had flown to one of my "feeding sticks" that hung about 5 feet above the ground, suspended by a wire from the branch of a cherry tree. Our feeding stick was a round, 3-inch-thick section of a tree limb about a foot long in which I had bored 1-inch-diameter holes and had filled with suet. The nuthatch now clung to this stick and fed quietly without being disturbed by the starling, which had not yet learned to cling to a swaying perch.

My neighbor, apparently impressed with the success of my bird-attracting program, went home and started one of his own. Later he proudly showed me downy wood-peckers and nuthatches feeding on the suet he had put out for them in his trees. He thought, even through that first summer, that the birds had helped him get a better crop of fruit. We are sure that they help to keep our fruit and shade trees and our garden shrubs healthy. Our most welcome bird guests are the woodpeckers, nuthatches, chickadees, creepers, and others that, besides eating our suet, spend most of their time eating the insects in our garden.

How Many Feeders Should You Have? More than fifty years ago, at Ithaca, New York, a bird scientist studied the sizes of the wintering territories and the feeding habits of black-capped chickadees and white-breasted nuthatches. From the results of his careful work, we know today exactly how many feeders you need to take care of all the nuthatches and chickadees that will winter in and around your back yard.

You need just one feeder.

One feeder will attract and feed all of the twenty-five or thirty chickadees that the bird scientist discovered will winter on eighty acres of partly wooded country in upstate New York. One feeder will take care of the needs of the *one pair* of white-breasted nuthatches that live on each twenty-five acres of woodland near Ithaca. Therefore, one feeder easily accommodates our one pair, or rarely the two pairs of white-breasted nuthatches that come to our quarter-of-an-acre yard on Long Island. It, also, easily supplies enough food for the three to a dozen chickadees that we feed every winter.

But we are attracting far more birds than a few nut-hatches and chickadees. We are also host and hostess in winter to blue jays, grackles, cowbirds, juncos, tree sparrows, white-throated sparrows, song sparrows, starlings, house sparrows, goldfinches, and others—about fifty to one hundred individuals of twelve to fifteen different kinds of birds each day. Our back yard and our free lunch are open to all and so we need more than one feeder to provide for those small, shy birds that will not come to a feeder crowded with larger birds.

All birds need food frequently in cold weather to keep alive, especially when the temperature is at freezing or lower. You probably will have only one feeder in the beginning. Later you may want several to prevent your chickadees, song sparrows, and other small birds from standing by on a cold, snowy day while your lone feeder swarms with a scrambling mob of starlings, blackbirds, house sparrows, and others of the more aggressive birds.

Even though you are anxious to attract as many birds as possible, you should not have too many conspicuous grain feeders in your yard or it will be what some people describe as "junky." Space your feeders at least 30 feet apart and set them up temporarily until you can look them over to see that they are neat and appropriate in their places and can be seen from one of your windows.

The Number of Feeders in Our Yard

Our yard from the rear of our house to the back property line is about 80 feet deep and 60 feet wide. On the window sill of one of our living room windows, overlooking the garden, we have a window shelf feeder. Beyond it, in the middle of the lawn within view of this window, we have set up our large open feeder on a 4-foot post. At both rear corners of the garden we have roofed or partly enclosed feeders, set on cedar posts. In these four feeders we always have a supply of our bird seed mixture, some grit, and small pieces of bread or toast which most birds like.

On the trunks of three trees that are at least 30 to 40 feet apart we have nailed suet cages that we keep filled with white beef suet, which birds like best. We have two feeding sticks hung from the branches of trees growing in opposite corners of the garden. We fill the 1-inch holes of these feeding sticks with beef suet and peanut butter.

From a branch of a small cherry tree we have suspended a green-painted metal feeder which we keep filled with sunflower seeds only. These are for the chickadees, goldfinches, purple finches, and the occasional flocks of evening grosbeaks that visit us in winter and prefer sunflower seeds to all other kinds of food.

In an apple tree I have hung a wooden feeder, which we also keep filled with sunflower seeds. All of our feeders, which are suspended by heavy wire from the branches of trees, are at least 5 feet above the ground. You should

THE FEEDING STICK. These can be made from roughened wood, about 2 inches square and about 2 feet long. Drill 1-inch holes through the stick, a few inches apart, and drill a small hole in the top of the stick for a wire loop to suspend it. If you don't want to make your own, you can buy feeding sticks from dealers in bird-attracting supplies. See list of dealers on page 241.

always hang your suspended feeders this high to be out of reach of cats and dogs that will try to catch birds on feeders any nearer the ground. Be careful, too, that you do not hang it any closer than about 8 feet from a fence or a post from which a cat or a squirrel can jump to the feeder.

I have hesitated to mention the costs of bird foods because, like the prices of human foods, they may vary considerably from year to year. One winter some years ago was a season of relatively high prices. If I tell you what it cost us to feed our birds, you will have an idea of the greatest expense that it might be to you. Although we feed birds all the year round, we consider our "winter feeding" to last from about October 1 to April 20 of the following spring. During that time, in 1951-1952, the birds in our yard ate 200 pounds of our mixed small bird seeds at a cost to us of 7½ cents a pound, or $15. They also ate 1 pound of white beef suet a week, or 30 pounds for the winter. At 10 cents a pound that we paid for suet, the 30 pounds cost us $3.00. Our total feeding bill, to keep our yard alive all winter with at least fifty birds each day, was exactly $18. We do not add the cost of bread or toast to our winter feed bill because this is usually stale leftovers that would be thrown away if we didn't feed it to the birds.

One economical way to feed birds is to offer them your table scraps. A friend of mine who has fed birds for many years attracts most of the starlings, grackles, blue jays, and others of the larger birds away from his feeders to a far corner of his back yard that is protected from winter winds by a few small cedar trees. Here, on about six square feet of ground which he keeps clear of snow, he puts leftover food scraps. As long as he doesn't put too much on the ground at any time, the birds can eat it before it freezes and becomes useless to them.

We don't put our table scraps out because they often attract stray dogs and we don't like the idea of having garbage in our yard. A single, open feeding station set

The Cost of Bird Foods and the Amounts Birds Will Eat

on a post above the ground might be a good place to put table leftovers, but never place them in a feeder in which you put your bird seed mixture. Greasy garbage covering the clean seeds that appeal to the juncos, sparrows, and other seed-eaters might discourage these little birds.

Sunflower Seeds and Your "Extra-Dividend" Birds

In late fall or early winter if you one day get a flock of the beautiful, pale-gold evening grosbeaks or the scarlet and rose-colored pine grosbeaks at your feeding station, rejoice in your good fortune. These and the crossbills, birds with beaks oddly crossed like a pair of scissors, are beautiful strangers that usually nest in the North Country, from the Adirondack Mountains of New York far into the Canadian wilderness. They come down to us only in winter.

We call these birds our extra dividends because we don't get them regularly every winter, nor do they come to everyone's feeding station. To get these extra-dividend birds we invest a little more money in a special food for them. These northern grosbeaks, the crossbills, and the purple finches that sometimes stop with us on their way farther south are especially fond of sunflower seeds. The evening grosbeaks will not come to our feeding stations unless we have these seeds available for them, but sunflower seeds are expensive.

In 1986, sunflower seeds at some grocery stores were 50 to 60 cents a pound, depending on the quantity bought; bird seed mixtures were about 50 cents a pound—but write to dealers in bird-attracting supplies to get their catalogue prices. Suet at one grocery store was 59 cents a pound.

Besides the large flocks of evening grosbeaks, purple finches, and crossbills which may visit you and eat 100 pounds or more of sunflower seeds in one winter, redbirds (or cardinals), blue jays, chickadees, tufted titmice, nuthatches, goldfinches, grackles, and even red-winged blackbirds, as we discovered, will eat them.

Fortunately, some of the wild-bird seed mixtures that you can buy fairly reasonably from local feedstores or from dealers in bird-attracting equipment contain from 15 to 25 per cent of sunflower seeds. These will take care of most of the birds that eat them and ordinarily winter in your back yard. We like to have an extra quantity on hand just to feed those beautiful evening grosbeaks if a flock of them suddenly sweeps down into our garden. We know they will stay for a while, *if* we keep our feeders filled with sunflower seeds every day.

There is another way, besides buying in bulk, to bring down the high cost of sunflower seeds. If you have a sunny, open area in your yard, you may wish to grow your own sunflowers. They are not difficult to raise and the seeds will sprout quickly in almost any good garden soil.[2] We have raised ours by planting several rows of seeds along our back-yard fence. When the heavy-stalked plants grow up ten or twelve feet tall, their big, green leaves and large golden flower heads, a foot or more across, make a colorful and effective background for other kinds of flowers. Unfortunately in a small yard the few rows of sunflower plants that you will have room for will only supplement your sunflower seed supply. It requires about half an acre of ground to raise several hundred pounds of sunflower seeds.

Grit for Seed-Eating Birds

I remember, when I was a youngster, my father had an expression that used to puzzle me. Whenever oranges or some other fruit or vegetable weren't to be had in winter, he would say that they were, "scarce as hens' teeth."

"But haven't hens got teeth?" I would ask him, and then we would both laugh at the foolishness of my question. Of course, hens didn't have teeth! Anyone knew that if he'd just trouble himself to catch a chicken, open its mouth, and look at its smooth-edged bill.

That was long ago, before I knew much about birds. Since then I learned that some of them do have teeth, but they are in the stomachs of these birds, not in their mouths.

[2] Write to your state college of agriculture for information about growing sunflowers.

In 1937 I collected from sportsmen in upstate New York about fifty stomachs, or gizzards, of pheasants that they shot during the hunting season. That was when I was a government biologist and I wanted to get an idea of what kinds of fruits, seeds, and grains pheasants ate in autumn. If I knew, it would help me to tell farmers the kinds of trees, shrubs, and grains they should plant to attract pheasants. What I found did no more than prove what I already knew of their feeding habits from the studies of other biologists. But after cutting open fifty of their tough, muscular gizzards and looking inside of them, I knew, better than ever before, that grain and seed-eating birds do have teeth.

Every one of those gizzards, each of them about the size of a flattened lemon, had masses of muscles overlying the thick, horny, ridged, grinding surfaces of their inside walls. In almost every one I found, besides grains of whole corn and weed seeds, small pieces of limestone and gravel. These were the "teeth," or millstones, which ground up the corn and seeds under the pressure of the gizzard muscles and so helped the birds digest their food. I never forgot that experience and it helped explain a pathetic little drama that Ernest Harold Baynes, a noted bird-attractor of an older generation, told of many years ago.[3]

Mr. Baynes, one cold snowy day, watched a flock of crossbills, bird-visitors from the Far North, swarm over a ruined building where they spent hours nibbling at the mortar that held the bricks together. He got some of this mortar, pounded it up, and scattered it on the snow he had trampled down in his garden. Down came the crossbills to the mortar and they spent every day there for weeks eating it. The crossbills became so fearless that they permitted Mr. Baynes to walk about the flock while they fed. Some of them alighted on his hands and head, and even allowed him to pick them up. All the while they ate the mortar as if they were famished.

Mr. Baynes did not say why he thought these birds were so fond of this particular kind of grit, but mortar for bricks

[3] See *Wild Bird Guests*, by Ernest Harold Baynes, page 141, E. P. Dutton & Company, New York, 1915.

is usually made from calcium, or lime. There is supposed to be a mineral deficiency in the foods of northern finches and other birds, which, like the crossbills, usually live in the Far North. I believe that Mr. Baynes's flock of birds was just as starved for calcium as they were for the grit.

We buy finely crushed oyster or clam shells which are high in calcium, and mix about 5 to 10 pounds of this grit with each 100-pound lot of our bird-seed mixture. Coarse sand from the seashore makes a good grit for birds. The breeders of cage birds, particularly of the budgerigars, or "budgies," as they are popularly called, have discovered the value of suitable grit for these seed-eaters. They recommend grit not only for the budgies to grind their food and aid their digestion but to provide them with minerals of which calcite, or lime, is most important. One noted breeder of seed-eating cage birds uses a grit containing 90 per cent calcium carbonate (lime). He says that old mortar also makes good grit because it contains a lot of lime and certain helpful salts.

Salt for Birds

Birds need salt for their health and well-being just as we do. Usually they won't eat table salt put out for them, but they will eat certain kinds of salty foods. Peanut butter and bread, both of which are favorite foods of birds, seem to have all the salt in them that a bird normally needs.

A few years ago, I made two small compartments in our open feeder by nailing two strips of wood on the inside about 2 inches from each end. I keep the middle section of the open feeder filled with our seed mixture, but I fill these narrow end-compartments with peanut butter.[4] Chickadees prefer it to suet, and tree sparrows and juncos are fond of peanut butter in winter, especially during extremely cold weather. The peanut oil is high in protein and gives energy and warmth to birds that eat it.

Water

Most of us, when we first begin to attract birds, forget that they need water, for both drinking and bathing. In some parts of the United States, particularly in Arizona, New Mexico, and other sections of the dry Southwest,

[4] Mix with corn meal and bacon fat to avoid choking birds.

water may be more difficult for birds to find than food. People who attract birds there have told me that all they ever put out is water, which draws birds to their gardens more readily than seeds and suet.

One winter day, a few years ago, I measured the approximate distance which a bird in our back yard would need to fly to get a drink of fresh water.

It was two miles.

This meant that our birds, after eating the dry grain, bird seeds, salty peanut butter, and other foods that we offer them, must fly four miles—two miles each way—to get a drink and then return to our yard. After that I never had to remind anyone in our family that our birdbath needed thawing at least once or twice a day when our out-of-doors thermometer registered below freezing.

Many years ago, shortly after I had put up my first window shelf feeder, I decided to keep a saucer full of water on it during the winter. It was a very cold day with the temperature below zero when I filled the saucer with boiling hot water and placed it for the first time on the feeding shelf just outside my living room window. I hadn't any more than closed the window when a chickadee alighted alongside the saucer. The little fellow shivered as I had often seen birds do in cold weather and stood there for a moment eying the hot water from which steam was rising in a small cloud. Then he stepped into it, shivered again (I thought with pleasure), and stood for some time without moving. He did not drink, but finally hopped out of the warm water, took a sunflower seed, and flew away. In a few minutes he came back and again stepped into the saucer of water which was still very warm. For a while he stood there as though enjoying the warmth of the water or the steam arising from it. Then out of the saucer he hopped, took another sunflower seed, and flew up into a tree to eat it.

Since that day we have seen many other birds stand in our saucer of hot water, just as that chickadee had done many years ago. Of course they drink the warm water too, but on cold days they remain in it for such a long time that we are convinced they like to warm their feet quite as much as they enjoy drinking.

If you don't want to walk out in the back yard to thaw your birdbath on cold, freezing days, you can easily set up a small birdbath on your window shelf feeder. There it will be quite simple for you to open the window and bring the small shallow pan or dish indoors where you can thaw the ice in it and replenish it with hot water in the comfort of your home. Always put *hot* water in the birdbath in winter because you may find, as we did, that birds like it as a foot warmer.

Should You Feed Birds in Summer?

The first winter that I started to attract birds I didn't feed them through the following summer. I was told that birds don't need our suet and seeds in warm weather because there are plenty of insects and fruits in our parks, fields, and gardens for them to feed on. From what I had already learned about birds, I knew this was true, and I decided that putting out food for them in summer would probably be wasteful and fail to attract birds.

In June of that year I spent two weeks in southern New Jersey with my parents. One day someone who knew of my interest in birds told me of a man a few miles away who attracted them. I called him on the telephone and to my delight he told me that he fed birds in summer as well as in winter. At his invitation I went to see him the next day. I shall never forget that visit and what it taught me about the fun one can have from feeding birds in summer.

My host had only one large feeder in the center of his yard, but he had planted along his property lines several shade trees, thickets of shrubs, and dense clumps of honeysuckle and grapevines in which birds could hide their nests. Cardinals, catbirds, robins, thrashers, and many other birds sat in his treetops or shrubbery, whistling, calling, or flying from thicket to thicket. While we watched, a flaming red cardinal flew to the bird feeder, fed there for a few moments, then flew to a honeysuckle bush in a corner of the yard.

"Watch this," my host said quietly.

He walked to the bird feeding station, took some English walnut kernels from his pocket, and spread them on the tray of the open feeder.

Instantly a clamor of young bird voices came from the honeysuckle thicket. The male cardinal popped out of the bush, flew directly to the feeder, and picked up a walnut kernel almost from under my host's hands. Quickly the bird turned about and flew back to the honeysuckle bush where I could see it poke the piece of walnut down the throat of one of several noisy young cardinals, not long out of the nest, that crowded about the parent bird. Still the young birds called, perhaps more loudly than before. The female cardinal now came to the feeder. She, too, picked up some of the walnut meats, flew back to the young birds, and fed them. Both parents now worked feverishly to feed the clamoring young ones until all of the walnut kernels on the feeding tray had been carried away. The young birds still called loudly, but when the man moved away from the feeder and we walked out of their sight behind the house, they were silent.

"Don't let anybody tell you that birds aren't smart!" my host said smilingly. "Shortly after those young cardinals left the nest, the parents, in addition to feeding them insects, gave them walnuts that I had been putting in the feed tray for the old birds. The young birds took a liking to them and soon learned that whenever they saw *me* at the feeder, that meant *walnuts*. So all they have to do now is to make a lot of noise and the parents fill them with walnuts to shut them up."

It takes only one experience like this to convince you that birds in the back yard are interesting at all times of the year, and that feeding them in summer can be just as entertaining as in winter.

Foods That Attract Birds in Summer

In June we have had downy woodpeckers bring their young ones, just out of the nest, to the chopped suet we keep in our open feeding tray. It is a delight to see the parent woodpeckers pick up pieces of suet and poke them down the throats of the young birds. Ovenbirds, a small warbler that nests in woodlands throughout most of the northeastern states, bring their youngsters from a nearby woods to feed them some of our suet. The pine warbler and other small birds like suet in summer, and even wrens will sometimes eat it.

We have been feeding birds in summer for many years now and we have added very few things to the seeds, suet, and peanut butter that we offer birds in winter. We have discovered that our birds seem to like peanut butter on warm days just as well as on cold ones. Friends of ours put out oatmeal or rice with raisins in it for the summer birds; bread, cake, and biscuits are always attractive to them at any time of the year.

Birds like walnuts, both in winter and in summer, but nuts are expensive. We have gone to the woods in fall and collected black walnuts which we crack open and lay on our feeding trays where catbirds, sparrows, brown thrashers, and wrens will come to eat them, even during hot weather. Blue jays will eat roasted unshelled peanuts which we put on our feeding trays for them, but they seem to prefer these in winter. Many birds like peanut hearts which you can buy in some of the ready-prepared bird seed mixtures sold by feed companies. In fall and spring, crushed pecan nuts will attract many kinds of birds, including migrating warblers that may visit your back yard.

Of all the foods that will attract summer birds—robins, bluebirds, catbirds, thrashers, thrushes, mockingbirds, and others—fruits seem best. Sliced apples, raisins, soft cherries, bananas, and even oranges will bring these birds to your feeders. During the summer, we often put out half an orange on our feeding shelf to attract a pair of golden Baltimore orioles. A pair of these birds attach their nest every year to one of the trailing outer branches of our neighbor's tall, wild black cherry tree.

One summer my mother fed a pair of catbirds steamed raisins. Each morning she put out a dish filled with them on the back porch feeding tray, and by noon the catbirds and robins had eaten every one of them. One day she also put

Unusual Foods That Birds Will Eat

out some leftover sour cream for them to see if they would eat it. When the catbirds discovered it they couldn't seem to gulp it down fast enough. Later, on a morning when my mother didn't have sour cream, she put out milk for them instead.

The catbirds came to the saucer of milk, tried to eat it, and then gave it up. There they sat on the feeding shelf, crying their displeasure and peering at my mother through the window glass of the kitchen door a few feet away.

A man I knew who taught me a lot about birds once told me that "birds are like children, easy to love and easy to spoil." The more you get acquainted with them and cater to their wants, the quicker you will discover the truth of this man's observation. Even so, you won't like them any the less for it. In fact, I think you will admire birds as we do, for their ability to learn quickly who their human friends are, and then to let us know what they like and what they don't like in this world.

The Bird That Liked Pie Crust

One of the most interesting stories about a back-yard wild bird that I ever heard was that of a tufted titmouse, a small gray bird related to the chickadee. This bird was in the habit of alighting on a man's hand for the pie crust he fed it each day. Now lots of birds like crisp pie crust if it isn't saturated with fruit juice, but this particular titmouse not only ate it himself, but fed it to his mate during the twelve days that she sat incubating her eggs.

The female titmouse was too shy to come to the man's hand. Whenever he appeared in the yard and she wanted some of the pie crust, she came to a nearby shrub and called until her mate appeared. The male would fly directly to the man's hand, get some of the pie crust and then carry it to his mate. Each time the male faithfully fed her before he ate some of it himself.

Strangely, after the young birds hatched, the female titmouse no longer would eat pie crust, but her mate apparently wanted her to eat it again. He would fly to the man's hand, get some pie crust, and then follow her about, trying to feed it to her, but she was utterly indifferent to his offers. Perhaps during the incubating period she may have had a craving for a certain kind of food, and the pie crust satisfied her need.

I have no doubt that birds, like ourselves, have strong desires for certain foods at times when their bodies particularly need it.

Blue jays, in the spring of the year, will eat the eggs of smaller birds, and probably those of larger birds, too. It is quite possible that the egg shells, as well as their contents, supply a mineral need of blue jays at this time of the year. We save the broken shells of hens' eggs, crush them, and mix them with grit in our bird feeders during the spring and early summer. Many birds come to eat both our egg shells and grit, particularly the blue jays, and the supply disappears quickly. We hope that this helps to keep blue jays from eating the eggs of some of the robins, catbirds, song sparrows, and other birds that nest in our back yard.

The more we hear of experiments with the feeding habits of birds, the more convinced we are that they will eat almost any kind of food, if it satisfies a need. A bird-attractor in North Carolina watched a pair of song sparrows feed their youngsters corn, wheat, rye bread, bread and milk, cottage cheese, mashed potatoes, sausage, hominy, and walnuts that he had put in his feeders. A pair of brown thrashers fed their youngsters all of these foods and canned salmon besides!

Other Unusual Foods of Birds

Another bird-attractor found that catbirds liked soda crackers and bread and butter, blue jays ate the skins of baked potatoes, and some birds ate cheese when other foods didn't seem to interest them.

We are satisfied to stick to those foods that are more natural for birds to eat, which scientists have discovered will provide them with a well-balanced diet, both in summer and in winter.

If you wish to keep pigeons out of the feeders, staple or nail several ¼-inch-diameter brass or copper bars (they won't rust) horizontally across the open sides of the bird

Additional Information About Feeding

feeder. Place the bars so that the spaces between them are about 1½ inches wide, which is enough to admit chickadees, juncos, nuthatches, and other small birds to the feeder. Do *not* use wire instead of bars; birds will get their heads entangled in the wires and may injure themselves. (See page 190.)

* * *

Birds that eat wet and moldy feed may become infected with *Aspergillus fumigatus*, a deadly fungus. Use only a clean bird seed mixture, free of dust and dirt, and do not allow too much of the seed or grain to accumulate in the feeders (or on the ground), especially if the feeders are open to rain and snow. About once a day, allow the birds to eat all the feed in the open feeder. Keep the feeder clean. At least once a week, unless you have several feeders in operation, and rotate their use, clean, scrub, and disinfect the feeder with Lysol or some other disinfectant. (See page 265.)

* * *

In feeding and caring for orphaned baby birds, give them plenty of canned dog food (meat), along with the chopped yolks of hard-boiled eggs, and mashed walnuts.

* * *

Young hummingbirds or injured adults in captivity should be fed the following (feed young hummingbirds with an eye-dropper; allow adults to sip food from a small vial): To four ounces of water, add and stir until dissolved 1 level teaspoon of Mellon's food (or Pablum), ½ teaspoon of condensed milk, 1½ teaspoons of honey, 2 or 3 drops of "Vipenti" (a vitamin), and 1 drop of beef extract.

The Well-Balanced Diet for Birds

We have a menu for our back-yard birds that seldom varies. If you include some of the following in your feeders all the year round, as we do, birds will get most of the vitamins, proteins, fats, carbohydrates, and minerals which will enable them to survive the winter and will attract them to your feeders in summer. We feed our birds:

yellow corn—crushed or cracked for smaller birds—to supply vitamin A and carbohydrates

proso millet, sorghum, and wheat for carbohydrates
and energy-producing vitamins
peanuts, peanut butter, and hemp seeds for protein
sunflower seeds for especially high-quality protein
suet, peanut butter, pecan meats, and other nuts for
fats
bread and peanut butter for salt
grit and egg shells for calcium and phosphorus
fruits for carbohydrates, fats, and vitamins

The well-balanced diet will help keep your birds healthy
and contented; but, when spring comes, some of them that
have been coming to your feeders will be faced with a
problem far more critical than that of finding food. The
breeding cycle has started and those birds in your garden
that mate early will already have chosen their mates and
will be looking about for nesting places.

If you have thickets of shrubbery in your yard, you are
fortunate, because in them the catbirds, robins, chipping
sparrows, and other birds that return in the spring usually
build their nests. But to ten or twelve kinds of birds in the
eastern United States, including many that eat garden
insects, your shrubbery is useless at nesting time. These
birds—some of them the chickadees, titmice, nuthatches,
and woodpeckers that came to your suet feeders all winter
—*prefer to nest in holes in trees.* Now in these days of
clean gardening we seldom allow the trees in our gardens
or those along our suburban streets to have dead limbs or
dead trunks in which these birds can, with their sharp
beaks, excavate a nesting hole. We either cut off those dead
tree branches, or seal the hollow tree cavities with cement.
This means that the hole-nesting birds must seek a nesting
place elsewhere, unless you provide them with homes.
Most of us can keep some of these birds about our gardens
all summer. It is the purpose of the next chapter to tell
you how to do this.

3

Birdhouses in Your Garden

IN THE SMALL southern New Jersey village where I spent my boyhood, I remember a male flicker that, one spring, apparently went crazy. This big woodpecker nests in holes that he usually drills in dead trees. At that time, I didn't know why he sometimes drums with his beak on resonant, hollow limbs, rooftops, or any other sounding board that he can find. Later, I learned that his long, rolling tattoo is said to be a challenge to other males, attracts the attention of his lady love, and plays some mysterious part in the flicker's courtship and mating.

Early one morning, this particular male flicker rapped a few times with his bill on one of our neighbor's metal downspouts that carried rain water from the roof of his house to the ground. The flicker must have liked the sound of his beak striking metal. Suddenly he attacked the downspout furiously until his thunderous rolling call awakened echoes from the houses all along our quiet village street.

"B-r-r-r-r-r-r-r-r-r-r-r-t-t-t-t-t-t-t-t!" the sharp tattoo rang out like the rattling of a snare drum. People came out of their houses curiously and then laughed when they found that the noise came from a love-sick woodpecker.

After several days of this racket, our neighbor didn't

laugh. The flicker had drummed a hole right through his galvanized rain spout. Then someone said that the bird hadn't been drumming after all, that he had been drilling a nesting hole for his mate. Apparently the flicker discovered his mistake, because he flew away and no one heard him drumming on the downspout after that.

There is both comedy and tragedy in this story. The flicker is a wonderfully useful bird about our gardens where he destroys colonies of ants in our lawns, and insects that eat our garden crops. Like other woodpeckers, this bird has been deprived of nesting homes wherever people cut down dead trees or trim off the dead branches of living trees. Perhaps that flicker of my boyhood had attacked the metal downspout because there were no hollow limbs about in which he might have carved a home. It might explain another story about a flicker that I once heard.

A farmer in southern New Jersey built a new barn which he completed in the fall of the year. The following spring, a flicker came to the empty barn and drilled so many holes in its sides that it looked as if it had been cannonaded. I am sorry that I wasn't there to see the look on this foolish bird's face when he finished drilling each hole and poked his head inside the barn. What a big room he had cut into! He must have had great faith to keep on with his drilling.

In a way, I am glad that I *wasn't* there when the farmer saw those holes in his new barn. I might have had a lot of trouble convincing him that the flicker didn't know his barn from a dead tree. It might have been even more difficult to make him believe that he, himself, had invited the flicker to his barn by cutting down all the dead trees in his woods in which this poor bird might have built its home.

The Adaptability of Hole-Nesting Birds

One of the wonderful things about the flicker is his adaptability. He and more than thirty other kinds of hole-nesting birds in the United States have learned to accept a man-made home—the bird nesting box. He will now raise his family in one of these in place of the holes that he ordinarily digs for himself in the rotted limbs and the trunks of dead, or partly dead, trees. Perhaps if my boyhood neighbor had known this, and had put up a flicker nesting box in his yard, he might have prevented that flicker from damaging his rain spout.

Flickers are not usually difficult to attract. Of the nine kinds of woodpeckers that breed in our northeastern states, the flicker seems most likely to nest in our city parks and suburban gardens. Nesting boxes for them, unless you choose to buy one from a dealer in bird-attracting equipment, must be built according to a specified size or the birds won't nest in them. The circular entrance hole must be large enough for the bird to enter and to leave the nesting box easily, yet not so big that a larger bird can get in and drive the flicker out.

I know of a flicker nesting box in which the builder cut the entrance hole so large that it would admit a screech owl. Now the screech owl is a beautiful and interesting bird which has nested in my own back yard. We like screech owls and welcome them, but sometimes they will kill and eat flickers. That is why we make the entrance hole to our flicker nesting box exactly 2½ inches in diameter, and no larger.

The man who made that extra-large hole to his flicker box was fortunate. A screech owl that had been dispossessed from her own home in a hollow tree nearby decided to adopt the young flickers, instead of choosing to eat them as she might easily have done. Frequently this frustrated mother owl came to the flicker box to squat like a setting hen over the young flickers. Once she even brought them part of a mouse, perhaps intending to feed it to them. All this time the parent flickers were feeding their young ones ants and other insects which a normal young flicker requires. Eventually, the screech owl left the nest box, leaving the baby flickers unharmed.

A scientist interested in bird behavior might have explained this screech owl's unusual actions. I think he would have said that her instinctive desire to feed and mother young birds, even though they weren't her own, was stronger than her normal hunting instinct. Ordinarily, screech owls feed on mice, beetles, moths, and other creatures of the night, but occasionally they will kill and eat small birds. When I heard this astonishing story it taught me a simple lesson: *Always make the entrance hole to a flicker nesting box, or to any other birdhouse, the exact size required for the particular bird and no larger.*

The Flicker Nesting Box

Make your flicker nesting box 7×7 inches square (inside dimensions) and 16 to 18 inches high, from bottom to top. Bore the 2½-inch-diameter entrance hole in the front panel about 14 to 16 inches above the floor of the box and drill several ¼-inch holes just *above* the entrance hole for ventilation. Drill several 1-inch holes in the bottom of the box to drain away any rain water that may get inside. Complete the bird box by putting a roof on it. The roof should slant toward the front of the box to shed rain water. It should also project from the front of the box several inches, like a porch roof, to shelter the entrance hole in the

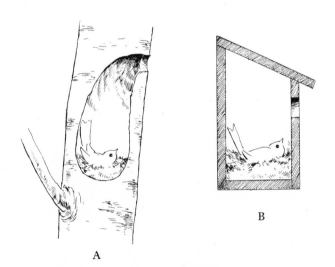

A

B

BLUEBIRDS, CHICKADEES, AND OTHER SMALL BIRDS that have nested in the abandoned nest holes of woodpeckers (*A*), probably for thousands of years, will accept the man-made nesting box (*B*), if it is designed correctly. The man-made nesting box should be built to approximate the design originally carved out of a tree by a woodpecker.

front panel from wind-driven rain. Be sure to fasten the roof or one of the side panels with hinges so the box may be easily cleaned out once each year.

After the box is assembled, select a board about 1 inch thick, 12 inches wide, and 24 inches long. With screws, fasten it to the back of the birdhouse, with its 24-inch length pointing from sky to ground. This "mounting board" will be useful to nail, or preferably to screw, the assembled birdhouse to a tree or the side of a post.

Last—and this is most important—put a 2-inch-deep layer of moist earth and sawdust, or moist earth and wood shavings, on the inside floor of the box. Apparently all woodpeckers need this material to hollow out a bed in which to lay their eggs. Ordinarily, when they dig a vertical hole in a dead limb for their home, they use chips and rotted wood from their excavations to line the bottom of the nesting hole. Unless you put a layer of sawdust, wood, or cork chips in the bottom of a woodpecker box, these birds may not nest in it.

The first year that I put up a flicker house, I lived in the country. I had several large apple and pear trees growing in the back yard and it would have been easy to nail the flicker box to the trunk of one of them. If I did, the nesting box would have been too heavily shaded by the leafy boughs. Most birds like their nest boxes to be in full sun or at least in a place where it will get sunshine most of the day.

I knew, too, that hole-nesting birds are sometimes wary of nesting in a bird box on the main trunk of a tree. Perhaps they have learned from experience that cats can climb to such bird boxes and kill the young ones, and the parents too, if they catch them in the nest box. I might nail a 30-inch-long sleeve of tin or sheet metal tight around the tree trunk to keep cats from sinking their claws in the bark and, thus, from climbing the tree, but the metal guard might injure or kill the growing tree by cutting into the bark.

A post seemed best and so I cut one about 12 feet long and 6 inches in diameter from the trunk of a cedar tree that I had to cut down because it grew too close to my

Where to Place the Flicker Nesting Box

43

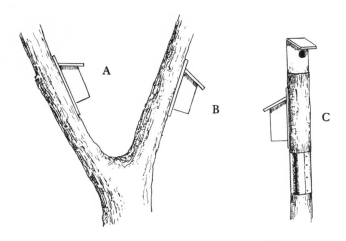

HOW TO PUT UP A BIRD-NESTING BOX. *Wrong way at
A*. If box is to be attached to a tree, do *not* put it up with the entrance hole facing upwards, which would allow rain to enter the
box. *Correct way at B*. Attach box to the tree so that the entrance
hole faces slightly downward. When attaching the bird-nesting
box to a post, (C) put it either on the top or on the side of the
post. Be sure to wrap a metal sleeve around the post below the nest
box to prevent cats and squirrels from climbing to it.

house. After I had fastened the flicker nesting box very
firmly to the side of the post, near its top, I dug a hole 3
feet deep near the edge of my lawn at the rear of the yard
and set the post in it. Before I filled the earth in around the
post and tamped it solidly, I turned the post until the
entrance hole of the nest box pointed toward the southeast
which was *away* from the prevailing winds. This would
keep rain from driving into the birdhouse in bad weather.

Here, in the open, my flicker box had plenty of sun, it
was 9 feet up in the air and above the surrounding shrubbery. Flickers like to nest in boxes that are from 6 to 20
feet above the ground. When they are placed fairly low,

one can stand on a 6-foot stepladder and reach the box to inspect it occasionally, or to clean it once a year.

Last of all, I wrapped a metal sleeve, 30 inches wide, around the nest-box post to keep cats from climbing it. I nailed the cat guard snugly in place, then I sat back to wait for my first pair of nesting flickers.

My notes say that it was about May 1 when I put up that first flicker nesting box many years ago. Flickers usually begin to nest in New York state about the middle of May. Although I didn't realize it at the time, it is best to have all bird boxes in place in late summer, before the leaves fall from the shrubs and trees. This will prevent you from putting them in places that are too densely shaded, especially if you put up the boxes near or under trees or shrubbery. Setting them up early in fall will also permit them to weather over winter, and probably be more acceptable to birds in the following spring. More important, wintering flickers, nuthatches, downy woodpeckers, chickadees, and other hole-nesting birds will have a sheltered place to roost on cold, stormy nights. If you can't get your birdhouses up in the fall, you can put them up any time during the winter. Your chances of getting birds to nest in them will be improved if you have them in place before March 1.

That first flicker house I put up was an exciting adventure. A pair of flickers came to it one day and inspected it carefully. The male bird, which I knew from the female by his black facial markings, came first; and, after a great deal of going in and out of the box, the female joined him. I don't know when she finally accepted this home of his choice, but from that day on they were in and out of the box regularly.

I felt a lot of pleasure in knowing that the birds had accepted my handiwork. Yet, knowing what I know now about birds, I shouldn't have been surprised if I hadn't got a pair of flickers nesting there the first year. I have learned that birds, during the first nesting season that a box is up,

When Should You Put Up Bird Nesting Boxes?

may not use it. Sometimes they may for several years ignore a nesting box that meets every requirement of size, height above the ground, apparent safety, and required position in full sunshine or in part shade.

The Fight Between the Flickers and the Starlings

Birds of different kinds, like the flicker and the starling, do not usually fight when they are feeding near each other on your lawn. You will see a flicker stand in one spot and probe deep into an ant hill to eat these insects. While he does so, a starling a few feet away may be strutting about and stopping occasionally to thrust his sharp beak deep in the grass. The starling is probably digging out the white Japanese beetle grubs which move up near the surface of the ground in spring. Apparently there is little, if any, competition between the flicker and the starling for insect foods or for territories in which to live. But when they go apartment hunting, especially when "bird apartments" are scarce, a lot of things can happen.

One day trouble came to the flickers in my nesting box. I heard them screaming and, when I ran out into the yard, I saw the male flicker pulling at the black wings of a starling that had gotten inside the flickers' nesting box. Starlings nest in holes in trees and in bird boxes, too. They are smaller than flickers and can easily get into flickers' nesting holes and nest boxes. The fight for the house was furious. The flicker pulled the starling out of the hole and wrestled it to the ground, but while they were battling, the mate of the fighting starling slipped into the bird box and held it by pecking sharply at the female flicker whenever she tried to get in the entrance hole.

The starlings and flickers, both male and female, fought for a long while, but I did not interfere. I have learned it is a hopeless struggle to try to keep starlings away, and I have never discriminated against any of the birds in our yard. All are welcome to our feeders, and the birdhouses belong to the birds that want them and can hold them. Later that day the starlings were in full possession of the nest box and the flickers had disappeared.

I was angry at the starlings because I wanted flickers in my yard, but starlings have the useful habit of feeding themselves and their youngsters on army worms, potato beetles, white grubs of the May beetle, billbugs, and other insects that eat our garden crops. I thought about the problem of getting the flickers to come back and finally came up with what I believed was an answer. A few days later I built another flicker box and put it on a post in another part of the yard. I was confident that the new box would soon have tenants because of the bird housing shortage, but that spring and summer passed and no flickers came to nest.

The following year, flickers, perhaps the same pair, came back, not to the newest nesting box, but to the one which the starlings had dispossessed them of the previous spring. I had cleaned it out after the starlings had finished their nesting and the flickers were soon quite at home. When a pair of starlings decided to nest in our yard, they pleased me by going to the new nesting box. As far as I knew, they had no quarrels with the flickers that summer and both pairs successfully brought up their broods of young.

Your Building Materials for Birdhouses

If you build your own birdhouses, a fascinating indoor project for winter evenings, you will want your houses sufficiently well made to last five years or longer. Use wood ¾ inch to 1 inch thick, in preference to thinner wood, metal, clay, or building paper. Wood is the best insulator against heat and cold; a wooden bird box will generally be cooler in summer and warmer in winter than one made of metal or pottery.

Soft woods—cypress, white pine, cedar, yellow poplar, whitewood, and Philippine mahogany—are easy to "work." The cypress birdhouses will be the most durable of all. Do not use green or wet lumber because it will split and warp after it dries. We always use well-seasoned wood to build our bird nesting boxes.

For long-lasting houses, you should put the parts together with brass screws, brass hinges, and galvanized or brass nails (steel nails will rust). Bird boxes put together with screws are always more solid and durable than those that are nailed. Sharp changes in temperature will cause nails to loosen and pull out of the wood.

On the following pages is a table of dimensions for bird-houses and nesting shelves, with a drawing of a typical birdhouse and a typical nesting shelf, for most of the birds that will use this kind of nesting place.

THE DESIGN OF A BIRD NESTING BOX. The simple design of this birdhouse will suit *all* birds that will nest in bird boxes, but the *size* of your birdhouse and its dimensions must be made to suit each kind of bird as shown in the table. If you want to attract bluebirds, you must build a bluebird house; if you want to attract house wrens, you must build a house wren box. Make the roof of the house or one of its sides detachable or hinged to allow you to inspect the inside or to clean it. (See also page 182.)

Dimensions for Birdhouses [a]

(See accompanying illustration for corresponding lettered parts.)

Kind of Bird	A Size of Floor (inches)	B Depth of Bird Box (inches)	C Height of Entrance Above Floor (inches)	D Diameter of Entrance Hole (inches)	Height to Fasten Above Ground (feet)
Bluebird	5×5	8	6	1½	5-10
Chickadee	4×4	8-10	6-8	1⅛	6-15
Titmouse	4×4	8-10	6-8	1¼	6-15
Nuthatch	4×4	8-10	6-8	1¼	12-20
House wren and Bewick's wren	4×4	6-8	4-6	1-1¼	6-10
Carolina wren	4×4	6-8	4-6	1½	6-10
Violet-green swallow and Tree swallow	5×5	6	1-5	1½	10-15
Purple martin [b]	6×6 [b]	6 [b]	1 [b]	2½	15-20
House finch	6×6	6	4	2	8-12
Starling	6×6	16-18	14-16	2	10-25
Crested flycatcher	6×6	8-10	6-8	2	8-20
Flicker	7×7	16-18	14-16	2½	6-20
Golden-fronted woodpecker and red-headed woodpecker	6×6	12-15	9-12	2	12-20
Downy woodpecker	4×4	8-10	6-8	1¼	6-20
Hairy woodpecker	6×6	12-15	9-12	1½	12-20
Screech owl	8×8	12-15	9-12	3	10-30
Saw-whet owl	6×6	10-12	8-10	2½	12-20
Barn owl	10×18	15-18	4	6	12-18
American kestrel	8×8	12-15	9-12	3	10-30
Wood duck	10×18	10-24	12-16	4	10-20

[a] This and the next table are from *Homes for Birds,* Conservation Bulletin 14, U.S. Department of the Interior, Washington, D.C. For sale by Superintendent of Documents, U.S. Government Printing Office, Washington 25, D.C.

[b] These are dimensions for one compartment, or a martin house for one pair of birds. It is customary to build martin houses eight compartments at a time, which constitutes a section. See pages 66-72.

Dimensions for Nesting Shelves with One or More Sides Open

(See accompanying illustration.)

Kind of Bird	Size of Floor (inches)	Depth of Bird Box (inches)	Height to Fasten Above Ground (feet)
Robin	6×8	8	6-15
Barn swallow	6×6	6	8-12
Song sparrow	6×6	6	1-3
Phoebe	6×6	6	8-12

BIRD NESTING SHELF. This simply designed nesting shelf for robins, phoebes, etc. should be built according to the size specified for each bird in the table.

Many people paint or stain birdhouses after they build them, but you will preserve yours longer if you first treat each part of the house with a wood preservative before you put the bird box together. Some of the new chemical wood preservatives contain a water repellent, a fungicide to protect the wood, and a penetrating oil. These combine to keep your birdhouses in excellent condition for at least five years and will protect them from weather and decay more effectively than paint. (Treat outside of box only.)

If you don't use a wood preservative on the boxes, paint will be better than no protection at all. If you don't want to stain the box to keep a natural wood finish, three or four days after you apply your wood preservative, paint the birdhouse any color you wish. Dark green, gray, and brown seem best because they are more like the colors of the tree trunks and limbs in which birds build their nests. White houses are also accepted by birds. If houses are placed in full sunshine, white paint, which reflects the sun's rays, will help keep them cool.

Painting or Staining Your Birdhouses

If you live in the eastern states and aren't too far from a park or a woodland with big trees, it is possible for you to attract downy and hairy woodpeckers, chickadees, nuthatches, and tufted titmice in addition to flickers. In many regions, these are resident birds which do not migrate but live in your area all the year round.

Some of them may be the ones that came all winter to your feeders for suet, peanut butter, and sunflower seeds. If you continue your feeding of these birds through spring and summer, it may encourage them to stay in your yard and raise their families in bird boxes, instead of going to the woods to hunt for a natural cavity, or to drill a hole in a tree for themselves.

One spring a pair of downy woodpeckers nested in a bird box I had put up in an apple tree in my yard to attract nuthatches. The male of this pair had a deformed bill. It curved upward as if he had broken it and by this sign I knew him. He, and his mate that I assumed to be the same bird, nested in this bird box for two consecutive years.

Other Hole-Nesting Birds You May Attract

Bird scientists have proved by trapping and banding birds that pairs of downy woodpeckers and pairs of black-capped chickadees often remain mated and live together continuously for two or three years. Our male downy woodpecker with the crooked bill disappeared after the second year, as many small birds do. The death rate among them is high.

Nesting Boxes for Smaller Birds

Some birdhouses that you can make, or buy if you wish, will suit several kinds of the small birds that nest in holes in trees. If you prefer to buy your bird boxes, always tell your dealer the kind of a nest box you want. Ask for a *chickadee* nest box, a *house wren* box, or a *flicker* box, because each one is made in different sizes and of certain specifications to suit each kind of bird. See the dimension table and typical drawings earlier in the chapter.

The kinds of birds that you will be able to attract to your nest boxes will depend a great deal upon where you live. If you live near a park or woodland where large trees grow, you may be able to have chickadees, nuthatches, and titmice living in your back yard. If you live out in the suburbs or country where open fields surround your property, you may be able to attract bluebirds, tree swallows, and purple martins to your nest boxes.

Chickadee, titmouse, nuthatch, and downy woodpecker boxes. For the smaller hole-nesting birds I build a simple birdhouse that is designed similar to the flicker nesting box, but is not nearly so large. The entrance hole of 1¼ inches in diameter, the inside dimensions of 4×4 inches, and the height of 8 to 10 inches from the floor of the box to the inside bottom of the roof will accommodate titmice, nuthatches, and downy woodpeckers. The entrance hole of this box should be 6 to 8 inches above the floor of the box. A box built to these specifications will also suit chickadees if you make the entrance hole 1⅛ inches in diameter, instead of 1¼ inches.

Chickadees, titmice, downy woodpeckers, and nuthatches are birds of the woodland. They seem to prefer rustic nesting boxes made of slabs of wood with the bark on them, which resemble the outside of the cavities in trees where these birds usually nest. They also will nest in birdhouses made of weathered lumber. If your yard is close to a wooded park or an old orchard, you may attract these birds. Chickadees and titmice will nest from 6 feet above the ground to 15 feet or higher; downy woodpeckers, 6 to 20 feet above the ground; and nuthatches, 12 to 20 feet.

A   B

THE "LOOK-IN-ON-THEM" NEST BOX. Edward H. For-bush, a New England ornithologist, made his first observational bird house (A and B) some time in the 1870's, about the time he first began to attract birds. Forbush, probably the originator in America of many of our methods of bird attracting, built this simple nesting box to try to keep near his home a pair of chicka-dees that had been coming to his window-sill feeder all one winter. Forbush rabbeted the edges of the side of the box to receive a pane of glass (B) through which he hoped to observe the progress of egg-laying, hatching, and the growth of the young. Over the pane of glass he fitted a side panel, hinged at the bottom (A), and held tight at the top by a hook and eyelet. This was only to be opened (B) for brief observations. Forbush mounted the chickadee nest box on a short board that he nailed to his window sill and sat back to watch. The pair of chickadees came, accepted the nest box, and raised their families there for three successive years. In this way, Forbush was able to make scientific observations on the home life of chickadees, which might have been impractical or even impos-sible to make had they been nesting in a hollow in a tree.

These are among the few birds that may be attracted to a nesting box put up in a shaded place, because they ordinarily nest in woodlands and woods borders.

Place each box preferably on a post, and put a metal sleeve around each post to keep cats from climbing it. It is a wise precaution to set the post and bird box at least 8 feet away from a fence or tree from which a cat might jump to the nest box. When we put up a nesting box in a tree or post, we face the entrance hole away from the direction of the prevailing summer winds.

How Many Birdhouses Should You Put Up?

Some of our hole-nesting birds will live surprisingly close together, and peaceably, *if they are of different kinds.* I remember, years ago, a telephone pole in Massachusetts that was an apartment dwelling for a pair of flickers, a pair of redheaded woodpeckers, and a pair of chickadees. The families of these three different kinds of birds lived in separate "flats" or holes that were only a few feet above or below each other. Each pair of birds hatched and brought up their young without a single quarrel as far as anyone knew.

Now if all three pairs of these birds had been of one kind—say, flickers—they might have spent most of their time fighting over their territorial rights instead of raising their families. As a general rule (excepting swallows and certain other birds that nest side by side, in colonies) *birds of the same kind* will not usually nest close together. This means that in your small yard in the suburbs, or in the country, it would be best to put up no more than one birdhouse for each kind of bird you want to attract.

For example, in our suburban New York city back yard, we have had flickers, downy woodpeckers, starlings, house sparrows, and house wrens nesting in our bird boxes during the same year. We have had a woodland nearby and it is theoretically possible to have the woodland hole-nesting birds—crested flycatchers, hairy woodpeckers, chickadees, titmice, and nuthatches—also nesting in our yard. Like the fisherman, who baits more than one hook, we put up a box for each of these kinds of birds, hoping to attract them.

Some of our bird nesting boxes, for different kinds of birds, are in the same trees, but at different heights above the ground. We make it a general rule to space them no closer together than about 25 feet. Although birds of different kinds will sometimes live peaceably much nearer to each other, we like to keep our boxes as far apart as a neat arrangement of them on posts or trees in our yard will allow.

More than seventy years ago when I first began to notice birds, the one that seemed strangest to me was the great crested flycatcher. Each spring, in late April or early May, when I heard its loud cry of "w-h-e-e-e-e-e-p!" ring through the southern New Jersey woodlands, I knew that it had returned to spend the summer.

The crested flycatcher had one habit that puzzled me and lent a deeply mysterious air to this hole-nesting bird of the woods. In most of its nests I found almost invariably a piece of dried snakeskin. Usually there were only a few pieces in each nest; sometimes an entire castoff snakeskin lay draped over the outer edge and trailed outside of the cavity in the tree in which the nest had been built. Some of the older and wiser people of my home village had a solution to this problem. They said that crested flycatchers put snakeskins in their nests to frighten away any animal that might try to eat their eggs or young ones.

Long before I got interested in crested flycatchers, naturalists had puzzled over this strange habit and had a much more logical explanation for it. One man in West Virginia who studied the ways of crested flycatchers identified the castoff skins of at least five kinds of harmless snakes which these birds had woven into their nests. Yet, in some nests, crested flycatchers hadn't used the moulted skins of snakes at all. Instead they had added pieces of the shiny, outer skins of onions, waxed paper, paraffin paper, strips of cellophane, and other materials that resemble dried, castoff snakeskin. Apparently the shininess of snakeskin makes it attractive nest material to crested flycatchers, not any supposed protective value it gives its nest.

Crested flycatchers will nest in bird boxes that are not

too far away from woodlands. The same pair came to a nesting box in a Pennsylvania back yard for three consecutive years and one of the pair lived to be at least eight years old.

Make the entrance hole of the crested flycatcher nest box 2 inches in diameter, the inside dimensions of the box 6×6 inches square and 10 inches deep from floor to inside top of box. Cut the entrance hole about 8 inches above the floor of the box. Crested flycatchers like their nesting boxes set on a post or tree between 8 and 20 feet above the ground. See the dimension table and typical drawings earlier in the chapter.

The hairy woodpecker, a highly useful woodland bird, like its smaller cousin the downy woodpecker, will also accept a bird box with an entrance hole 1½ or 2 inches in diameter. The box should be 6×6 inches square, inside dimensions, and about 14 inches deep from floor to inside top of box. Cut the entrance hole in the front panel about 11 inches above the floor. Put your nesting box for the hairy woodpecker on a pole or in a tree between 12 and 20 feet above the ground.

Nesting Boxes for Wrens

Of all hole-nesting birds, wrens are the ones you are most likely to attract to your city, suburban, or country back yard. Several kinds will nest in bird boxes. There is hardly a section of the United States where one of the hole-nesting species isn't found. These tiny, explosively energetic birds bubble with song and nervous excitement. If you put up a nesting box for them and get a pair of perky little house wrens, Bewick's wrens, or Carolina wrens nesting in your garden, they will entertain you endlessly. The Carolina wrens, resident birds, will usually remain with you all the year round. The house wren and the Bewick's wren are migratory. Each fall the little house wren leaves the northern states and spends the winter in Louisiana, Georgia, Florida, and other southern states. It returns north again in the spring.

Before our country was settled, the house wren nested

in a cavity in a tree or stump, usually in natural openings or burned-over lands in the wilderness. Today, these little birds are the most eccentric in their choices of nesting places of any that I know.

One spring, at a bird sanctuary on Wallops Island, Virginia, the caretaker picked up twenty-four bleached cow skulls that he found lying about on the island. At various places he hung them up in trees and shrubbery. Almost immediately house wrens moved into twenty-three of the skulls, and reared their families in them.

They have built their nests inside the abandoned paper nests of the white-faced hornet, in the deserted nests of barn swallows, robins, and orioles, in a fishing creel hung on the side of a fence, in rusty tin cans on garbage piles, in the pocket of a pair of overalls hanging from a clothesline, in an iron pipe railing, and in many other unusual places.

With the wrens we make an exception about putting up only *one* nesting box for each species of bird. I have hung three in my back yard because of the tremendous nest-building urge of the male bird. The males usually arrive in the North several days ahead of the females and at once start to build their nests. (See also page 264.)

One spring a male built three nests in our bird boxes and then built another in our neighbor's wren nesting box, all before the female arrived. The following day the female followed him about to each nesting box which he showed her, between bursts of singing. When she finally decided upon one that seemed to please her, she immediately began to throw out every stick that he had worked so hard to put into the box. We thought the male wren would explode with anger, but later we saw him helping the female build a new nest in the box of her choice.

Occasionally the industry of the bustling house wren catches him an extra wife. While his mate is incubating her first set of five to eight eggs, the male, between bursts of singing, may carry sticks into a nearby nest box. There his singing and nest-building sometimes attract another female. Friends of ours thought they had two pairs of wrens in the two boxes in their back yard. One day they watched and discovered that only *one male* was helping the two females feed the youngsters that filled each nest box.

One of the most pathetic bird stories I have heard was that of an unmated female house wren in Maine. This little bird, by herself, built a nest in a wren nesting box. After that, she allowed no other bird to alight on her house or to come near the nest. If they did, she was ready to fight them, no matter how large they were. She remained at the nesting box all that summer until August when she disappeared. During that time, the housewife who watched the wren never saw a male house wren about, nor heard one sing. After the female left, the woman took the box down. Inside it she found an exquisitely built nest containing twelve eggs which were all sterile.

Bewick's Wren

Carolina Wren

Another wren, the Bewick's wren, a gentle and confiding creature, is also a familiar bird in gardens. It is a little larger than the house wren and has a white stripe over each eye. Its range overlaps that of the house wren in parts of our northeastern states, excepting in New York state and New England where this bird is practically unknown. This little wren and its close relatives are widely distributed over the United States from central Pennsylvania to the Pacific coast. The Bewick's wren has a sweet, tender song, considered one of the finest of all bird songs. Many people would rather have the Bewick's wren about than the house wren, but both are interesting, attractive, and useful. Both use the same size nest box and will compete with each other for nesting places where they both occur. If you live within the range of the Bewick's wren or one of its many subspecies, you will surely want to put up nesting boxes to attract it to your yard.

The Carolina wren, which also has a distinct white stripe over each eye, is larger than the Bewick's wren, which it resembles. Like the Bewick's wren it sings beautifully and will often nest in bird boxes put up for it in our yards and gardens. Many years ago in a country place near Philadelphia, a pair of Carolina wrens entered the sitting room of a house through a window that was left partly open, and built their nest in the back of an upholstered sofa. They got inside the upholstery through a hole that had been torn in the covering material. The owner of the house was so delighted with his bird guests that he did not disturb them and they brought up their young successfully.

The Carolina wren is a more southern bird than the house wren and the Bewick's wren although all three birds together occur over certain areas of our country. In the eastern United States the Carolina wren seldom nests commonly north of New York city, although it has nested as far north as Maine. In the fall of 1949, I watched one of these birds flit about in a wooded thicket on Point Pelee, the southernmost tip of Ontario, Canada, where it had nested.

Boxes for house wrens, Bewick's wrens, and Carolina wrens. For house wrens and Bewick's wrens, make the entrance hole a slot, instead of a round hole. We make ours from 1 to 1¼ inches high and about 3 inches long. This slot, which looks like a letter drop in a city mail box, gives the wrens more room to maneuver the long twigs that they carry into the box as a foundation for their nests. For the slightly larger Carolina wren, cut the entrance slot 1½ inches high and 3 inches wide. For all three kinds of wrens make the inside of the house 4×4 inches square and about 7 inches high, measured from the floor of the box to the inside bottom of the roof. Cut the entrance slot in the front panel of the wren boxes from 4 to 6 inches above the floor. See the dimension table and typical drawings early in the chapter.

In *all* bird boxes, I always drill several ¼-inch holes in the front panel, *between the roof and the entrance hole.* These will ventilate the box and keep the young birds cool on hot days. Do *not* drill air holes below the entrance hole. These will create a draught on the young birds in the nest and might endanger their lives. Besides ventilation holes, I also drill ¾-inch holes in the floor of all nest boxes, just as I did in the flicker nest box. These will drain off any rainwater that may get in. (See also page 264.)

In the eastern United States, it is usually necessary to live outside of the limits of large cities to attract bluebirds. If *Bluebirds* you live in suburbs bordering open country you may get bluebirds, tree swallows, and purple martins to nest in your bird boxes. People who live in rural villages or on farms have the best chances of attracting them.

Of all our native birds, none is so widely loved as the bluebird—our true "bird of spring." With its sky-blue back, reddish breast, and soft, sweet, warbling song, it has always been a favorite of country people. I remember from my childhood the thrill that my father and I got from discovering, not the first robin, but the first bluebird of the year. We always looked forward to its return to us on a mild day in March from the southern states where it winters.

During the past fifty years, old orchards, where bluebirds once nested so frequently, have almost disappeared. Either the old hollow apple trees have been pruned of their dead branches and their cavities filled, or the trees have been cut down. Farmers have replaced the old orchards with new young trees which they prune and spray regularly. This has improved the apple crop, but has discouraged crops of bluebirds, tree swallows, and other hole-nesting birds the old orchards once produced. Fortunately for these birds, as the old orchards disappeared, farmers and others started to put up nesting boxes for them. Bluebirds quickly adapted themselves to nesting in bird boxes, which may have saved them from disaster.

If you treat bluebirds with kindness and patience, these beautiful creatures may become very tame and friendly. A man I know of, who lived on the edge of a country town, trained a family of bluebirds, young and old, to be friends with his wife and children. He began by coaxing the birds to his window sill for mealworms,[1] of which they were very fond. Soon they learned to feed from his hands and to perch on his shoulders.

In one of his many books, Enos Mills, the Rocky Mountains naturalist of a generation ago, told the story of his

[1] Mealworms, the immature or larval form of a beetle, can be bought in pet shops that sell cage birds and other animals.

companionship with a family of bluebirds. These birds lived in and around his cabin for several years. Mr. Mills learned many things about these mountain bluebirds. One day he was delighted to discover that the five youngsters of the first brood, after they were able to fly, remained with the parent bluebirds to help feed their brothers and sisters from a second brood. Bluebirds usually start to lay their eggs in April in the northern states, but in the South, they may have laid their first clutches of eggs by March.

Make the round entrance hole of your bluebird nest boxes exactly 1½ inches in diameter. The slightly larger starling, the bluebird's strongest competitor for nesting places, cannot get into a bird box with an entrance hole this size. Build the box 5×5 inches square, inside dimensions, and 8 inches deep from top of the floor to inside bottom of the roof. Bore the 1½-inch entrance hole 6 inches above the floor of the box. See the dimension table and typical drawings, pages 48–49. (See also page 264.)

Tree Swallows

Along the Atlantic coast, this is the earliest swallow to move northward in spring. Many tree swallows winter in the South and arrive in the northeastern states in March and April. Like other hole-nesting birds, it has learned to rear its families in nesting boxes we put up for it. The tree swallow seems to prefer man-made nest boxes, although it hasn't altogether given up nesting in holes in trees and other natural cavities. If you have never put up nest boxes for them, you may not realize how badly they suffer from a "housing" shortage.

At Cape Cod, Massachusetts, a scientist interested in birds wanted to see if he could attract more tree swallows in his area. Early one spring, he had ninety-eight nest boxes put up on posts and all ready for the swallows when they arrived from the South. That spring, his local nesting population of tree swallows rose from four pairs to sixty pairs, or fifteen times what it had been!

To test the choice of tree swallows for various kinds of nesting environments, he put up boxes on posts in open fields, in the salt marshes, and in densely shaded woods. Of these different kinds of surroundings, the tree swallows much preferred to nest in the boxes put up for them in or along the edges of open fields.

Usually, pairs of tree swallows nest by themselves, somewhat away from other pairs of their kind. Although pairs occasionally nest close together in hollow trees, especially around marshes, it is best on small properties to put up only one or at most two nest boxes for these birds.

Make the entrance hole to the tree swallow box 1½ inches in diameter, the inside dimensions of the box 5×5 inches square, the depth, from top of floor to inside bottom of roof, 6 inches, and cut the circular entrance hole in the front panel any distance from 1 inch to 5 inches above the floor. See the dimension table and typical drawings earlier in the chapter.

The entrance hole to the tree swallow box will admit bluebirds. The boxes built for these two kinds of birds are almost identical so that it isn't surprising that each will nest in the box of the other. This causes some competition be-

---

THE KINNEY TREE SWALLOW NEST BOX. This new and successful kind of tree swallow box (A) was designed by Henry E. Kinney of Massachusetts. Mr. Kinney's new nest box is especially designed to protect young tree swallows from starving and from exposure during spells of rainy and cold spring weather when they need considerable insect food, which may be difficult for the parents to find. The front of the Kinney nest box has four holes in it; the largest is 1½ inches in diameter, which is the main entrance for the adults. The other three holes (each of *1-inch* diameter) and the entrance hole for the adults allow the young swallows to accept food without the parents' having to enter the nest box. This gives the adults more time to spend hunting insects. Mr. Kinney discovered that more nestlings survived in his new nest box, and that more adults returned to nest in them in spring than in the standard tree swallow boxes with a single hole. The "T" perch nailed to the nest box (A) gives the male tree swallow a perch on which he likes to stand guard close to the female, especially while she is incubating the eggs. The cleats on the roof are for the adults to cling to on windy days.

The scale of the detail drawing (left) is ⅛ inch = 1 inch. Use wood ¾ inch thick. Drawing adapted from *Bulletin of the Massachusetts Audubon Society*, March 1952.

tween them, but both are very desirable birds to have in your yard and garden. When we lived in the country, where we could attract these birds, we always allowed them to fight it out for possession of a nest box. We never interfered but we *did* try to be peacemakers by putting up extra nest boxes for them. Sometimes, if the tree swallows were driven out, they would turn to one of our extra boxes. At other times the bluebirds lost the fight and accepted one of the extra nesting boxes. For both tree swallows and bluebirds, we put their boxes on posts about 5 feet above the ground. To reduce the number of fights between these birds, we spaced their nest boxes at least 100 feet apart.

Violet-Green Swallows   In Seattle a man built a nesting box for violet-green swallows and fastened it under the eaves of his house. For sixteen consecutive years after that, a pair of these birds nested in the box.

This beautiful hole-nesting swallow lives over a wide area of the western United States, west of the Great Plains from Alaska to Mexico. It is as common in the mountains of Colorado as the house sparrow is in our eastern cities. Although it lives about houses and gardens of the West, it ranges far up the mountain slopes and into wild forest lands to build its nest.

Make your nesting boxes for violet-green swallows of the same size and specifications as those for tree swallows.

Barn Swallows and Cliff, or Eaves, Swallows   These two kinds of swallows, like the tree swallows, have learned to live in our yards and about our buildings, especially in country towns and on farms. When North America was a vast wilderness, barn swallows built their nests on the shelves of rocks in rock crevices or in caves. Cliff swallows attached their bottle-shaped hollow mud nests to the walls of deep gorges in remote mountains and, sometimes, against the trunks of giant trees.

Today, the cliff swallow is often called "eaves" swallow because it has almost deserted the cliffs where it usually built its nest. It now nests under the eaves of our barns and houses. Likewise, the barn swallow has gotten its name from its habit of nesting in barns. Usually there are never more than six to eight nests of this swallow in one building, but there are records of up to fifty-five in a large barn at Ipswich, Massachusetts, nearly all of which were occupied or "active" nests. These were built in the old-fashioned New England barns of many years ago when it was the custom to leave the doors open and swallows were free to fly inside to build their nests. Modern dairy barns and neatly painted farm buildings have closed doors and no open windows so that barn swallows need our help if we want to keep them around our homes.

Barn and cliff, or eaves, swallows, do not nest in bird boxes. They need a horizontal ledge or some other support on the side of a building on which to build their nests. When I lived in the country where I could attract these birds, I fastened several rough, unplaned 2×4-inch joists, with the 4-inch sides flat against the building walls, on the outside of a small barn and of a garage in back of our house. I nailed these about 6 to 8 inches below the eaves to give the swallows that might nest there some protection from rain. The first year that I put them up, two pairs of barn swallows came and built their nests of mud, straw, and feathers on one of the joists.

One of the most interesting projects to increase a "backyard" bird in this country succeeded brilliantly because of a chance discovery. At Deerfield, Wisconsin, the owner of a large barn had only one pair of cliff swallows nesting under its eaves in 1904. Appreciating the nesting requirements of these birds, he encouraged them to return the next year by nailing several strips of wood horizontally across the sides of the building to which they could more easily attach their mud-built, flask-shaped nests.

The Great Cliff Swallow Experiment

The following season, several pairs of cliff swallows nested on the sides of his barn. Each year, the owner nailed up extra wooden strips to provide nesting places for more cliff swallows. Gradually he built up his colony until by 1911, several hundreds of these birds returned to nest on his barn each spring. This seemed to be the greatest number of them that he could attract for thereafter they did not increase.

Then came a wet year. After the cliff swallows had flown south for the winter, steady rains drove hard against the sides of the barn all that fall. The dried mud nests of the cliff swallows slowly crumbled and finally dissolved until not a one was left. The following spring when the swallows returned, each pair had to build a new nest, but instead of their usual numbers, almost twice as many nested on the barn. Was this purely chance—a happy coincidence? The barn owner decided to experiment.

Late that summer, after the swallows had left, he *knocked down every one of their nests*. When they returned the following spring, again they nested in greater numbers than ever before. By this time, the owner of the barn had the answer.

Each spring, previous to the wet year, many of the old swallow nests, instead of housing cliff swallows, had been invaded by house sparrows. Living in Deerfield throughout the year, these aggressive little birds got established in many of the old cliff swallow nests before the rightful owners returned in spring. But with the old nests gone, the house sparrows no longer drove a competing wedge into the swallow colony. They had to look elsewhere for nesting places and the cliff swallows could now build their nests and raise their young ones in peace.

In June, 1942, more than four thousand cliff swallows lived in the 2,011 nests they had built that spring on the sides of the Wisconsin barn. In thirty-eight years, the owner had increased his cliff swallow population four thousand times! As far as I know, this is the greatest back yard bird-attracting project to help a single species of bird in this country. It is also a model of patience and enduring kindness by the man who made it possible.

Purple Martins   Each summer we went to Cape May, New Jersey, for a few weeks. In this quiet, old-fashioned resort on the southern New Jersey coast, I saw more colonies of purple martins nesting than I have seen elsewhere at one place in my lifetime. One spring day I counted more than two hundred martin houses and most of these seemed to have martins nesting in them.

Almost every yard had its neat, white-painted martin house set up 15 to 20 feet above the lawn on a white post. Usually, glossy, blue-black martins were flying gracefully about over the grass or settling on the rooftops of these big birdhouses. Many of them perched and chattered conversationally on the porches or galleries that surround each of the floors of their "bird apartments." The rich, cheerful warbling of this largest of our swallows is one of the familiar sounds you will hear any summer day along the shaded streets of Cape May. Some of these martin colonies are so old that the birds that first came to nest in them have long since passed away.

One of the oldest colonies of martins I know of is in Greencastle, Pennsylvania. There, in the public square, in boxes put up for them by the townspeople, martins have been returning to nest since 1840. In more than a century, it is said, they have failed to return to Greencastle only during one period of time. For fifteen years after the Civil War the martins did not come back. Up to now no one has been able to explain this mystery.

Martins become deeply attached to their nesting houses and have a remarkable sense of accuracy in returning to them, which makes the Greencastle story even more puzzling. One spring, a man in Houston, Texas, had taken down his martin house to paint it. Some household chore diverted him from getting the martin house and its pole reset in his garden before his birds returned. Early one morning he heard a great chattering in his yard. When he went outside, his martins were flying in circles around the *exact* place in the air where their martin house should have been.

To keep house sparrows and starlings from nesting in the houses ahead of martins, some people don't put them up until the day that the martins usually arrive. A man in Massachusetts had just started to raise his martin house on its pole on the day he expected his birds to return. At that moment, some of his martins came flying into his yard. So eager were they to get into the house that they alighted on it and rode up with it while the man pulled and hauled it into place!

The Martin House

A single-room martin house, 6 inches square and 6 inches high, inside dimensions, with a 2½-inch entrance hole cut in the front panel 1 inch above the floor, will comfortably house one pair of martins. See the dimension table and typical drawings earlier in the chapter for a single pair of martins to nest in. It will be more satisfactory, however, to get more than one pair of them in *one large birdhouse*, because they will nest together in colonies. The big, roomy "apartment" house can have 20, 30, or even 200 rooms, but an 8-room house will make an excellent start.

It is only fair to warn you that building a martin house is a bigger and costlier job than building the small, single-room houses that you may have already built for other birds. If you prefer to buy your martin house, the cost of a good one of 8 to 24 rooms will vary between $10 and $35,* depending upon how many rooms there are in the house and the quality of the materials with which it is built.

Before investing your time and money in a martin house, it would be desirable for you to inquire in your neighborhood and section of the state to see if martins have ever nested there, or if it is *probable* that they might nest in your community. In the Far West, I know of only two colonies of martins that learned to nest in birdhouses instead of in hollow trees. These were both in California, one in Loyalton, the other in Pasadena. Perhaps other colonies of martins have learned to nest in bird boxes on the Pacific Coast, but they haven't done so like the martins of the eastern United States. Perhaps they will in time, particularly when more people put up martin houses.

If martins are already nesting close by, your chances of

---

* For the latest prices of multi-room martin houses, write to dealers in bird-attracting supplies listed in the Appendix.

attracting them will be good, especially if you live near open fields and have a pond or stream. Even though your yard and garden may be ideally situated to lure martins, you might put up a house and still fail to attract them. If you are willing to risk the disappointment of not getting a colony of these birds, your neatly painted martin house, on its 15- to 20-foot high pole in the center of your lawn or garden, will be a handsome accessory.

Start your martin house modestly, with one section of 8 rooms. Follow the directions for building it and for setting the pole on which to mount it as given in the illustrations. Build your martin house of the same kinds of wood and fittings recommended under "Your Building Materials for Birdhouses," see page 45, and follow the advice given there for treating birdhouses with a wood preservative. Paint all martin houses white, including the pole to support it, and paint the roof and possibly the moldings around each section green or black. Either of these is an excellent color combination and makes a neat, attractive, and *cool* house because white paint reflects the sun's rays.

Some boys in a mining village in West Virginia had different ideas about color combinations for birdhouses. One boy painted his one-room martin house a bright yellow, another painted his red, another chose orange, and one boy painted his house red, white, and blue! Yet, each boy had a pair of martins nesting in his house, which suggests that these birds may not be finicky about the colors of their homes. Nevertheless, be sure to paint your house white, if only for the comfort of the martins in warm weather. Martins like their houses well up in the air and in an open place where they get sunshine most of the day. In such a place, a large martin house, even with its central ventilating shaft and air space beneath the roof, can become very hot in summer.

Gourds Make Economical Martin Houses

In the spring of 1939, while driving along a country road in Georgia, I saw a colony of martins nesting in gourds. I had heard of gourds being used for birdhouses

BUILDING THE MARTIN HOUSE (*opposite page*). Sections, or floors levels, may be built and added separately to the martin house (*A*) as the bird colony grows. A central air shaft and elevated roof allow air to circulate within and to cool the house. A molding strip around the under side of the roof and under each floor section (see detail *E*) holds them in alignment. The sections are held together by hooks and screw eyes (*E*). Use ¾-inch pine or other soft wood for walls and floors; use ½-inch wood for the roof and the interior partitions.

Roof Detail B. Roof with one side removed. The 6 × 6-inch opening of the central air shaft which should be cut out of the center of the attic floor is not shown. A 1-inch-high shoulder on the roof supports allows air to pass up under the eaves and into the attic, which has a ventilation hole at each end that is screened to prevent birds from getting in. The roof is 29½ inches along the ridge top and 16 inches from peak to eaves level. The distance from outside to outside of the end ledges is 22½ inches.

Nesting Compartments, Detail C. Make outside dimensions of floor 26½ inches square. If you use one piece of wood for the floor, the metal angle irons shown will not be needed. Make each nest compartment 6 × 6 × 6 inches, inside measurements. Cut out the floor of the central chamber which is the central air shaft. Make outside dimensions of nesting compartment 20½ inches square, ¾ inch thick. Use ½-inch pine for walls of *inside* of each nesting compartment. Cut the 2½-inch entrance holes along a line 2¼ inches above the floor.

Foundation Frame Support, Detail D. This is the 20½-inch square foundation, 2½ inches high, for the bottom section. It has a center cross built of a double-thickness of ¾-inch oak boards, 2½ inches wide. Attach four heavy angle irons, bolted to the oak frame as shown, which can be spaced to bolt to a supporting post 4 × 4 or 6 × 6 inches square, or to a round pole.

Detail E of Porch. When porch extension, instead of being part of floor, is attached separately, fasten with angle irons. Attach molding trim and angle irons with screws, as shown.

Detail F of Pole Supports. The 8-foot-long supports 4 inches square are set 4 feet deep in the ground. A heavy bolt or section of pipe serves as a hinge (*G*) and the base of the pole is held locked by two hardwood blocks or iron plates bolted together.

Detail H of Pole. Cross section of a post 4 × 4 inches square, built of ⅞-inch hardwood. Supporting poles or posts for large martin houses should be 6 inches in diameter or 6 inches square.

in the southern states, but this was the first time I had ever seen them in use. In the side yard, near a low plantation house, stood a white-painted pole 25 or 30 feet tall. From four, x-shaped crosspieces nailed to the pole at different heights above the ground, hung about 20 hollowed-out gourds, which are the fruits of plants closely related to the pumpkins and squashes. Each of the gourds had a pair of martins nesting in it. The variety most used for martin houses is the "bottle" gourd. Other varieties of the Lagenarias, or hard-shelled gourds,[2] can also be used as houses for larger or smaller birds.

Robins and Phoebes

Robins usually build their nests in trees, but like many other birds they are quick to use places that our civilization offers them. I have found their nests on fence posts, window ledges, the eaves of porches, and garages, on fire escapes, and other supports that seem secure to them.

Apparently a robin's idea of a safe place wouldn't always agree with your judgment and mine. I know of one nest that robins built in a city on top of the overhead running wire of the streetcar line. Every time that a street car passed beneath the setting bird, and the trolley wheel ran by a few inches below her nest, she stood up, then settled back on her eggs after the car had passed!

Both robins and phoebes will build their mud nests on a shelf or bracket put up for them on an arbor in your back yard or nailed to the side of your house, garage, or tool shed. These shelves may have all sides open, or only three, two, or one side open; but whatever type of shelf you build or buy, it should have a sloping roof to keep rain off the nesting bird, unless you can fasten the nesting shelf well up under the eaves of a building or other protective shelter.

For the robin, make the nesting platform about 6 inches deep, from front to back, 8 inches wide, and 8 inches high from floor to inside bottom of roof. Drill several small

---

[2] If you are interested in growing gourds to make your own birdhouses refer to Farmers Bulletin 1849, *Useful and Ornamental Gourds*. This publication tells how and where gourds may be grown, and how to prepare them for birdhouses.

holes in the bottom of it to drain off rain water, just as you did with the bird nesting boxes. Place it anywhere from 6 feet to 15 feet above the ground. See the dimension table and typical drawings earlier in the chapter.

Pattern the phoebe's nesting shelf after the robin's, but make it 6 inches square, inside dimensions, and 6 inches high from floor to inside bottom of roof. Place the phoebe shelf between 8 feet and 12 feet above the ground on the side of a building, arbor, or location similar to that of the robin's nesting platform. If you build your nest shelves, use the same kind of wood and other materials that you use for birdhouses, but it is better not to paint them. Leave the wood a natural finish, but treat it with a wood preservative before you assemble it.

Phoebes like to nest near water. In the country they often build their nests on the timbers under bridges and trestles and on rock ledges in caves and ravines. This gentle, attractive little bird also nests under the eaves of porches and on the joists of barns, garages, and other buildings. Occasionally it even builds its nest below the ground in mine shafts and in abandoned wells.

One of the most perilous nesting places that I ever saw a phoebe choose was on the inside of an I-beam under the carriage of a steam shovel that was idle for a few weeks. When the shovel started digging again, the parent phoebes continued to bring food to their young ones by following the slowly moving machine. Eventually they brought them off the nest successfully.

Screech Owls and Sparrow Hawks (American Kestrels)

Both of these interesting and useful birds will nest in boxes built for them, especially in suburban and even in city yards and gardens. Although these predatory birds usually feed on insects and wild mice, they occasionally kill and eat songbirds. This may make them objectionable in the small suburban garden, but there is no reason why screech owls and American kestrels shouldn't be invited to the country place. On a property of several acres or more, they should be encouraged to nest in bird boxes. I know of few birds that are more interesting and useful, and they should

73

be welcomed as valued members of your bird community.

The American kestrel hunts largely for grasshoppers, crickets, and mice by day; the screech owl feeds upon beetles, moths, mice, and other creatures at night. Each feeds on almost the same *types* of food, except that one is on the day shift; the other the night shift. Both of them can enter a nesting hole down to about 3 inches in diameter, which means they are occasional competitors for nest sites.

One of the most interesting stories that I ever heard about these birds concerned a nesting hole in the dead limb of a eucalyptus tree in California. A pair of American kestrels were making frequent trips into the nest hole, obviously to feed their young ones. A man climbed the tree and found four young American kestrels and *one young screech owl!* The adult American kestrels were feeding the young screech owl, along with their own youngsters, and all of the young birds were in excellent condition. Possibly a screech owl had laid one egg in the nest hole and then had been dispossessed by the American kestrels, or the screech owl may have gotten to the nest of the kestrels and laid an egg in their absence.

At any rate, the kestrels had accepted their strange foster child and continued to feed and care for it until it, too, flew from the nest.

Build your screech owl and American kestrel nesting boxes exactly the same size. See the dimension table and typical drawings earlier in the chapter. Make the inside dimensions 8 × 8 inches square, and about 15 inches from the floor of the box to the inside bottom of the roof. Cut the 3-inch entrance hole in the front panel about 12 inches above the inside floor of the box. Drill small ventilation holes in the front-panel *above* the entrance hole and make drainage holes in the bottom as prescribed for other nest boxes. It is better not to paint these boxes, but be sure to treat them with a wood preservative before assembling them. Fasten the nest boxes of these birds from 12 to 15 feet above the ground, preferably on the main trunk or on one of the upper vertical branches of a tree. An apple orchard is an excellent place to put up screech owl nest boxes. For American kestrels, locate the nest boxes in trees along the edge of a woodland or in a tree in an open field.

I don't like to disturb the birds that occupy our backyard nesting boxes, but we keep a close watch on their progress from the time that they lay their first egg until their last young one leaves the nest. We are eager to see them raise their families successfully, and so I look in the nest box occasionally to be sure that all is well with the eggs or young birds. I have done this without frightening the parent birds by waiting until I am sure that neither of them is in the nest box. Our boxes have hinged tops that lift up. It is easy to climb a stepladder and raise the roof of the box for a quick look inside while the adult birds are somewhere about, feeding themselves or gathering food for their youngsters.

One night I wanted to see which bird of a pair of flickers nesting in our yard spent the night in the nest box. At the time they had newly hatched young and either one or the other of the parent birds would be brooding them. Several hours after dark I took a flashlight and ladder, climbed to the box, and looked in. In the beam of the flashlight the sleeping flicker started, turned its head, and looked up. Quite plainly I could see the black mustachial marking on the side of its face. It was the *male* bird.

To see if the birds changed off in night brooding, I looked in the box on the following night. Again the male bird looked up at me. On successive nights, while the youngsters were small and required brooding, I always found the male flicker in the box. Later, when the young birds were well-feathered and no longer needed the warmth of brooding, the male did not sleep in the nest box.

Long after the nesting season was over and the young flickers had gone away, I discovered what I believed was the same male flicker sleeping in the nest box at night. Flickers go to bed early, before most other birds. One evening, while I waited to see the male go to bed, a female flicker flew to the box and entered it. A few minutes later the male came. Cautiously he looked into the box before entering it, then in a fury he drove the female out. Before winter I put up an extra flicker box and saw a female enter it one evening about an hour before dark. A few weeks later when I looked into the box at night, I found that another male flicker had taken possession of it.

Roosting Shelters for Hole-Nesting Birds

Hole-nesting birds need roosting shelters, particularly on cold, winter nights. I once read about a man in the state of Washington who had put up a 6×6-inch birdhouse in his yard in which a pair of violet-green swallows nested in summer. One evening in fall, after the swallows had gone south for the winter, he saw thirty-one winter wrens crowd into this bird box to spend the night!

A woman in Nebraska who attracted birds kept nesting boxes up for their use all year around. After a heavy February snowfall, she watched one evening while eight bluebirds entered a flicker box, one by one. The ninth and tenth birds could not squeeze into the box and had to leave the garden to find a roost elsewhere on that cold and stormy night.

A safe warm place to sleep may save the lives of many birds that are wintering in your back yard. Although our birdhouses give roosting shelter to screech owls, flickers, downy woodpeckers, nuthatches, chickadees, wrens, and other birds, there is not always room in them to accommodate all the birds that try to use them. Even blue jays and certain others that do not nest in bird boxes will sleep inside a roosting shelter.

In the fall we put up four roost boxes in addition to our eight birdhouses that are always in place and available to birds both in summer and in winter. These roost boxes are easy to build and are designed to make use of the body heat of the birds themselves to keep the boxes warm.

Building the Roosting Box

Make bird roosting boxes of the same kind of wood, hinges, screws, and other materials recommended for nesting boxes. For small birds, make the roost box about 10

76

inches square, inside dimensions, and about 3 feet high
from floor to roof. Cut the 3-inch entrance hole in the
front panel *only about 2 inches above the floor of the box.*
This will allow the accumulated warmth from the bodies
of birds sleeping in the box to rise to the top and to be
held there. If the entrance hole in the roost box were cut
high up near the roof, as in nesting boxes, the body heat
of the roosting birds would be lost and the birds less able
to keep warm.

Make round perches about ¼ inch in diameter for the
small birds to roost on, and fasten them with carpenter's
glue into small holes drilled into the inner walls of the
roost box. Stagger, or offset, the perches as shown in the
illustration to prevent birds from roosting directly above
or below each other. Do not paint roosting boxes but treat

A   B

THE ROOSTING BOX. Make it of the same kind of wood,
hinges, screws, and other materials recommended for nesting boxes.
Have a "lift-up" top (*A*) for periodic inspections or cleanings.
The open section of the box (*B*) shows the placement of the roost
perches inside.

each part—roof, sides, etc.—with a wood preservative before putting the boxes together.

After you have built your roosting box, place it 8 to 10 feet above the ground on a tree or post, as recommended for birdhouses. Be sure that it is in a sheltered place, with the entrance hole toward the south, away from the winter winds that usually blow out of the north or northwest. Use cat guards on the trees or posts like those used to protect birdhouses.

Screech owls, American kestrels, flickers, and other larger birds that nest in holes seem to prefer roosting by themselves. If you have built nesting boxes for them, these will also provide them with roosting places.

Will Nest Boxes Raise Your Bird Population? In 1926, at Bell, Maryland, W. L. McAtee, a government naturalist, started a fascinating experiment to increase songbird populations. Our federal government had planted Asiatic chestnut trees that showed a remarkable resistance to the blight, an incurable fungus disease that had doomed most of our American chestnut trees. Even though the Asiatic trees were immune to blight, the *chestnuts* were not safe from the attacks of an insect called the nut weevil, which sometimes eliminated fifty per cent of the chestnut crop. The government needed just as many sound chestnuts as they could reap to perpetuate this promising tree. What would destroy the nut weevils?

Birds would help, because at least eighty-four kinds feed on nut weevils. Among these, downy woodpeckers, chickadees, titmice, crested flycatchers, and other hole-nesting birds that eat nut weevils might be lured to the chestnut tree planting by putting up nest boxes for them.

McAtee, an expert in attracting birds, put up a sixteen-room martin house, a large birdbath, and ninety-eight nesting boxes on the 3½-acre tract, or about twenty-eight nest boxes on each acre of land. The boxes were kept in place for about six years and a careful record kept of the kinds of birds that nested in each box and how many broods of young they raised. Eight different kinds of hole-nesting birds—starlings, house wrens, house sparrows, purple martins, bluebirds, crested flycatchers, flickers, and tufted titmice—came to live in the boxes. Although the birds did not completely eliminate the nut weevils, they helped to control them and added considerably to the bird life of the area. Just the adult hole-nesting birds, without counting the hundreds of broods of nestlings they raised, swelled the local bird population by about four times.

You may duplicate McAtee's accomplishment on your own property and you might achieve an even greater increase of birds. A woman in Minnesota put up nesting boxes and, by attracting a large colony of martins and other hole-nesting birds, raised her bird population to two hundred nesting pairs on 3½ acres of land. This is about 57 pairs an acre, which is almost a record for attracting songbirds in this country. There are many ways by which you can attract, in large numbers, an interesting variety of useful birds to your yard and garden.

Before I started to attract birds, I never thought they might suffer from a shortage of nesting materials. Perhaps most birds don't ordinarily, but the story of the materials that a house wren once put in her nest would make you believe so.

A Bird's Need for Nesting Material

After the nesting season was over, a curious housewife living in Ames, Iowa, examined a house wren's nest in her yard. She found the following items, which she separated and counted:

Fifty-two hairpins, 68 large nails, 120 small nails, 4 tacks, 13 staples, 10 straight pins, 4 pieces of pencil lead, 11 safety pins, 6 paper clips, 52 pieces of wire, 1 shoe buckle, 2 fish hooks, and 3 garter fasteners!

This pair of house wrens seemed to have had a taste for hardware, but their choice was unusual. We can supply birds with natural nesting materials and we can have a lot of fun doing it, as described in the next chapter.

Some years ago, on our Bluebird Trail at Chapel Hill, North Carolina (see Chapter 10), I revisited a house sparrow's nest in one of the bluebird houses I had nailed

Other Man-made Materials in Birds' Nests

to a roadside fence post. The nest, containing four of the sparrow's eggs, had been deserted by the female four days before when a cat from a nearby farm had climbed the post. It had scratched about the box and had so severely frightened the incubating sparrow within that she left and had not returned.

Curious to see what nesting materials the sparrows had used, I opened the front panel of the box, lifted out the nest entire, and carried it in my car to my cottage at Chapel Hill. There, on my stone doorstep, I carefully sorted out the items, photographed them, and wrote an article about it—"Anatomy of a Nest"—published in the November-December 1964 issue of *Audubon*. There were 1,063 pieces of dead grasses; 126 strips of grapevine bark; 15 paper items (mostly candy wrappers, also some filter tips of cigarettes, a torn piece of an envelope postmarked, "New York, 17, N.Y.," and fragments of a typewritten letter with the visible words "difficult struggle," "philosophers," and "attempts"); 10 pieces of cellophane; 13 pieces of Kleenex; 16 pieces of blue cotton thread; 28 blue, red, and gray feathers of blue jays, cardinals, and catbirds; 9 pieces of cotton; 1 piece of twine; and 1 used Band-Aid. Total: 1,282 items.

In California, Emerson A. Stoner discovered a warbling vireo's nest built almost entirely of Kleenex. In 1955, Enoch Peterson, a Minnesota farmer, sent me an astonishing record. It was a photograph of a brown thrasher's nest that had been built in a rose bush, and inside the bottom of the cup on which the female lays her four or five, brown-dotted, pale blue eggs, the pair had woven a crisp, new five-dollar bill.

4

Helping the Birds at Nesting Time [1]

THE MORE I WATCH birds, the more some of them astonish me with their adaptability. In human beings we might describe this as a practical quality through which certain people always "make the best of things." In the same way our house wrens, even if our back yard were completely bare of plants, would probably pick up nails, pins, wires, or any other odds and ends with which to build their nests, provided we put up nesting boxes for them. Fortunately we have trees, shrubs, and a lawn, and from these the wrens gather the coarse dead twigs and dried grasses they ordinarily use to build their nests.

Bullock's Oriole

When our house wrens start to build, we often pick dead twigs from our spirea and dogwood bushes and put them in neat little piles on the lawn. The sharp-eyed wrens soon find them and carry them hastily into the nest box, as if they feared that some other bird might find this treasure and make off with it before they did.

Once, to see if they always preferred dry, dead twigs, we mixed in a few fresh green ones from which we had

[1] This chapter appeared in the July-August 1952 issue of *Audubon Magazine*, pages 262-266, copyright 1952 by the National Audubon Society.

stripped the leaves. One of the wrens immediately picked these out of the pile, one at a time, flew to a corner of the yard, and dropped them. Then both birds went to work on the remaining dead twigs and quickly carried them into the nest box. Apparently they rejected the green twigs because a nest built of these would undoubtedly make the inside of the nest box damp. Such is the guiding instinct of birds.

We have a pair of northern orioles that nest either in our suburban New York city yard or in our neighbor's yard every year. They don't find on our properties the milkweed plants from which they usually gather long fibers to weave into their nests. Instead of going on a long hunt for these materials they have learned to use bits of string, cotton yarn, and strips of cloth that we put out for them. The instincts of these adaptable birds have told them that our gifts are acceptable substitutes.

A Bird Tragedy   One spring, when I first started to experiment with the willingness of birds to accept man-made nest materials, I was living on a farm in upstate New York. A pair of northern orioles were building a nest in the drooping end-branches of an elm tree in my front yard. Each morning, I put out strings, finely torn strips of rags, and cotton waste on the lawn for them, and by noon, the orioles had taken every bit of it to their growing nest. By the time they had completed it, they had used about seventy-five feet of white string, which I had cut into twelve-inch lengths for them.

Then came the tragedy. One afternoon I looked up in the tree and saw the bright yellow and black body of the male bird hanging limply from the side of the nest. With an extension ladder I reached him and found that he had gotten his neck entangled in one of the strings. The string, like all those I had cut for the orioles, was so long that it had not been completely woven into the nest. A loop in it had trapped the bird. He was dead—strangled to death by one of my good intentions.

I had heard of orioles, robins, chipping sparrows,

swallows, and other birds dying from getting enmeshed in horsehairs, plant fibers, and other natural nesting materials, but I never quite understood how, until I saw the treacherous loops in those long strings. Since then I never put out string, yarn, flax, thread, horsehairs, or strips of cloth any longer than about six to eight inches. As far as I know, none of the birds that have used them have been injured.

One hot July morning a few years ago we cut short pieces of white and dark-colored yarns and simply dropped them on the grass in the center of our lawn. A female robin, building a nest for her second brood that summer, quickly discovered the pieces and carried them away as fast as we put them out for her. The next day, we dropped short pieces of cotton twine on the lawn and watched her carry these to her nest.

How to Offer Nesting Material to Birds

Because it is safer for birds, we ordinarily hang nesting materials on the limbs of trees and shrubbery. There, robins, orioles, and vireos can pick these up without being stalked, and perhaps caught, by cats which might sneak up on them while they were absorbed in gathering nest materials from the ground.

Some of our friends prefer to put the stringlike materials in a small wire basket hung from the branch of a tree, or to nail a wooden container to a tree trunk and fill it with nesting material. Later, the wire basket and wooden container can be used to hold suet in winter.

We have taken the mesh-bags that oranges are sold in, and have filled these with yarn, strips of cloth, horsehair from old upholstery, bristles from worn-out paint brushes, cotton batting, pieces of wool, non-absorbent cotton, chicken feathers, pieces of soft cloth, rags, paper, bits of fur, excelsior, and dried grasses. We have watched robins, orioles, yellow warblers, chipping sparrows, song sparrows, goldfinches, cedar waxwings, and other birds come to the bag to make their own choice of nest materials from this hodgepodge.

We try to keep these bags or other containers filled with nest materials available to birds from May through August.

Some birds, like the robin, may build two, or possibly three, nests during the summer. Others—goldfinches and cedar waxwings—do not nest until late summer, usually in July and August. Certain other birds require even different nest materials, which we also offer them.

Mud for Birds   One of the queerest robin nests that I ever heard of was built in a tree in a Boston back yard in the early 1900's. The female robin usually builds most of the nest, and the male helps by bringing her materials. This female, with an extraordinarily feminine touch, had woven into her nest two red satin ribbons worn by people who attended the 1903 convention of the National Education Association. Trailing partway out the side of the nest, the gold-lettering on one of these ribbons read plainly:

"New York N. E. A. at Boston, 1903."

Near the nest rim the bird had embedded a piece of coarse white lace through which she had neatly threaded two white chicken feathers. The remainder of the nest she had decorated with brown string, yellow string, a piece of blue embroidered silk, the hem of a handkerchief, and a bit of white satin ribbon! But inside the nest she had unfailingly built a hidden lining of mud. Without mud, no robin nest is complete.

Wood thrushes, phoebes, barn swallows, and cliff swallows are other birds that use mud in building their nests. In one corner of our garden, near the tomatoes, parsley, and other vegetables, we have sunk a shallow cake pan about 2 inches in the ground. In it each spring we put a mixture of clay and garden soil. To this we add enough water to make it wet and sticky. When it is about the consistency of wet putty or modeling clay, we know it is about right for the birds. Robins come to the pan regularly while they are nest-building. They stand over the wet mud, peck down into it vigorously until they get a beakful, then fly off with it to the nest. There the female molds the mud into an inner, cup-shaped lining by settling down in the nest and turning her body around and around. During fair weather, soaking our "mud pan" with water each day seems to keep the material sufficiently moist to suit the birds.

Mud is so important to some birds in nest-building, particularly to cliff and barn swallows, that it may be impossible for a colony to remain established without a dependable supply. The man who encouraged the great cliff swallow colony to nest on his barn in Wisconsin kept large pools of water and mud near the barn all during the nesting season. He claimed that the swallows could not have built the 2000-nest colony without this large and reliable mud supply.

One spring morning, a woman in a New Hampshire farmhouse sat at an upstairs window looking out over the sunlit fields. She had been very ill all winter and her recovery had been discouragingly slow. As she looked gloomily down into the farmyard, a breeze picked up a white chicken feather and whirled it into the air. Higher and higher it hoisted the feather until it had lifted it to the height of the woman's window. There the feather floated motionless, but only for a second. Suddenly an arrow shaped steel-blue form struck it, darted toward the ground, rebounded high into the air, and with the feather in its beak raced toward the barn a hundred yards away.

Feathers for Swallows

The woman gasped with admiration. A barn swallow had snapped the feather out of the air and without a pause had flown swiftly with it to the barn and through the big, open doors. Somewhere within, on one of the big crossbeams, it had taken the feather to its mud nest. There it would add it to the soft lining of feathers and grass that would cradle the eggs and later the young ones.

The woman called her husband and excitedly told him the story. She asked him to bring her feathers—lots of soft, fluffy feathers—from the chicken yard. Her husband knew that barn swallows seemed to prefer white feathers and so he gathered only white ones. When he returned with a small sack filled with them, the woman leaned from the open window and dropped one on the air. A breeze caught it, sped it upward and outward. A pair of swallows came racing from the barn, one caught the feather and turned deftly to carry it to the nest. The other bird, chippering excitedly, raced alongside its mate and both birds disappeared inside the wide-open barn doors.

Again the woman dropped a feather on the air and this time, *two* pairs of swallows came swiftly from the barn in a race to catch the feather. Within a week, nine pairs of barn swallows were taking the feathers that the woman dropped out of the window for them each day. Several of the swallows became so tame that they snatched the feathers from her fingers as they flew past her window.

One morning she arrived at the window fifteen minutes later than usual. When she looked out she was atonished to see the barn swallows flying back and forth, calling in a way that she took to be a loud demand for more feathers! When she tossed one into the air, they all dived for it at once.

For three weeks the swallows came for feathers, until the end of May, when their nest-building seemed to be over. To the woman this had been a new experience with birds—one that had helped her regain her strength and had speeded her recovery. She vowed never to forget the swallows and said that, thereafter, they would never want for white feathers at nesting time and her barn doors would never be closed to them. They never were, as long as she lived.

5

Offering a Drink and a Bath [1]

ABOUT SIXTY years ago Ernest Thompson Seton, a famous American naturalist, wrote an article, "Why Do Birds Bathe?" which was published in *Bird-Lore*, now called *Audubon Magazine*. Seton listed three kinds of baths that birds commonly take—sun bath, dust bath, and water bath. He told of having seen eagles, hawks, owls, grouse, quail, and buzzards taking sun baths, of game birds and sparrows that took dust baths, and of other kinds of birds that liked a water bath. Of all the water-bathing birds he had seen, robins were the greatest bathers of all. One of them that he had watched soaked itself until it could barely fly.

But the question of *why* birds bathe he could not answer. He supposed that most birds did because it is healthful for them to do so, and he cited as an example the house sparrow. This is a vigorous and normally healthy bird which takes sun baths, dust baths, and water baths, and will even wallow in the snow when no other baths are available.

[1] This chapter appeared in the *Atlantic Naturalist*, January-February 1953, pages 116-123, copyright 1953 by the Audubon Society of the District of Columbia.

As a result of Seton's article, many people wrote to him about the kinds of baths they had seen birds take, but not one could answer the question: "Why do birds bathe?" Dr. Arthur A. Allen, Professor of Ornithology at Cornell University, wrote that dust baths usually help to kill bird lice and other insect parasites that sometimes get in a bird's feathers. These, by the way, are not the kinds that will infest human beings. As for other bathing, he could find "no biological reason for sun-baths or water-baths except as it seems to bring a pleasurable sensation to birds."

The Pet Hawk That Liked Her Bath

Many years ago I had a peregrine falcon, or duck hawk, a pet that seemed more fond of bathing than any bird I have ever known. Near her perch in my back yard I scooped out a shallow hole in the ground. In it I sunk the inverted galvanized lid from a large garbage can, which made a bath about 30 inches across, 5 inches deep in its center, and about 2 inches deep along its edges.

Even on cold winter days the pet hawk bathed, and she was so vigorous about it that she usually splashed most of the water out of the bath. The following day I might find her standing expectantly in the center of the dry pan. There she sometimes went through all the actions of bathing—squatting down, ruffling her feathers, lifting her wings, and ducking her head, even before I had poured a drop of water into the pan!

Garden Birds Like Shallow Water

I have seen at least sixty-five different species of birds use the baths in our garden. After watching them year after year, I am convinced that they enjoy bathing quite as much as human beings do, particularly in warm weather.

Although the birds in our yard enjoy bathing, they come to our birdbaths far oftener for a drink. On hot summer days robins and other birds that move about on our lawn hold their wings out from their sides and pant from the heat. These are the times when they drink and bathe most often. In July and August, we have had ten or twelve of several different kinds perched side by side on the edges of the baths, all drinking together. When many of them are drinking and bathing frequently, we clean the baths and refill them with fresh water each day. The strong flow of water from our garden hose does this quickly and effectively.

Birds will use the same water both for bathing and for drinking; but, in order to get the birds to bathe, the birdbath must be shallow. It should be no deeper than about 3 inches at its center and even less at its edges—perhaps no more than ½ inch to 1 inch deep where the birds enter the water. The deepest part of a bath of this kind will suit the larger birds—jays, grackles, and robins—and the shallows will be right for the smaller goldfinches, song sparrows, chickadees, and others. Small birds are afraid of deep water. You will notice that when they bathe along a stream's edge or in a woodland pool, they invariably hunt for places where the water trickles thinly over the rocks or the shallows close to the bank.

The birdbath with a bottom that slopes downward from the outer edges toward the center, like the gradual descent of a sea beach or pond bottom, will attract the most birds. In it they can wade to the depth of water that suits them before they start bathing. They also like baths that have roughened bottoms which their feet can grip without danger of slipping. That is why concrete baths or those with a rock bottom seem to inspire them with greater confidence.

The Birdbath with the Sloping Bottom

A   B

THE BIRDBATH MUST BE SHALLOW. Birds will drink from and bathe in the same bath (*A*). Follow the dimensions given in the text for making this birdbath (*B*).

I made our first birdbath of concrete, at a cost of about $1.00 for materials. I chose a sunny place on the edge of our lawn, next to a border of rhododendrons and other shrubs into which the birds could fly to preen and dry their feathers after bathing. There I scooped out a circular area about 3 feet in diameter. Along the outer edges of the circle I dug down only about 2 inches, but in the center I went down about 4 inches deep. Next I mixed with a hoe about 4 parts of sand to one part of cement, then added enough water to make a sticky, plastic mass which I spread evenly in the hole to a thickness of about 1 inch. This made a cement-lined depression in the ground which sloped from ground level to about 3 inches deep at its center. It made an excellent, economical-to-build bath which lasted for a number of years. I could clean it out easily with a hose and broom, but it did fill up with leaves and other debris that the wind blew into it occasionally. Although it served its purpose satisfactorily, I prefer the birdbath that is above the ground because it is safer.

The Birdbath Above the Ground

One day, as I walked down our garden path, I saw a big, gray cat move out of the shrubbery and bound toward our ground-level birdbath. I yelled, but I was too late to prevent the swift tragedy that followed. Even as I shouted, the cat leaped into the birdbath and struck down a robin that was too wet to fly quickly. With the robin in its jaws, the cat raced through our property-line hedge and disappeared behind a building in our neighbor's yard.

That was the only time that I had ever *seen* a cat catch a bird in the ground-level bath, but I could no longer let the birds use it. It was too close to the shrubbery for their safety. I could have made a new cement ground bath in the center of the lawn where the birds could see a cat approaching and easily fly to safety, but I had a better plan.

A few days later I made a shallow concrete bath, 36 inches in diameter, and set it on a concrete pedestal and base that raised the bath 40 inches above the ground. I put the bath out in the open lawn, directly under the low-swinging branch of an apple tree into which the wet birds could fly at the first sign of danger. From their elevated position, they also could see any cat approaching long before it got within striking distance. Our back-yard birds have now been drinking and bathing in this bath for the past twelve years in undisturbed peace and enjoyment.

I especially recommend that you have an elevated bird-bath in your garden, but it isn't necessary to build your own. Attractive ones, made of concrete or tile, may be bought from dealers in bird-attracting equipment, or from manufacturers of garden benches, chairs, and other back-yard accessories.

I don't know if it is still there, but in 1933 I saw what I believed was one of the strangest birdbaths on earth. On the lawn of the National Museum at Ottawa, Canada, a stone foundation, resembling a watering trough for horses, supported a flat rock in which a dinosaur had made a giant footprint millions of years ago. The footprint, a few inches deep, had been made originally in soft mud which later turned to rock. The giant reptile that made the big track had once lived in that part of western Canada we now call British Columbia.

The Birdbath from a "Lost" World

On the day that I saw this unusual bath, a catbird sat in the water that filled the big footprint, fluttering water over its back and ruffling its wet feathers. Scientists believe that birds are descended from a prehistoric reptile that lived millions of years ago, at a time in our earth's history that has been popularly called "the lost world." If you believe in evolution you will understand the strange thrill that ran through me as I watched this comparatively tiny creature bathing in one of its ancestor's giant tracks!

You may have several different types of birdbaths in your yard, but none will attract a variety of birds like the drip bath, a device that you may add to any birdbath.

The Magic of Falling Water —the Drip Bath

Birds are strongly attracted by dripping water. So powerful is its lure that an occasional falling drop in your birdbath—perhaps only one or two a second—will attract warblers, flycatchers, some of the northern thrushes, and others that without falling water might never come to your bath. Many of these birds will not come to feeding stations. The drip bath is necessary if you would like to see as many species in your yard as it is possible to see in your particular region.

THE DRIP BIRDBATH.

One of the simplest drip-bath arrangements you can make requires only a 10- to 12-quart wooden bucket or metal pail. Drill a small hole in the bottom so that only an occasional drop of water will seep out. Suspend the bucket from a tree limb or some kind of artificial support no more than about 2 feet above the birdbath (any higher and the wind may blow the drops outside the bath).

Although this is a simple arrangement, you may not like its appearance. I once hung a pail with a spigot near the bottom of it from a tree on our open lawn about 15 feet away from the birdbath. To the spigot I attached a ¼-inch copper pipe and ran it downgrade, through a series of iron eye hooks that I sunk in the lawn. I ended the copper pipe at a point about 18 inches above the birdbath. I filled the pail with water, then turned the spigot on just enough that a drop of water issued from the end of the pipe and fell into the birdbath about every second. Although this worked, I found it unsatisfactory because it looked like a mad inventor's dream and did not add to the attractiveness of our yard. Later I moved the whole assembly of bucket and pipeline into our side-yard shrubbery and then shifted the elevated birdbath to the edge of the lawn near it. From spring until fall when leaves are on the trees and shrubs, they conceal the bucket and pipe from view, which makes it quite satisfactory. In winter I store the assembly in the cellar because it would freeze and fail to operate in cold weather. Also, its effectiveness would be wasted on the *wintering* birds in our Long Island back yard, which don't need the drip of falling water to attract them.

For ten years now the sharp *plink!* and *plop!* of falling water has sounded out in our back yard. Altogether it has attracted forty-five species of migrating birds that I am sure we wouldn't have seen without it.

The Birdbath in Winter

Like many of our friends who attract birds, every winter we have had the problem of keeping the water in at least one of our birdbaths "operating" during cold weather. To make the birdbath usable for birds, we have had to thaw the ice with boiling water, sometimes three or four times a day on those days when the temperature dropped to 20 degrees above zero or lower. We have never minded doing this. What worried us most were those occasional periods when we had to be away from home for a few days. Our hopper feeders filled to the brim with grain would feed our birds until we returned, but what about water?

One winter that problem was solved very capably for us by a reader of *Audubon Magazine*. He introduced me to the "submersion" water heater for the birdbath. Here is what it is, and how it works:

Submersion, or waterproof, electrical heaters are usually made for fish aquariums in various watt sizes that will keep the water at a certain, even temperature. The warming power of these heaters will vary according to the wattage size of the heating unit. These are manufactured in 25-, 40-, 50-, 75-, and 100-watt heaters which are sold by dealers in aquarium supplies in New York city for about $2.00 each. We use a 75-watt heater which is probably ample for most birdbaths. The heating unit, sealed within a tube made of chrome, nickel, or pyrex glass, is supplied with electric current by a short length of insulated, waterproof wire. For your birdbath, this can be plugged into whatever length of extension wire you need to reach from your house to the birdbath (see sketch below).

If your birdbath is some distance from your house, you might, as we did, run a durable type of extension cord to

THE BIRDBATH HEATER. Bury the lead-covered wire (from the house to the birdbath) at least six inches below the ground surface. Lead-covered wire is expensive—from 15 to 20 cents a foot. To reduce the length of cable to the birdbath heater (which is in use only in winter) move the birdbath close to the house, in a sheltered place, at the beginning of cold weather, but not too far from shrubbery where birds can fly for protective cover.

it. We used a lead-covered wire that we buried a few inches below the ground, but make sure that you do not bury your wire where you may be digging in your garden at some future time. We ran ours (see the sketch above) from the house, under our lawn, to our north property line fence, then east, underground, close to the fence and beneath shrubbery all the way to the birdbath. Under shrubs and close to the fence there will be little danger that we will ever disturb or break the wire by digging, and there is not much chance of our doing so where it is buried under the lawn.

To contain a water heater a birdbath must be at least six to eight inches deep at its center. For a bath of this depth we use a large wash basin—a dish pan would do just as well —which we set in our dry concrete birdbath. We don't fill concrete or tile birdbaths with water in winter because freezing and thawing of the water will crack them.

How to Install the Water Heater in Your Birdbath

Using a birdbath this deep seems contrary to all I have said about using a shallow birdbath but the heater needs weighting down with a few stones or ordinary red building bricks. These cover the heater and provide a roughened false bottom only a couple of inches below the surface of the water, which gives the birds their shallow bath after all.

We drilled a hole through the bottom rail of the sash of one of our basement windows (see sketch, page 94) and ran our lead-covered extension cord inside. We then called in an electrician to finish the job, because we didn't want to risk any wire work that might be a fire hazard. You can see from the sketch that the electrician installed a switch box near a base plug outlet inside our house, just below our living room window from which we watch the birds in our back yard. When the switch is "on" and the heater is operating, a red jewel light on the face of the switch box glows; when the switch is snapped off and the heater it not working, the light goes out.

Connecting the Birdbath Extension Cord at Your House

Early in the morning during freezing weather we switch on the heater which soon thaws the ice in the birdbath. Our heater, turned on for only a few hours each day of the ordinary cold weather in our area, keeps the birdbath water thawed. If we have bitterly cold nights or days when the temperature drops near zero or below, we may keep the water heater operating all night and all day. The cost of operating the heater is so slight that since we have been using it, we have noticed little difference in our winter electric bills.[2] The length of time that you need your water heater operating to keep your birdbath water thawed will depend on how cold or how mild the winters are where you live. You will soon learn, with a little experimenting, how frequently you will need to use it, and you will be more than repaid by the trips it will save you or your wife in cold weather, carrying hot water to thaw the ice in your birdbath.

Our good friend, who introduced us to the easily installed and practical, submersible water heater, now has what he believes is an even better idea. He has learned about a thermostatic heater on the market which can be set to maintain any desired water temperature. He believes that in winter his birdbath water can be kept at a temperature higher than 40 degrees by using this heater; and that it will use less electricity because the heater would go on automatically only when the water temperature in the birdbath dropped below the setting of 40 degrees.

We have learned that this thermostatically controlled water heater is on the market. It has a water submersible heating unit sealed inside a metal tube eight inches long and 1¼ inches in diameter, which is placed in the birdbath water. Attached to it is a six-foot-long weatherproof electrical cord that can be plugged into an extension cord, which in turn can be plugged into an outlet, either inside or outside the house. This assembly can be arranged exactly like that of the submersible aquarium heater illustrated on page 94, and can be connected from the house to the birdbath in the same way. It differs from the fish aquarium heater in that it operates automatically. After

[2] Our local utility company says that our 75-watt birdbath heater, if it operated an average of 3 hours daily, for a 30-day month, would cost us only about 30 cents to 50 cents a month for electricity.

the metal tube of the water warmer has been placed in the birdbath water, and the cord plugged into the house current, the warmer goes on automatically when the water temperature drops to 45 degrees. When the water temperature in the birdbath rises to 50 degrees, it shuts off.

You can buy one of these heaters from a company that sells supplies to people who raise poultry. It is manufactured by the Smith-Gates Corporation, Farmington, Connecticut, who supply it to dealers in poultry supplies all over the United States.

The Strange Practice of "Anting"

One October morning, some years ago, my wife and I were seated on a rustic bench overlooking our garden on Long Island, New York. We were watching three house sparrows taking their dust baths. They were lying flat on a sunny place in a flower bed with their body feathers slightly puffed out. Each had settled about a foot apart in its own small hollow, scratched out of the soil with the feet. They were shaking their wings and shifting their bodies about as they sifted dust through their feathers. Their eyes shone, they chirped, and every motion showed their pleasure.

The dust bath not only seems to suffocate body lice and other parasites in a bird's feathers but, according to one scientist's experiments, realigns the interlocking barbs of the body feathers and removes oil and moisture from the bird's plumage. Suddenly the sparrows got up, vigorously shook dust from their feathers, and flew off.

Then we saw a starling alight on our lawn. It seemed about to squat, and we assumed that it was going to sunbathe as robins and so many of our garden birds do on a hot day, sprawled flat, sometimes on their sides, gazing up at the sun. Through my binoculars, I could see the starling suddenly begin to pick up pale objects from the ground and dab them under its wings.

"That bird is anting!" I said excitedly. It was the first time in my thirty years of bird study that I had ever seen this strange phenomenon. The starling continued to pick up ants and to dab them under each wing. Then it flew, and we walked quickly to the place where it had been standing. As I knelt on the grass, I smelled a familiar sweet odor, like that of the crushed leaves of our spicebushes in the garden border. In the starling's freshly dug holes, I saw several active golden-bodied ants, known to scientists as *Lasius claviger*. The starling had disturbed them at the entrance to their underground gallery, and they had emitted their strong spicy odor in self-defense.

I found no dead ants on the ground, and I had not seen the starling eat them, although it may have crushed the ants in its bill before putting them in its feathers. One of the theories about this behavior is that birds benefit from the ants' defensive spray of formic acid.

Formic acid and other ant-fluid chemicals have certain insecticidal values when sprayed in the anting bird's feathers. These are thought to kill or repel bird lice, mites, and other annoying parasites that live on a bird's body or in its feathers. However, recent investigators believe that anting, usually practiced by birds during their summer and fall molt, is especially effective in soothing irritations of the bird's skin caused by its new feather growth.

At least 160 kinds of birds are known to practice anting and observations of it extend around the world. Besides ants, birds rub at least 40 kinds of substitute materials into their feathers, such as chokecherries, juice from the hulls of walnut shells, cigarette and cigar butts, hot chocolate, soapsuds, sumac berries, etc. Most of these materials are acid and may serve birds as effectively as the formic acid of ants.

If you want to invite anting, put out mothballs as a woman did in her garden in Milwaukee, Wisconsin, to prevent cottontail rabbits from eating her young green plants. Grackles soon discovered them, and each would take a mothball in its bill and deliberately rub it under its wings and over its body feathers. In Central Park, New York, I have seen grackles, scavenging in trash baskets, pick up orange peels and dab them through their feathers.

Some of the North American garden birds known to ant, besides starlings, are blue jays, catbirds, robins, tanagers, towhees, and cardinals.

6

The Care and Feeding of Young Birds

EVERY SPRING and through the early summer we got a flood of telephone calls at Audubon House, headquarters of the National Audubon Society in New York City. The question most frequently asked was: "What should I feed a young bird that has fallen out of the nest?" Before these kind-hearted people told me their stories, I could have told them what had happened.

Someone in the household saw an apparently helpless, half-feathered young bird on the lawn. The parent birds weren't in sight and it looked as if the young bird had been abandoned. So they brought it into the house to save it from starving or sudden death from the neighbor's cat. Perhaps these kindly people did rescue the young bird, but there is a better way to save it, with far less trouble to themselves.

When young birds leave the nest, they don't always fly away. Sometimes they "walk" from the nest and by a series of hops climb out into the bush or tree in which they were hatched. There they sit and call loudly; the parents, attracted by their cries, or "food calls," come to the youngsters at regular intervals to feed them. The young but feathered robins we see on the lawn, even if they can't fly strongly, are usually able to flutter up into the lower limbs of a bush and up into trees until they are safely out of the reach of dogs and cats. If you will remember this the next time you see a young robin on your lawn, and place it in a bush or tree out of reach of its enemies, you may save yourself a lot of trouble. You will also be sure that the young bird will be well-fed with wireworms, white grubs, and cutworms from your garden, and earthworms from your lawn.

If you have already brought the young bird into the house and have accepted your responsibility of feeding and caring for it, here is what this will mean to you.

You are now a foster parent and once you start feeding the youngster you will be astonished at how quickly he will learn what your relationship means to him. To the young bird, you have become his world, and a young bird's world is *food*.

Accidents May Thrust Young Birds upon You

Because she did such an excellent job of raising young birds, I especially remember a Missouri woman who raised four baby robins a few years ago. Someone in her neighborhood cut down a tree in which a pair of robins had a nest filled with young ones. When the tree crashed to the ground, the recently-hatched robins were thrown out of the nest and scattered over the lawn, but were unhurt.

The woman gathered up the four helpless creatures and put them in a sewing basket about eight inches deep, which she had lined with excelsior to simulate the lining of grasses in their former nest. Then she wired the basket securely on top of a branch of a tree near the tree that had been cut down, hoping that the parents would return and feed the young ones.

Sometimes if a fallen nest and its young ones are replaced in the exact site from which the nest fell, or within a few feet of the original spot, the adult birds will return and continue to feed their young as though nothing had happened. But all birds, like all human beings, cannot be depended upon to behave in the way we think they should. If the adults are disturbed or frightened at the nest when the eggs are newly laid or the young just hatched, they may desert it and start building a new nest elsewhere.

The robins that the Missouri woman found were extremely young, scarcely more than a day old. Keeping some distance away, so as not to alarm the parent birds if they came back, she watched for a while over her improvised basket-nest. When the adults did not return, she realized they had abandoned their family. She was frightened at the prospect of raising the tiny young birds, but determined that she would not allow them to die without trying to save them.

Knowing that robins sometimes feed themselves and their young ones on earthworms, she got her two children to dig in the garden until they had a large jar filled with them. Meanwhile she had cooked some oatmeal. With a pair of old sugar tongs, she dropped small pieces of the earthworms in their mouths, which they opened wide whenever they were hungry. When the oatmeal had cooled, she fed them some of it, along with small pieces of whole wheat bread, moistened slightly with milk. To this diet she added pieces of scraped apple and small bits of cherries. Regularly, at least once every half hour, she fed the young robins that first day, and at night she covered the basket with a cloth to keep the birds warm.

Feeding the Young Robins

As the birds grew older, their appetites grew larger, and she increased her feedings to once every fifteen minutes. Within two weeks the young robins had feathered out and were so active that they would no longer stay in the basket. Then the woman had a chicken-wire cage, 10 feet long and 3 feet high, built for them in her back yard.

For a week the young birds lived there, flying from one branch to another of the limbs of trees she had put in the cage for them. They were now learning to hunt for worms and to pick up insects from the ground. The woman had become deeply attached to her four young birds, but legally [1] she had no right to keep them once they had proved they were able to care for themselves.

[1] All songbirds are protected by federal and state laws, excepting house sparrows and starlings. If you raise these birds, you may legally keep them, but every wild bird should be allowed its freedom after proving it is capable of caring for itself.

When her robins were strong enough to fly, the woman allowed them to go free in the yard. For a few days they returned at her call to be fed pieces of bread and ripe blackberries. One day they flew off to a nearby woodland and she never saw them again. Presumably they survived and, though she regretted to see them go, she had acted commendably and sensibly. She had granted them their natural right to live the rest of their days wild and free.

The Attachment of Some Birds to Their Eggs and Young

Not all birds will desert their young or their eggs when they are disturbed on the nest. I have stroked the backs of red-eyed vireos and chestnut-sided warblers as they sat on their nests, incubating their eggs or brooding their young ones to keep them warm.

One of the most remarkable examples of a parent bird's devotion to its offspring came to me from a man in Michigan. A pair of northern orioles built their nest one summer in an apple tree in his yard. When a cat killed the female, the male took over the feeding of the young. One day this bird broke its wing and when the man discovered that the oriole was crippled, he saw that it was still carrying food to its youngsters!

A grapevine had grown up into the lowest branches of the apple tree to a point where a pole leaned at an angle against the limb, where the nest was hung. This formed a continuous pathway from the ground to the nest and up and down this "road" the poor bird searched for food. He never went far from the grapevine and kept a keen watch for enemies. After filling his beak with caterpillars and other insects, he started his tedious journey up the grapevine—one hop at a time. In this way he cared for his family until the birds were able to fly and care for themselves. The crippled oriole disappeared soon after that, perhaps a victim of the same cat that had killed his mate.

The Substitute Nest for the Young Bird

After you have raised quite a number of young birds, you get a local reputation for being a "bird doctor." People believe you can perform all sorts of miraculous cures. In the spring, our neighbors have brought us many kinds to be helped—from hour-old naked sparrows, with their eyes not yet open, to sick and crippled adult jays and crows. We always try to help these unfortunate creatures. If we have so many in our care that we can't possibly take on more, we are glad to tell our friends how they may care for them until these waifs are able to shift for themselves.

When an extremely young songbird, which is usually quite naked or only sparsely feathered, is brought to us, we immediately put it into a box. A shoe box, or any container deep enough to keep it from falling out or scrambling out later, will do. We line the box with a mat of grass, excelsior, or torn up bits of paper. This substituted nest material helps to keep the young bird clean, can easily be replaced when it is soiled, and gives the bird something to grasp with its feet. The material also helps it to keep its balance when it raises its head high and opens its mouth to be fed.

For the first few days after they are hatched, young songbirds are "cold-blooded." When you touch them they will feel cool because their bodies are adjusted to the temperature of the surrounding air. When they are five or six days old, their body temperatures go up to what is near normal for an adult bird. The youngster is now "warm-blooded" and will feel warm to your touch. It is important, until your charge is fully feathered, to keep its nest box covered with a cloth, especially at night and *always* to keep the bird out of a draft.

The parents instinctively know this. For example, the female robin, during the first few days after her youngsters are hatched, will brood them frequently, that is, settle down in the nest with her feathers spread over the young birds to keep them warm and dry. This is the way she guards them at night, and if the weather remains cool and damp, she may spend time brooding them every day and up until the moment when they leave the nest.

I think one of the most touching and yet most amusing sights in all nature is a parent bird trying to cover a nest

*Keeping the
Young Bird
Warm*

filled with young ones so large that when they shift about under her they lift the brooding mother into the air and almost off the nest.

What to Feed Young Songbirds   Our basic food for all songbird nestlings, other than hummingbirds, is equal parts of the finely mashed yolks of hard-boiled eggs (the yolks are more nourishing and easier for the birds to digest) and finely sifted bread crumbs, *slightly* moistened with milk or cod-liver oil. This mixture will agree with starlings, blue jays, cardinals, towhees, robins, catbirds, orioles, sparrows, blackbirds, waxwings, bluebirds, thrushes, and other small birds.

Good supplementary foods are canned dog food, bits of grapes, cherries, raisins, bananas, soft apple pulp, pieces of earthworms that have been "squeezed out," and bits of scraped or finely chopped beef.

Many years ago I knew of a woman in Amsterdam, New York, who raised one of two young flickers entirely on bananas! The other flicker, besides eating bananas, ate boiled veal, strawberries, cherries, and boiled green peas. She also raised a young bank swallow on bread, milk, and hard-boiled egg yolk. When the swallow got older, and refused these foods, she hired children to catch flies foi it. In one afternoon the bird ate eighty-five large flies, but in our experience flies are not good for captive birds, which often become weak and ill after eating them. Possibly the house and blue bottle flies have too many germs on them.

It will greatly strengthen the young bird to supplement its egg-bread-milk-cod-liver-oil diet with the chopped green leaves and stems of watercress and nasturtiums, which are rich in calcium and vitamins. Feed it also a little cottage cheese now and then for added protein.

Young woodpeckers (flickers, downy woodpeckers, etc.) should be fed a mixture of canned dog food and the basic, finely mashed egg yolks.

Feed a young hummingbird a mixture of 28 ounces of white cane sugar in one gallon of water with ¾ ounce of Super Hydramin powder, as recommended by Paul W.

Colburn, Director of the Tucker Bird Sanctuary in Orange, California. After about ten days give it its first protein by adding some finely sifted, dried dog food to the sugar water and Super Hydramin powder. (See page 36 for another successful formula.)

What and How to Feed Hawks and Owls

Hawks and owls, both young and adults, require raw meat, preferably with the fur or feathers on it, for these aid their digestion. Feed them on freshly caught mice, or poultry, and raw beef sprinkled with cod-liver oil, with which chicken feathers may be mixed.

To get a newly acquired hawk or owl to start eating, cut small strips of raw beef, a few inches long, and lay them across the bird's feet. This seems to attract its attention and it will usually reach down and pick up the meat. It may drop it and you may have to lay the meat across the bird's feet several times before it will bolt it down. Once it starts feeding it will usually continue until its crop or craw in the lower part of its neck is bulging with food. After its crop is filled, it will not accept more until the food has digested and passed into its stomach. Feed the young hawk or owl about three times a day, adults once a day.

Some Sources of Foods

If you want to get a large number of earthworms for your young robin without digging in the ground for them, go out into your yard at night with a flashlight. Take along a mason jar partly filled with soil in which to put the worms. In the beam of the light that you direct ahead of you on the grass, you will see the glistening skin of an earthworm that has come up out of its underground burrow and is lying stretched out in the grass. Fishermen call these "night crawlers," but they are the ordinary earthworms that you can dig out of the garden in the daytime.

Approach the worm softly and pounce on it quickly, because it can move with incredible speed back into its hole, especially if you walk heavily and it feels the slightest tremor of the ground as you approach.

I know a woman who had a captive yellow-billed cuckoo.

Like swallows, these birds feed almost entirely on insects. The woman's biggest job was to get a large daily supply. She solved this by attracting insects each night to a light in her window where she easily caught them.

Other supplementary foods for young songbirds may be bought in pet shops. Meal worms, mockingbird food, and ant eggs, which aren't really the eggs of ants at all but undeveloped young, are usually available in stores that sell cage birds, tropical fish, and other animals.

How to Feed the Young Bird

A baby bird, with its eyes not yet open, will usually raise its head and automatically open its mouth for food whenever it hears you come near its box. Put the chopped egg yolk and bread crumbs in a small dish and use a narrow wooden spoon or, better, a small paint brush to pick up food on the tips of the bristles. Poke the food well back in its throat but don't give it too much at one time, or it may choke. Continue feeding until it will not accept any more food. It should be well fed, especially at nightfall, just before it goes to sleep.

Why Birds Can't Be Overfed

When a bird has had enough to eat, it will usually refuse to swallow. I have often watched parent robins feeding their young in the nest. They do not rotate their feeding among the birds, but push food down the throat of the one with its neck stretched highest, and its mouth opened widest. As soon as this youngster has had enough to eat, it will refuse to swallow. If the parent robin puts a worm or bug down the throat of the young one several times and it does not swallow, the parent will give it to the next robin in the nest, and so on, until all are fed.

The rule to follow in feeding is: *Don't put more food down a bird's throat until it has swallowed the food you have just given it.*

When to Feed Young Birds

Handle a young bird just as little as possible because merely holding it in your hands may sap its strength and kill it. Feed the young bird only during the daytime, starting early in the morning and ending at dusk when you should cover the bird's box or cage to encourage it to go to sleep. The feedings should be frequent and *regular*, at least every fifteen to twenty minutes apart, or, at most, half an hour apart.

Many years ago a bird scientist wanted to measure how much a young robin would eat at the time that it was ready to leave the nest. A young bird's appetite is probably greater then than at any other time of its life. The young robin of his experiment ate fourteen feet of earthworms on that last day of its nest life!

Another scientist discovered that parent robins will bring a total of about three pounds of food to their average brood of four young ones during the two weeks that they stay in the nest.

People who don't realize what enormous appetites young birds have may unknowingly allow the ones they adopt to starve to death. Young birds don't eat much at one time, but their food digests so rapidly that their parents feed them almost continuously from dawn until dark.

Don't force a bird to drink! When I was a boy, the first bird that I ever tried to raise, a young blue jay, died because I opened its mouth and poured water down its throat. Apparently the water got into its lungs, for it died within twenty-four hours.

Small birds can be killed very quickly by forcibly giving them water. While they are in the nest, most young songbirds get sufficient water for their needs from the insects and wild fruits that the parent birds bring to them. In the same way, your young bird will get moisture from the food that you give it. If you occasionally feed it blackberries, mulberries, strawberries, and other small juicy fruits you will make certain that it gets enough liquid in its diet.

When the bird is old enough to sit on a perch, we offer it water in a shallow dish, from which it soon learns to drink. You may teach it to drink by dipping its bill in a cup of water and then holding the container of water in front of it, or by putting it somewhere within the bird's reach.

Give your young bird sunshine, but not too much of it. It is best to keep it shaded from the midday sun, which is usually too hot for a young bird and might kill it.

How to Care for Older Birds

When we first get an ill or injured adult songbird or a young bird that is so well-grown that it has already learned to fear man, we put it in a large cage or, preferably, in a room where it is free to fly. We give the grown-up the same kinds of foods that we give to a young bird because this will sustain it until it is strong enough to take care of itself. When we are sure that the bird can fly, we release it in our garden. There, unless it flies away immediately we can watch over it.

When they are first rescued, these older birds may not eat, even if we put food before them, because a bird that is already used to eating insects may not recognize our mixed egg yolk and bread as food. This means that we shall have to force feed it, perhaps for a few days, until it will eat the food by itself. Some adult birds that we have had never voluntarily took food as long as we had them. Others learned to eat our offerings very quickly.

We force feed these adults about three or four times a day because a full-grown bird doesn't require nearly as much food as a nestling, which may eat its own weight in food each day. For the well-grown young bird or the adult, we put a shallow pan of water on the floor of the room or of the cage in which the bird is kept, so that it can drink or bathe whenever it chooses.

Force Feeding a Bird

One of the first things to learn in force feeding a bird is how to hold it without injuring it. This is really easy. To learn the proper way to hold a bird, all you need to do is to pick up a large apple or an orange as if you were going to eat it.

Now look at the position of your fingers. They encircle the apple just in the way they should encircle the body and wings. Pick up the bird so that its back is against the palm of your hand and your fingers curve around its breast. The back of its head now lies comfortably in the V between your thumb and index finger. As you hold the bird, not tightly, but loosely in this position, you are holding its wings against its sides. It can't struggle, and it will automatically reach its feet out to grasp your little finger. It will now lie quietly and comfortably in your hand and you are ready to force feed it.

Using the thumb and index finger of the hand that is holding the bird, gently squeeze them together against each side of its bill, at the *base* of the bill, and the bird will open its mouth. When it does, you have your free hand to feed it. Make sure that the food is placed *in back of its tongue and well down its throat*, or it may spit the food out.

Withdraw the narrow wooden spoon from the bird's mouth and it will almost immediately swallow, unless it is badly frightened. If it doesn't swallow, hold it quietly until it does. Patience is a virtue in force feeding a bird. You must remember that this bright-eyed creature, whose wildly beating heart you feel pulsating in the palm of your hand, may be too terrified to swallow. *Be gentle, be patient, and be kind.* You will be surprised at how quickly the bird senses your good intentions and will respond to them.

7

Hummingbirds and How to
Attract Them

THE PROFESSOR of the summer nature study course at a
university in Massachusetts looked around his classroom.
He had finished his series of lectures about the life of the
honey bee and fifty students had closed their notebooks on
finished work. Freshly cut flowers, in vases on long laboratory tables, brightened the room.

Suddenly the professor raised his hand and pointed to the
window. A tiny bird hovered in the air over the sill, its
wings beating so rapidly that they were a blur on each side
of its body. In the astonished silence that fell over the
students, they heard the low hum of its wings as it poised
in mid-air, looking into the room. In the bright sunlight its
back glittered a resplendent green, and its throat feathers
flashed a deep, glowing red.

The bird hesitated only for a moment, then darted into
the room. With a sudden jerk, it stopped at a vase of
flowers and, while it whirred its wings rapidly to keep aloft,
it probed with its slender bill the hearts of each blossom.
When it had finished with these, it sped around a group of
students to another vase of flowers at the far end of the
laboratory, turned quickly, and darted to another. There it

searched several blossoms, gleaning from them such nectar and tiny insects as it could find, and in one swift movement flew out of the window and disappeared.

That happened in the summer of 1899. The uninvited but welcome bird-guest to that classroom of long ago was a male ruby-throated hummingbird, typical in its fearlessness of many of its kind. The beautiful little ruby-throat that comes to the flowers in our gardens will often come to feed from flowers held in the hands of people. Occasionally it flies fearlessly inside of houses, and has gently taken sugar from the lips of a man who knew the liking of hummingbirds for sweets.

The Fearlessness of Hummingbirds

The fearlessness of hummingbirds is all the more remarkable when we learn that some of their kind are the smallest birds in the world. There are no hummingbirds in Europe or anywhere in the Old World. They live only in North, Central, and South America; about three hundred and thirty different species, most of which are very small. A male ruby-throat, the hummingbird of the eastern United States, is about three and one-half inches long and weighs only three grams, or *one-tenth* of an ounce! Yet this Tom Thumb will attack crows, hawks, and eagles, which weigh from three hundred to sixteen hundred times its weight, if they fly anywhere near its chosen nesting territory.

I have never heard of a hummingbird attacking or chasing from its nest a human being, but one at a nest that I found gave me quite a start. The nest was on a limb of a beech tree in a woodland in western New York state. As I peeped into the nest to look at the two small white eggs that are no bigger than soup beans, the female suddenly appeared in front of my face, her wings droning like those of a large bee. (The female usually does all the work of building the nest, laying the eggs, incubating them, and raising the young ones.) As she hovered in the air a foot or two away from me, she appeared to be searching my face anxiously, as if to discover what my intentions toward her nest might be. About as big in diameter as a silver dollar, the nest was only about six feet above the ground, on a down-sloping branch of the tree. When I backed away from it a few feet, she settled down on her nest as calmly as if I did not exist and was brooding her eggs as I walked away.

The ruby-throat is one of at least nineteen kinds of hummingbirds from tropical America that spend some part of their lives in the United States. It is the only hummingbird that nests in our country east of the Mississippi River, and it nests both east and west of the Mississippi over a great area.

On a map of the United States, run your finger down the Atlantic coast from Ontario, Canada, south to Florida. Then trace a course from Florida west to Texas, then north through the Plains States to the Dakotas and Saskatchewan. Inside that area you have outlined, if you know the right places to look, you may find many nests of the ruby-throated hummingbird during its summer breeding season. After it has raised its family, it moves southward. Some ruby-throats winter in Florida and Louisiana, but most of them fly across five hundred miles of water in the Gulf of Mexico each fall to winter in Mexico and Central America.

Like other hummingbirds, the ruby-throat is especially pugnacious toward both its own kind and other birds during its nesting period. At this time it can usually intimidate most other birds, but not all of them. One spring morning near Hagerstown, Maryland, I saw a ruby-throat dart into the upper branches of a wild cherry tree. There it hovered threateningly in the face of a Blackburnian warbler, a bird with a beautiful, orange colored throat. The little warbler, scarcely larger than the ruby-throat itself, did not fly away from the threat of that sharp, slender bill pointed close to its face. Instead it lowered its head like a little fighting cock. Then it ruffled out its feathers aggressively, and followed with its own little bill every shifting movement of its tormentor. The hummingbird finally zipped away; the warbler lowered its feathers and went about its business of searching the leaves of the tree for small insects.

How Fast Can a Hummingbird Fly?

Both the tremendous flying speed of the hummingbirds and their superb maneuverability in flight give them an aerial advantage over many other birds. The little body of a ruby-throated hummingbird without its feathers is no larger than the end joint of one of your fingers, but the breast muscles that move the wings are enormous in proportion to the bird's size.

In 1934 a man driving an automobile along a highway leading out of Washington, D.C., saw a hummingbird flying alongside his car and moving in the same direction. He increased his speed to fifty miles an hour and the hummingbird stayed opposite him, as though it were challenging him to a race. Suddenly the bird put on a burst of speed and pulled steadily ahead of his car. As closely as the driver could gauge it, the bird appeared to be flying between fifty-five and sixty miles an hour. Another man living in Washington measured the speed of a ruby-throated hummingbird over a short flight of 53 feet in his yard. The bird traveled it in three-fifths of a second! This is a flying speed of about sixty miles an hour, which is far in excess of that of most songbirds and equals the cruising speed of some of the swiftest hawks.* Apparently the air speed and small size of hummingbirds make them safe from attacks by most birds of prey.

Flower Colors That Attract Hummingbirds

If you like flowers and have a garden, you should find it easy to attract hummingbirds. Red, orange, and other bright-colored flowers, and especially funnel- or tube-shaped flowers, usually lure hummingbirds.

The little ruby-throated hummingbird of our eastern states is so enamored of red that he has been known to hover in front of a man wearing a red necktie, over the head of a woman who wore a red ribbon in her hair, and has even inspected the red, sun-burned noses of people!

---

* For additional and more precise measurements of the speed of hummingbird flight see *The Audubon Society Encyclopedia of North American Birds* (Alfred A. Knopf, New York, N.Y., p. 541) by John K. Terres.

A bird scientist who studied the flower color preferences of hummingbirds discovered that it is the *brilliance* of the colors of flowers that attracts them—they prefer intense colors to pale ones. Red, being the color complement of green, is the most conspicuous color that a flower can show. Orange-colored flowers, although not so brilliant as red ones, are more showy in deeply shaded swamps and woods where hummingbirds are quick to find them.

Green flowers are inconspicuous among green leaves, but in certain contrasting desert backgrounds and on the prairies during the dry season green flowers stand out. As far as I know, there are no green flowers in the eastern United States that attract hummingbirds. In the West the large green flowers of a tobacco plant, *Nicotiana paniculata*, attract them.

Bush-

Hummingbirds also visit certain tubular-shaped flowers of blue, purple, and, of course, certain white ones that offer them nectar, small insects, and tiny spiders to feed on.

Near Cape May, New Jersey, trumpet vines, or trumpet creepers, grow wild over the hedgerows of the farms in that area. This vigorous-growing vine, which botanists and nurserymen call, *Campsis radicans*, has a powerful attraction for hummingbirds when the plants are in bloom. Almost any summer day we can see half a dozen ruby-throated hummingbirds at one time by just sitting quietly near a flowering trumpet creeper. Sometimes we see clashes between hummingbirds when two or three of them try to probe the same orange-red flower at the same time. With angry squeaks and buzzing "z-z-z-z-z-z-z-t-t-t-t!" notes, they dart about with amazing swiftness. Usually they chase each other so rapidly that the birds to us are just a streak as they zip in and out of the hedgerow trees and shrubs.

Flo-
Attr
Hun
in the

Trumpet Vin

In our Long Island garden, hummingbirds that arrive early in spring, first visit the scarlet flowers of our Japan flowering quince. They also like the orange and red flowers of our columbines and the brilliant red, early-blooming azaleas. As the season progresses they come to our tatarian

bush-honeysuckle (which has small, yellowish-white flowers), to our morning glories, early larkspurs, weigela
bushes, nasturtiums, Japanese honeysuckle vine, tiger lilies, bee balm *(Monarda)*, and scarlet sage.

You will also attract hummingbirds if you plant gladioluses, cannas, petunias, hollyhocks, geraniums, lilies, coral
bells *(Heuchera)*, cardinal climbers, scabiosa, and cleome,
or spider flower. All of these are favorite hummingbird
flowers. You can buy the seeds of them at nurseries, and
sow them yourself, or you may wish to buy the plants and
set them out in your garden.

When planting your flower bed, put the plants that will
grow tallest in the back, the medium-height flowers in the
middle rows, those that will be shortest in the front of the
bed. Try also to plant each kind of flower in clusters, or
solid groups. This will make your flower bed more showy
and more effective when the plants are in bloom.

Hummingbirds also like to visit the red, trumpet-shaped
flowers of the coral, or trumpet, honeysuckle, *Lonicera
sempervirens*. This is an attractive vine that grows wild
from Florida west to Texas, north to the New England
states, and west to Iowa and Nebraska. Hummers like the
purple flowers of buddleia, or butterfly bush, the pink and
white flowers of horse chestnut, or buckeye, trees, and the
yellow flowers of *Caragana arborescens*, commonly known
as Siberian pea-tree. A more extensive list of plants that
attract hummingbirds is given in the appendix.

Honeysuckle

*The Mystery
of the
Night-Flying
"Humming-
bird"*

I remember, as clearly as though I had seen it yesterday,
the honeysuckle vine that covered the east side of the porch
of my boyhood home in the country. Hummingbirds often
came there to sip nectar from the white honeysuckle flowers in the daytime, but at dusk another creature came that
for a long while puzzled me. On summer evenings, just
before the moon came up, I sat on our front steps waiting
for the whippoorwills to call, and watching for the mysterious stranger. While I sat there, I breathed in the sweet
fragrance of the honeysuckle and listened to the night
voices of crickets and katydids.

Suddenly—silently—the stranger came. In the pale light of the rising moon a tiny creature, whose wings moved so swiftly that they were a blur, hung before a white honeysuckle flower. Hovering, backing up, moving rapidly from one blossom to another, it probed each flower with what seemed, in the dim dusk, to be its long, slender beak. I had always seen hummingbirds flying about in the daytime. Could this be a hummingbird that flew at night?

One evening I waited by the side of the honeysuckle vine until the mysterious dusk-flyer came close. In one swift motion, I swung my cap and swept it out of the air. I trembled excitedly, for I was sure that I had captured some strange and unknown creature that I had never seen before. Carefully I opened my cap until I could pick it up in my fingers. I remember my amazement to this day at what I saw, for I had caught a moth! So strikingly did it resemble a hummingbird that if I hadn't caught it, I might have gone on believing that hummingbirds flew in the dark.

Morning Glory

Later a local naturalist told me that I had caught a hummingbird moth, that it was one of many of its kind, some of which fly about by day, others by night. What I had thought was its beak was its long, harmless tongue, with which it sips nectar. My mystery had been solved and I had held in my hands the only creature that you or I might reasonably mistake for a hummingbird.

If you live in the southeastern United States, you will find that ruby-throated hummingbirds will visit the pink, fragrant flowers of your mimosa, or silktree. Botanists and nurserymen call this tropical plant, *Albizzia julibrissin*.[1] It grows thirty or forty feet tall, and is hardy as far north as Washington, D.C. Hardier varieties of it can survive the winters north to Pennsylvania and New York, and in some of the New England states.

Some Hummingbird Flowers of the South

[1] The scientific names and their spellings follow *Hortus Second*, except the beginning letter of the specific name, which in this book *always* begins with a small letter. This is a modern practice of some horticulturists to avoid excessive capitalizing and to standardize names.

The red buckeye, *Aesculus pavia*, a small tree up to twenty feet tall, is another southern plant whose dark red or purplish flowers lure hummingbirds. It grows from Virginia south to Florida and Louisiana. The trumpet creeper, *Campsis radicans*, so much favored by hummingbirds in the northeastern states, grows south to Florida and Texas.

In southern Florida, the scarlet bush, *Hamelia erecta*, and the royal poinciana, or flame tree, *Delonix regia*, are noted especially for their attractiveness to hummingbirds. Others —the scarlet rose mallow, *Hibiscus coccineus*, that grows wild in the swamps of Georgia and Florida, the purple cestrum, *Cestrum purpureum*, common lantana, *Lantana camara*, fuchsias, cannas, butterfly bushes, and jasmines— are excellent "hummingbird plants."

*A
Hummingbird
Experiment*

In 1889, Caroline G. Soule of Brookline, Massachusetts, developed an idea for feeding hummingbirds that may have been the first experiment of its kind ever made. Her idea was so good and so practical that people who attract hummingbirds to their gardens have used the same method to this day.

For a week she had watched a ruby-throated hummingbird visit the red flowers of the trumpet creeper vine that grew luxuriantly over a dead tree in her back yard. Sometimes when nectar in the flowers may have been low, the hummingbird became so eager for the sweets that, instead of thrusting its head and slender bill *inside* the flower tube, it slashed open the petals at their bases and drank nectar while it hovered outside the flower.

How could the woman help the bird? Then it occurred to her: *Why not offer it a supplemental supply of liquid sweets?* But how could she offer food to the bird so that it would accept it?

One day she sketched a trumpet creeper flower on a piece of stiff paper that she had fashioned into the tubular shape of one of these flowers. Next, she painted the outside of the paper a brilliant orange-red to match the color of the living flowers. Inside the paper flower she set a small, open-mouthed vial and then wired her artificial flower in a natural position among a cluster of trumpet creeper flowers. Using a mixture of about one part of sugar to two of water, she filled the little bottle within the paper flower and stepped back a few yards to watch.

Soon a hummingbird came to the trumpet creeper. Deliberately it hovered before one flower cluster after another until it had circled almost completely about the vine. With its next move, if it followed its circling course, it would arrive before the cluster of flowers within which the woman had wired the artificial flower.

Would the hummer fail to be attracted by the paper flower with its sugar water, and pass it by, or would it stop to drink? Its humming wings had carried the little bird before the artificial flower. It hung before it in mid-air, then unhesitatingly dipped its bill into the sugar water. Again and again it drank, left the sugar water, and then returned, as if it could not quite believe that it had discovered such a rich food supply. Thereafter it preferred the sugar-water mixture to the nectar in the living flowers, and the woman had to fill the vial twice a day to keep the bird supplied.

One day the woman took the artificial flower with its sugar-filled vial off the trumpet creeper and stood nearby, holding it in her hand. When the hummingbird came to the vine it suddenly veered away and came fearlessly to the paper flower in her hand. There it hovered and drank its fill from the little bottle!

In that gesture of confidence the hummingbird assured the woman that her experiment had been an undreamed of, and probably a heretofore unheard of, success.

For thirty-five years a man and his wife had attracted birds to their estate in New Hampshire. They had operated feeding stations, put up birdhouses, and kept their birdbaths filled with fresh, clean water. They had planted on their property trees, shrubs, and vines that bore fruits which birds like and that offered them protective cover and nesting places. By their devotion to attracting birds and

What to Do When Flowers Won't Attract Hummingbirds

their common-sense methods of doing so, this New Hampshire couple had lured to their property almost every kind of bird that migrated through or nested in their region. They had attracted all of the locally common summer birds, *except one*.

Even though they had planted many kinds of flowers, they had been unable to attract hummingbirds to their garden.

In the summer of 1928, the man's wife read an article by a woman in Maine who had attracted hummingbirds to small bottles about 2 inches long, covered with bright-colored ribbons. The bottles, or vials, she had filled with sugar water as a food offering to the hummingbirds. The New Hampshire woman and her husband immediately followed this woman's example. The results were remarkable.

Eight years later, in 1936, a visiting bird scientist stood on the sunny veranda of this New Hampshire home. While he watched, twenty hummingbirds fed at one time from various small bottles filled with sugar and water that were fastened to the veranda railing and to twigs of shrubbery planted nearby. Within an hour he counted fifty hummingbird guests that came to the feeders.

What to Feed Hummingbirds

At first the New Hampshire couple had offered the hummingbirds a mixture of strained honey and water, but this fermented easily and became unpalatable. (Later, Dr. Augusto Ruschi, a Brazilian expert on hummingbirds, both captive and wild, discovered that honey, when fermented, produces a fungus that affects the tongues of hummingbirds and eventually kills them. He does not recommend honey as a food for hummingbirds, even if the honey has been centrifuged, because as soon as the bottle is opened it can become contaminated and immediately infect the food solution and hummingbird food containers.) The New Hampshire couple turned to sugar water as an offering to their hummingbirds; and even song sparrows, purple finches, orioles, chickadees, nuthatches, and downy and hairy woodpeckers came to drink from the vials. However, sugar water must not be offered hummingbirds in too rich a mixture as it may cause enlargement of the liver with harmful effects. Dr. Ruschi recommends sugar water as the only basic food to feed hummingbirds in the garden and he recommends 25 *grams of cane sugar dissolved in 200 grams of water, or about 1 part sugar to 8 of water.*

In the beginning the woman had covered the outside of the glass vials with differently colored ribbons, until she noticed that the hummingbirds emptied those vials first that were wrapped in *red*. After that she used red ribbon.

In 1936 she had thirty vials fastened at intervals all along the veranda. Some of them she had attached to twigs which she had clipped from shrubs. She had fastened these twigs with their attached vials to window frames and to the porch railing. Other vials she suspended on fine wires hung from an overhanging trellis. Each day the hummingbird and other songbirds that came to drink the syrup emptied the vials three or four times. Between May 9 of that year and September 14—about four months—the birds ate sixty-five pounds of sugar.

How Much Will Hummingbirds Eat?

A woman in Pennsylvania, who attracted hummingbirds to sugar water, used two-ounce bottles[2] with large mouths and no necks which she covered with red satin. She wired each vial at a 45-degree angle to the tops of 36-inch stakes, which she "planted" upright in her flower beds. Some of the vials she attached to shorter stakes, which she put in flower pots on a back yard terrace.

Hummingbirds came to the eight bottles of sugar water regularly and emptied them several times a day. From May 1 to about August 1 they ate ten pounds of sugar.

In a fascinating feeding experiment in Iowa, a woman bird scientist fed wild ruby-throated hummingbirds in her back yard for seven consecutive summers. She discovered

[2] Hummingbird feeders—vials and other glass containers of various sizes—are sold by dealers in bird-attracting equipment. See list of dealers in the appendix.

that each bird ate a level teaspoonful of sugar each day. This is about one and a half times the average weight of each.

If a man weighing two hundred pounds ate sugar at the same rate, he would eat three hundred pounds of sugar each day!

The Rivoli's hummingbird, about 5 to 5½ inches long, is generally considered the largest hummingbird in North America. It does not come into the United States very far north of Mexico. As far as I know, it nests only in Arizona and New Mexico, high in the mountains near the Mexican border.

The ruby-throated hummingbird of the eastern states is small, but the calliope hummingbird of the West, which is only about 2¾ inches long, is the smallest hummingbird in our country. If you live anywhere within that region from southern California north to Oregon and Washington, eastward to Montana, Wyoming, and Utah, and south to Baja (Lower) California, you may find this tiny bird nesting, or possibly migrating through your area in the spring. You are not likely to see it in the fall because it migrates southward through the Rocky Mountains region, instead of moving along the Pacific Coast slope, where it migrated northward in spring.

Rivoli's

The calliope likes to feed at the flowers of paint brush (*Castilleja*),[3] columbine, wild rose, orange tree, wild gooseberry, and hawthorn.

Ruby-Throated

Besides the calliope and the ruby-throated hummingbird of the East, six other hummingbirds—the rufous, black-chinned, broad-tailed, Allen's, Anna's, and Costa's—push

[3] The Indian paint brushes, or painted cups, are parasitic on the roots of other plants and depend upon them in part for their lives. That is why people, who have tried to transplant paint brushes to their gardens, have been unable to keep these plants living. If you dig up paint brush in a clump of sod, with some of its associated plants, you may be able to keep it alive in your garden for a little while, but it is far better to let paint brushes grow where nature has planted them. There hummingbirds will have the use of them, and these flowers will continue to brighten the countryside.

northward well into the United States in spring. The rufous breeds the farthest north—to Alaska—and is the most widely distributed and probably the most abundant hummingbird in the West.

The broad-tailed, a hummingbird that usually nests in the mountains, is *the* hummingbird of the Rocky Mountain region. It nests in Montana, Idaho, Wyoming, Utah, Colorado, New Mexico, and southwestern Texas, and westward to Arizona, Nevada, and eastern California.

Calliope

The broad-tailed follows along with the blooming period of its favorite plants, moving gradually up the mountain slopes to its nesting areas in spring, and down them in fall on the way to its winter home in Guatemala in Central America. In the San Francisco Mountains of Arizona its principal food plant is the beautiful scarlet trumpet flower, *Penstemon barbatus torreyi*. After this flower finishes blooming, the broad-tailed visits the flowering beds of a blue larkspur, *Delphinium scopulorum*. This wildflower grows high in the mountains, from southern California to Alaska. The broad-tailed is also attracted to different kinds of sage (or salvia), scarlet paint brush (*Castilleja parviflora*), nasturtiums, lupines, penstemons, and ocotillo, which botanists call *Fouquieria splendens*, a spiny desert shrub with scarlet flowers. Gilia, agave, and trumpet honeysuckle are others of its favorite flowering plants.

Broad-Tailed

I remember the instinctive reaction of a little girl the first time that I showed her a hummingbird. The tiny creature, on droning wings, hovered before a flaming-red canna flower. The child turned to me, her eyes wide with mixed wonder and fear. "But it's so *little!*" she whispered. "How does it live?"

That is the way I feel about a hummingbird every time that I see one. To me, one of the marvels of this natural world is that a creature so small, and seemingly so fragile, can stay alive from day to day. Hummingbirds have great flying speed, sufficient to make them safe from most birds or other animals that might eat them—if they could catch them. But there are other threats to their lives. Some of

Strange
Hummingbird
Accidents

them are so subtle, or innocent-appearing, that we wouldn't think of them unless we had our attention called to them.

Who would believe that a *flower* could be a trap for a hummingbird? One June day a man wandering along the edge of a field in Connecticut saw the purple blossom of a pasture thistle waving about on its tall stalk. There was no wind blowing. What caused it to whip about so violently? Walking closer he saw a hummingbird beating its wings furiously to free itself from the flower. Its breast feathers were entangled in the prickly, pointed bracts that grow at the base of the flower, and all its efforts to fly away were useless. The man carefully removed the bird from the flower bract, and it flew away unharmed.

Caught by a Praying Mantis

At Philadelphia in September, 1948, a woman walking in her garden saw a praying mantis, about three inches long, sitting on an orange-colored zinnia flower. This lanky, green, goggle-eyed insect is useful to mankind. It has an enormous appetite for flies, beetles, and other insects, and it will sit on plants or flower heads for hours, waiting for them to come near. Without moving it sits with its long, spiked forelegs bent, like a man resting his elbows on a table. When a fly, beetle, or grasshopper comes within reach, the mantis darts its armed forelegs out in a lightning-like stroke and snaps them shut on its victim. Then it eats the insect at its leisure.

While the woman watched, a ruby-throated humming-bird flew to the zinnia flower where the praying mantis waited. Swiftly and surely the strong forelegs of the mantis shot out and gripped the hummingbird. Without hesitating, the woman seized the mantis, which will not bite and is harmless to human beings. Firmly she forced the insect and the bird apart. A few moments later the hummingbird died, probably from shock.

A Dragonfly and a Hummingbird

In Ontario a man and his mother were walking through a woodland when they heard a peculiar rattling noise among the dead leaves on the ground. When they walked to the source of the sound, they found a hummingbird lying on the ground with a large dragonfly clinging to its back. The dragonfly had seized the little bird by the neck and had pinned it to the ground. The man chased the dragonfly, picked up the dazed bird, and held it quietly in his hand. In a few minutes the hummingbird recovered and flew away.

Hummingbirds and Windows

In Massachusetts a hummingbird dashed against the picture window of a home and broke its neck. The bird had apparently seen the reflected image of trees and grass in the large window. This had created the illusion that they were part of the yard and it had flown into the glass at great speed.[4] Another tried to fly through two windows that were opposite each other in a room. Apparently the bird thought that it could fly through them to the lawn and trees on the other side of the house. The windows were closed and the bird was killed when it struck the glass.

Large Fish and Frogs

One fall day a family in Santa Barbara, California, were seated by a lotus pool in their yard. A hummingbird flew to the pool and hovered momentarily a few inches above the water. Perhaps an insect struggling on the surface may have aroused the bird's curiosity. Whatever the cause, the slight distraction that held it over the pool brought the bird's life to a quick end. With a loud splash a bass broke through the surface of the water, flashed into the air, and swallowed the hummer. Large frogs in ponds and along stream banks also catch hummingbirds, perhaps when hummingbirds hover too near them in the same way.

The Spider Web Death Trap

One of the most ironic death traps for hummingbirds is built by the spider—a creature which unknowingly provides many hummingbirds with one of their most important nesting materials.

I once watched a ruby-throated hummingbird start to build her nest. First she built a foundation for it of cotton-like down that she gathered from fern stems and oak

[4] See pages 198–199 for a way to prevent birds from flying into windows.

leaves. Using lichens, bits of moss, and small pieces of bark, which she took from the trunks of trees, she built up the sides of the nest. I did not count the number of trips she made to bring strands of spider webs to her nest, but she used them frequently to glue her delicate materials together. It is risky for the little hummers to gather spider silk from the strong webs of the larger spiders because they sometimes get caught.

To gather spider silk from one of these big, vertically-built, wheel-shaped webs, a hummingbird must fly to within a few inches of it. There, suspended on its rapidly-whirring wings, it faces the web and plucks strands of it loose with its bill. This brings the bird dangerously close to the coarse, sticky web. One slight error in the bird's judgment —a swing too near—and those whirring wings are enmeshed, and the bird is helpless.

Ruby-throated hummingbirds in the East, and Costa's and Anna's hummingbirds in California, caught in spiders' webs, have died of exhaustion and starvation before they were discovered. People have found others in webs while the birds were still alive, and have released them unharmed. There must be many other hummingbirds caught in webs each year that we never hear about.

These are tragedies that our sympathy for hummingbirds makes us want to prevent. Excepting the window glass problem, we can do little about them. We must remember that most of these "accidents" arise from natural hazards that are a part of the hummingbird's world. They serve to skim off only a part of the hummingbird population, and are Nature's way of preventing the plight of "The Old Woman in the Shoe," who, you will remember, "had so many children that she didn't know what to do."

How Fate May Direct Our Interest Toward Birds

It is strange how destiny sometimes directs our interest toward birds, and how that interest may benefit not only ourselves, but the birds too. A number of years ago I heard of a businessman who was forced to move to Arizona because of ill health. He was not a bird scientist; but, when he settled in Phoenix, he almost immediately became interested in the black-chinned hummingbird [5] which nests in and around that city. For four years he studied these birds which are closely related to the ruby-throated hummingbird. His discoveries about their nesting and feeding behavior and social habits are interesting, and he has also given us specific information about attracting black-chinned hummingbirds to gardens.

For example, he discovered that the black-chinned, like the rufous, calliope, Costa's, and broad-tailed hummingbirds, which migrate long distances into the United States, seem to time their arrival with the blooming of certain plants. In spring, when the black-chins arrive in Phoenix after spending their winters in Mexico, some flowers at which they feed are already in bloom. One of these, the American aloe, or century plant, *Agave americana*, has white flowers that bloom on a tall stalk, and give off a scent like that of butterscotch caramel. These are an excellent source of nectar for several kinds of hummingbirds. Another, the tree tobacco, *Nicotiana glauca*, which grows up to twenty feet tall, is a native of South America. It has been naturalized in Texas, California, and in other states and hummingbirds like to visit its yellow, tubular-shaped flowers for their rich supply of nectar.

Others that the black-chins favor are the red, orange, or yellow flowers of lantana, and the blossoms of orange trees, of other citrus trees, and of the shrimp plant, *Beloperone guttata*. The black-chins also like the flowers of the paloverde, or littleleaf horse bean, *Cercidium microphyllum*, ocotillo, yuccas, morning glories, gladioluses, nasturtiums, hollyhocks, jasmines, and butterfly bushes (*Buddleia*.)

During his first summer in Phoenix, only one black-chinned hummingbird came to the man's yard to feed at the few canna flowers that a former tenant had planted.

How to Attract Black-Chinned Hummingbirds

[5] The black-chinned, which is about 3¾ inches long, breeds in California, Oregon, Washington, British Columbia, Canada, Idaho, Utah, Colorado, Arizona, New Mexico, and Texas, and south into northern Mexico. It is most abundant in southern California, southern Utah, Arizona, and parts of New Mexico.

The man wanted to attract more of them in order to study these birds. The following spring he added beds of nasturtiums and larkspurs to the cannas. A female, black-chinned hummingbird then came to his yard and nested. He also put up hummingbird feeders—small bottles filled with honey and sugar water that he attached to shrubbery or to sticks "planted" among the flower beds. Within a short time, five female black-chinned hummers came regularly to feed from them each day. By late summer at least eight others and a pair of southward migrating rufous hummingbirds were visiting his syrup and sugar-water feeding stations.

In the spring of the following year, two female black-chins nested in his yard, and six fed regularly from the feeders. Others, which had not discovered the honey and the sugar-water mixture, visited the flowers in his yard each day.

Hummingbirds are quick to defend their nesting territories against the intrusion of other birds. With so many hummingbirds coming to a yard where two of them were already nesting in bushes on opposite sides of the house, tension soon built up. It was to touch off some small explosions of hummingbird tempers.

The Right of "Private" Domain

That second spring, the first of the female black-chinned hummingbirds to build a nest in the yard had driven off all hummers except a handsome male that she had accepted as her mate. Daily the man watched her grow more aggressive as her instincts to defend her nesting territory grew with her urge to build her nest and lay eggs. She drank frequently of honey or sugared water and she guarded the feeders from other birds by watching over them from her perch on the twig of an ash tree in the front yard. From this point she could see all the feeders and chase away most birds, even before they got to the feeders.

To the man, it must have been obvious that the little bird considered these feeders and the yard about them to be hers! Any other bird that came near trespassed upon her private property! Her persistence in guarding the feeders had been so effective that the man determined to outwit her. He *did* want other hummingbirds to enjoy his hospitality, too.

Outwitting a Hummingbird

One morning he moved one feeder to the rear of the house, and another to the front of the house. He did not move the third one, which remained alongside the house near a row of oleander bushes. The aggressive little hummer could now see only the front yard feeder from her perch. And while she drank syrup from any one feeder, she could not see a bird drinking from either one of the others.

It seemed like a peaceful settlement, a division of the hummingbird feeders in which all birds could share. The trick worked—for a few days. Then the little female hummingbird, whose intelligence the man had underestimated, caught on.

Instead of keeping her guard post on a twig of a tree in the front yard, she suddenly shifted to a eucalyptus tree from which she could watch both the feeder at the rear of the house and the one in the sideyard! By shifting between the tree perches, she could now watch all three feeders and continue her dominance over the birds in the yard.

The Queen's Defeat

Day by day, the little female grew more domineering over her chosen territory. Now she chased away not only hummingbirds but house sparrows, which previously she had ignored.

Eventually, the reign of all tyrants, even small, harmless ones like hummingbirds, must end, for nowhere is the dominance of one creature over another more likely to shift than in the world of birds.

One day a strange female black-chinned hummingbird arrived in the yard. She had visited the flower beds, and flew to one of the hummingbird feeders. The little female, from her perch in the eucalyptus tree, saw the stranger for the first time. Like a tiny thunderbolt she hurled herself downward at the bird in a blazingly swift dive.

The newcomer, hovering at the feeder, seemed in danger

of being knocked out of the air by that fiery assault. At the last moment, she shifted to one side and the attacking female buzzed by, stabbing at the air. Again and again the little female dived at the stranger. Each time the newcomer changed her position ever so slightly, avoiding the attacks with a calmness that must have been maddening to the bird so determined to drive her away. After each unsuccessful dive the little female returned to her perch in the eucalyptus tree. There she fluffed out her feathers and chattered angrily at the stranger, but the unwelcome visitor continued to feed about the yard and to ignore her.

At last the female that had dominated the yard so successfully had met more than her match. As the stranger moved confidently about the yard from flower to flower, and from feeder to feeder, she showed that she intended to stay. Gradually, the little female's attacks upon her grew less and less frequent, until they ceased altogether.

The New "Yard Boss"   The little female now had little time to guard her territory. She had built her nest in one of the oleander bushes in the yard, had laid her eggs, and was busy incubating them. Her aggressive attacks on other birds had almost ended, but another feathered volcano had erupted in her place. The stranger, coming into her own breeding cycle, became another tyrant and drove away all other hummingbirds, just as the little female had. Between these two, however, there now seemed to be peace, for the man never saw any further skirmishes between them.

The newcomer mated with a male black-chinned hummingbird that came to the yard each day. She built her nest in a bush in a corner of the yard farthest from where the little female had hatched her family. Each evening at dusk, the man saw the newcomer's mate come to the bush where she nested. There he roosted on a twig not far from where she sat brooding her eggs.

The individual lives of birds, to those of us who study them, are filled with many vague, half-formed pictures that we are not always able to fill in. Even while we watch over them, things happen to birds for which we can give no accounting—no logical explanation. One day the new-comer disappeared and she never returned. Only her nest and its two small, white eggs remained, to remind the man of the swiftly changing fortunes of creatures that must take their chances in the natural world.

The little female, as far as the man knew, had a more fortunate summer. She continued to return to the feeders. With her now came two young hummers which, by her tolerance of them, the man took to be the youngsters she had raised in the oleander that spring.

Avoiding Ants

To keep ants out of hummingbird feeders, suspend the vials by thin wire from the top of a window frame or from the underside of the eaves of the porch or the house, in front of a window where you can observe them.

John V. Dennis, in his book *The Complete Guide to Bird Feeding* (Knopf, 1976), notes that an effective way of keeping ants from crawling along wires or other supports for hummingbird feeders is to coat the wires with salad oil; he also coats the feeders to keep bees and wasps from set-tling on them.

A friend at Chapel Hill, North Carolina, when much troubled by bees and wasps at her hummingbird feeders, moved her wire-suspended feeders out of the sun and hung them in the shade. Then, when insects gathered at the feed-ers, she turned on her vertically rotating lawn sprinkler, positioned so that the water spray, with each rotation, struck her hummingbird feeders. The water dispelled bees and wasps and helped wash away the sticky fluid adhering to the outside of the feeders. The spray did not bother the hummingbirds which not only continued to come to the feeders but seemed to enjoy bathing in the fine water spray by flying back and forth through it.

In California, Emerson Stoner reported that when he watered his garden a female Anna's hummingbird often darted through the stream of the hose. One day, she dis-covered that she could ride this solid stream of water. She alighted on it crosswise, as she would alight on a twig, and allowed herself to be carried forward. She kept repeating her newly learned trick in what seemed to Stoner a delightful spirit of play.

Maintenance of Hummingbird Feeders

At our Little Neck garden, we used simple vials to hold our sugar water and were very particular to keep them clean. Every day or two, we emptied any sugar water solution left in the vials, washed each inside and out with warm water and a small stiff brush, then refilled them with a fresh supply of sugar water.

More about Sugar Water

If you are just beginning to attract hummingbirds, it is best to use the rich solution of one part of sugar to two parts of water because hummingbirds prefer the sweeter mixtures. After mixing the sugar and water, boil it for several minutes. This will help to slow fermentation after the syrup is put outside in the feeder. After filling the feeders, the extra quantity may be safely stored in your refrigerator.

Once the hummingbirds are coming to your feeders, you can dilute the solution to one part sugar to four parts water and eventually to the one part sugar to eight parts water recommended by Dr. Ruschi to protect hummingbirds against the possibility of getting enlarged livers from the richer solutions (see pages 120–121 for a discussion of this). Hummingbirds can detect small differences in the sugar water formulas, and you may discover as others have that they will not drink a solution with less sugar than one part to eight parts of water.

Other Birds That Like Sugar Water

Besides hummingbirds, some fifty or sixty other kinds of birds, such as orioles, catbirds, brown thrashers, mockingbirds, and the red-bellied woodpecker, are fond of sugar water. One year, while I was editing *Audubon Magazine*, Ruth Thomas of Morrilton, Arkansas, wrote an article for us in our bird-attracting column about attracting orchard orioles to sugar water. Orchard orioles are fond of flower nectar, which they get by sipping it from the hearts of blossoms in their winter home in the tropics.

Mrs. Thomas discovered that at least seven pairs of these

birds, which nested in her area, often visited the humming-bird feeding vials. In alighting on the resting perches of these feeders, they jolted them so severely that they often splashed half the sugar water out of the feeders. She solved this problem and got the orioles away from preempting the hummingbird feeders by dressing a small cold cream jar in a red ribbon frill, necessary only in the beginning, to give it a semblance to a flower. She wedged the cup securely into a wooden frame nailed to a corner post of her garden. The orioles immediately accepted the cup and in late June, when the young, fledged orioles also discovered it, she set up an additional one to take care of her extra orioles and other birds that now found the sugar water attractive. Each spring, the migratory orioles returned to her garden around April 12th. Mrs. Thomas had the cup on her corner post filled with sugar water, and the orioles flew straight to it.

8

Ornamental Plantings for Birds

PLANTING YOUR YARD to beautify it and to attract birds is a lot like building a house. You start by planting your biggest, sturdiest plants—the shade trees and evergreens—which are the foundations. Then you plant small flowering trees and shrubs, which are the walls, and you finish off with the fill-in plants—vines and ground-cover plants—which give your arrangement a finished look, like the roof and the paint job on your house.

Of course, you don't need to plant in this order—trees first, shrubs next, vines and cover plants last, but trees and many shrubs take at least several years of growth to make a showing. The sooner you plant them, the sooner they will be in flower and fruit to add to the beauty of your yard. Another big point in their favor—once your trees and shrubs are growing well, you won't need to give them the attention or maintenance you must give to your flowers and lawn.

How We Began

A number of years ago my wife and I were faced with the biggest gardening problem of our lives. We wanted to plant—in our Long Island back yard—trees, shrubs, and vines that we knew would especially attract birds. To do so, we would have to dig up and discard many shrubs that had already been planted there, which had little or no value to birds. We would also have to move others that we wanted to keep, to make room for the shrubs in our new planting plan. It was a big job, far bigger than planting a yard where nothing was growing, but we wanted robins, thrushes, catbirds, thrashers, song sparrows, and other birds that visited our feeding stations to remain in our garden and nest there.

I won't go into the details of what shrubs we already had in the yard, and what we moved, because it would only confuse you as it confused us in the beginning. We decided to close our eyes to what we had, and to draw a plan of what we wanted, just as if our yard didn't have a tree or a shrub in it. In this way we were starting fresh, like a youngster with a new notebook on his first day of school.

My wife wanted to plant immediately several flowering dogwood trees that have showy, white blossoms in spring, dark green leaves throughout the summer, and red leaves and red fruits in the fall. She couldn't have decided on a better small ornamental tree for a small yard, or a better one to attract birds. Almost a hundred different kinds of birds feed on the fruits of the various tree and shrub dogwoods that grow west to the prairies and beyond to the Pacific Coast. A few dogwood trees in our yard would attract lots of birds when the fruits were ripe in the fall. But we also wanted, besides dogwoods, other trees and shrubs that would provide birds with fruits or seeds in early and late summer, and throughout the winter.

Fortunately I knew from government research which plants attract birds most to their fruits, not only in our suburban New York city back yard but in gardens across the country to Oregon, south to California, and east to the prairies, Texas, Florida, and Georgia. But first, before we planted anything, we had to make a plan, to put down on an outline drawing of our yard the exact *kinds* of trees, shrubs, and vines we wanted, how *many* the size of our yard would permit, and *where* they should be planted to grow best and to look most pleasing to us. Looking back on that first plan, I think we got as much fun out of it as we did in making our plantings.

We discovered that there is only one way to make an orderly planting. To do so you must figure it out on paper, before you start to plant. First we measured our yard to find out how much room we had. We found it to be 60 feet wide, from neighbor to neighbor, and 140 feet deep, from the beginning of our front lawn to our back property-line fence.

After we had measured our yard, we next had to draw our property lines of a size on paper that would, proportionately, represent the actual size of our yard. To do this, we used a 12-inch ruler, and let each space between every one of the little marks on our ruler represent a foot (there are 16 of them to an inch on most rulers). Then we could lay out our 60×140 foot plot quite neatly within the boundaries of an ordinary sheet of typing paper.

When we had our outline of the yard drawn (see the accompanying map), we began to choose our trees, shrubs, and vines from the list of those (in the appendix) which are most favored by songbirds in the Northeast.

Starting Our Plan on Paper

For many years I have been interested in the food habits of songbirds, particularly the wild fruits that they like to eat. In the Adirondack Mountains of New York one winter day I saw a flock of big reddish pine grosbeaks eating the scarlet fruits of American mountain ash. At another time I remember fifty cedar waxwings that spent a cold stormy winter in the shelter of a grove of dark-green cedar trees in southern New Jersey. There every day I watched them eat the pale blue fruits of the cedar trees. I have no doubt that the birds stayed in the grove not only because of the warm shelter of these evergreen trees but for the rich supply of cedar berries which they lived upon all that winter.

What Fruits Do Birds Like?

In August and September in Central Park, New York city, I have seen migrating robins, catbirds, cedar waxwings, rose-breasted grosbeaks, and thrushes strip wild cherry trees of their glossy black fruits. Later, in October, catbirds, brown thrashers, robins, and thrushes eat the scarlet berries of Amur honeysuckle that the Parks Department has planted there. This is a tall ornamental shrub introduced into this country many years ago from Manchuria and Korea.

I have other records of native and foreign plants—elderberries, hollies, dogwoods, and viburnums—whose fruits I have seen songbirds eating during the past twenty years. But if I were to attract the most birds, I could not choose the plants for my own yard based upon these few observations. I needed scientific information—thousands of records of bird food habits—such as the Fish and Wildlife Service, formerly the U. S. Biological Survey, had been gathering in many parts of the United States for more than fifty years. These would truthfully show the seasonal foods of birds—not only the berries and fleshy summer fruits, but the dry, hard seeds of birches and pines and the acorns of oaks that songbirds eat. Knowing what they favored through each season, I would be sure of planting the trees, shrubs, and vines that would offer them a food supply the year around.

60'

140'

① Ⓐ Ⓐ ② ③ ④ Ⓑ

Ⓐ ⑤ ⑥ ⑥ ⑦ Ⓑ

Ⓐ ⑧ ⑨ ⑫

⑦ ⑩

BACKYARD LAWN

N

⑪ ⑮

Ⓐ

⑫ ⑬ ⑯ Ⓐ

⑫ ⑰ ⑱

⑭ ⑬ ⑱ ⑲

⑱ ⑲

⑳

MAP SYMBOLS

▢▢▢▢▢▢▢
Flagstone walk

Brick terrace

▭▭▭▭▭▭
Stone wall

↓ ↓ ↓
Ground slopes
in this direction

Break in slope

Cement steps

Cement walk

Arbor

㉑ ㉑

Ⓓ ㉑ **ANNUAL & PERENNIAL FLOWER BED** ㉒ ㉒ **ANNUALS AND PERENNIALS** ⑥

⑤ ㉔ ㉔

㉑ ㉓ **TERRACE**

㉑ Ⓔ **TABLE** Ⓕ

㉑

㉕ **CEMENT WALK**

HOUSE

㉖

SIDEYARD LAWN

DRIVEWAY

㉖

FRONT LAWN

⑤

㉗

↓ ↓ ↓ ↓ ↓

GRASS **GRASS**

Ⓒ

THE AUTHOR'S PLANTING PLAN

KEY LETTER OR NUMBER ON MAP	HOW MANY PLANTED	COMMON NAME	FOOD [a] RATING	SCIENTIFIC NAME	TYPE [b] OF PLANT	HEIGHT WHEN MATURE (feet)
A	6	Red cedar	7	*Juniperus virginiana*	Large tree	90'

REMARKS

One of the best of all evergreens for songbirds because it provides food, shelter, and nesting cover. Also a fine ornamental. It is susceptible to rusts, which it can transmit to apples, hawthorns, mountain ashes, juneberries, and quinces, but these can be controlled on red cedar by spraying it early in May with a 1% solution of Fermate or Elgetol. It is best not to plant red cedars near apple orchards.

B	2	Eastern white pine	1	*Pinus strobus*	Large tree	100' +

REMARKS

One of the most beautiful of all pines, particularly useful as a background tree for flowering trees and shrubs. A favored nesting tree of robins, blue jays, and mourning doves. Susceptible to blister rust which is transmitted to white pine from currants and gooseberries. Blister rust can be controlled on individual trees, but they will be reinfected if currants and gooseberries are growing nearby.

C	1	White oak	5	*Quercus alba*	Large tree	90'

REMARKS

Slow-growing, but one of the longest-lived, sturdiest, and most picturesque of all oaks. It bears a crop of acorns each year, although the size of the crop may vary considerably. The black oak group, which includes the rapid-growing northern red oak, scarlet oak, pin oak, and others, requires two years to mature its acorns, instead of one year.

[a] The songbird food rating here applies to the Northeast and to each *group* of plants, not alone to the plant listed. For example, the rating of 1 (most important food tree or food shrub) opposite eastern white pine, is for the pines as a whole, and so the number 1 appears opposite red pine, as well as white pine. The dogwoods of which there are about 17 species in the United States, mostly shrubs, are ranked the fourth most important woody plant (tree, shrub, or vine) to songbirds in the Northeast. Therefore the rating 4 will appear opposite both flowering dogwood and Japanese dogwood, even though flowering dogwood fruits are probably more eaten by birds than those of Japanese dogwood.

[b] This is a classification of whether the plant is a large tree, small tree, tall shrub, medium shrub, low shrub, or vine. Large trees are here classified as those that when full-grown, are 50 feet tall or more. Small trees are here classified as those that usually have a single trunk and grow from 15 feet to 50 feet high; tall shrubs are those that have two or more main stems and grow between 10 and 15 feet high; medium shrubs are those

KEY LETTER OR NUMBER ON MAP	HOW MANY PLANTED	COMMON NAME	FOOD[a] RATING	SCIENTIFIC NAME	TYPE[b] OF PLANT	HEIGHT WHEN MATURE (*feet*)
D	1	Red pine	1	*Pinus resinosa*	Large tree	75'

REMARKS
Handsome, rapid-growing, generally resistant to diseases, this hardy pine is adaptable to most of the Northeast region. There is a dwarf, rounded form, called variety *globosa*, that was discovered in New Hampshire about the year 1910.

E	1	American, or white, elm	16	*Ulmus americana*	Large tree	120'

REMARKS
One of the handsomest of all American trees. Orioles nest in its end branches, finches and grosbeaks eat its buds and seeds. Unfortunately, it is susceptible to both the deadly Dutch elm disease and phloem necrosis for which there is, at present, no cure.

F	1	Box elder,[c] or ash-leaved maple	7	*Acer negundo*	Large tree	60'

REMARKS
Not a good ornamental, but the winged seeds are so important to wintering, evening grosbeaks that one should be included in every songbird planting in the Northeast region.

1	1	Russian mulberry	8	*Morus alba tatarica*	Small tree	25'

REMARKS
Not an attractive ornamental, but one of the very best trees to attract birds in early summer. Birds are so fond of mulberries that they will pass up cultivated cherries, strawberries, and other fruits in favor of them. Every yard should have a mulberry tree, but you may need both a male and female tree to be sure that the female tree will set fruit. Do not plant mulberry trees near your sidewalks or in places where you might sit under the tree. The fruits that fall will stain your clothing and discolor your walks.

that grow between 5 feet and 10 feet high; low shrubs are those that grow less than 5 feet high. Vines are any climbing, woody plant that naturally clings to walls, arbors, etc.

c The box elder is one of the maple trees and so is rated with other maples as the seventh most important food-tree to songbirds in the Northeast.

KEY LETTER OR NUMBER ON MAP	HOW MANY PLANTED	COMMON NAME	FOOD[a] RATING	SCIENTIFIC NAME	TYPE[b] OF PLANT	HEIGHT WHEN MATURE (*feet*)
2	1	Fire, or pin, cherry	3	*Prunus pensylvanica*	Small tree	35'

REMARKS
This is a better tree for the small yard than its much larger relative, the wild black cherry, *Prunus serotina*. The fire, or pin, cherry is extremely hardy, and grows from Newfoundland south to North Carolina, and west to Colorado. At least 23 kinds of birds eat its small red cherries. It flowers in early May in New York State, and has beautiful red shining bark.

3	1	Washington hawthorn	26	*Crataegus phaenopyrum*	Small tree	30'

REMARKS
Thorny branches and dense foliage make hawthorns preferred nesting trees for many birds. Fruit persists on the branches of Washington hawthorn through the winter and makes good, emergency bird food. This is one of the best ornamentals of all the hawthorns and is the one most resistant to the cedar-hawthorn rust.

4	1	American elder	13	*Sambucus canadensis*	Tall shrub	12'

REMARKS
Not a particularly attractive ornamental, and rather coarse-leaved and vigorous growing, but birds are very fond of its purple or blue-black berries. The white flower clusters are attractive and bloom when most other shrubs have finished flowering. Try to buy the variety *maxima*, which has much larger flower clusters. Some of these may be 12 inches to 15 inches in diameter.

5	2	Flowering dogwood (white)	4	*Cornus florida*	Small tree	15'–35'
	2	Flowering dogwood (pink)		*Cornus florida rubra*		

REMARKS
This is the finest ornamental tree of all natives in the northern United States. It grows slowly, is long-lived, and will live either in sun or shade, dry or well-drained soils. It is usually best to buy good sturdy nursery-grown specimens, rather than to transplant it from the wild. The pagoda dogwood, *Cornus alternifolia*, is a good substitute for it and grows farther north.

KEY LETTER OR NUMBER ON MAP	HOW MANY PLANTED	COMMON NAME	FOOD[a] RATING	SCIENTIFIC NAME	TYPE[b] OF PLANT	HEIGHT WHEN MATURE (*feet*)
6	3	Thayer's yew	..	*Taxus cuspidata thayerae*	Shrub evergreen	8'

REMARKS
Roosting, nesting, and wintering cover for birds. Attractive red fruit on the *female* plants. Up to every five female plants, buy one male, or staminate, plant, to be sure that female, or pistillate, plants bear fruit. Thayer's yew, and variety *densa* are low and wide-growing; excellent for small yards.

7	2	Allegany serviceberry	20	*Amelanchier laevis*	Small tree	35'

REMARKS
This is better for the small yard than *Amelanchier canadensis*, which grows much taller and is commonly sold by nurseries. If you can find it in a nursery, try to get *Amelanchier grandiflora*, which is a cross between *laevis* and *canadensis*. It is a smaller tree (up to 25 feet) than either of its parents, and has larger flowers. Birds like the fruits of them all.

8	1	Maries doublefile viburnum	..	*Viburnum tomentosum mariesi*	Medium shrub	9'

REMARKS
Beautiful white flowers that bloom shortly after flowering dogwood has finished. Red berries in summer that birds eat. May grow as wide as tall; Maries variety has larger flower clusters than *V. tomentosum*, the species itself.

9	1	Gray, or poverty, birch	15	*Betula populifolia*	Small tree	30'

REMARKS
This small beautiful tree, besides the seeds it offers chickadees, redpolls, and pine siskins, has a tremendous attraction for the small, brightly colored warblers. These birds come to the tree to feed upon birch plant lice, which occasionally infest birches. When these insects are numerous on these trees, they will attract all of the local warblers, and the migrating ones, too, in spring and fall.

KEY LETTER OR NUMBER ON MAP	HOW MANY PLANTED	COMMON NAME	FOOD[a] RATING	SCIENTIFIC NAME	TYPE[b] OF PLANT	HEIGHT WHEN MATURE (*feet*)
10	1	Siebold's viburnum	..	*Viburnum sieboldi*	Small tree	30'

REMARKS
One of the most attractive of all viburnums. Makes splendid specimen plant in garden. Beautiful in flower and fruit, and birds like the red and black berries, borne on red fruit stalks in late summer and early fall. Hardy in most northeastern states.

11	10	Gray dogwood	4	*Cornus racemosa*	Tall shrub	15'

REMARKS
A dense, native shrub that endures city smoke and withstands shearing or clipping. It can be cut back to 6 or 8 feet high, and it makes a good thicket for birds to nest or hide in. Its white berries on red stalks are ornamental, and at least 22 kinds of birds eat them. It will grow in dry, well-drained or moist soils, and in the sun, or in shade.

12	3	Orange-fruited viburnum	..	*Viburnum setigerum aurantiacum*	Tall shrub	12'

REMARKS
We have watched migrating hermit thrushes in our backyard pull the orange berries from our bushes to eat them. The only viburnum with beautiful orange-colored fruit. They remind one of mountain ash berries.

13	2	Linden viburnum	..	*Viburnum dilatatum*	Medium shrub	9'

REMARKS
One of the best of the ornamental viburnums for its abundant bright red fruit. Migrating thrushes eat the berries from our bushes in the fall.

14	8	Arrowwood	..	*Viburnum dentatum*	Tall shrub	15'

REMARKS
Fine ornamental for city or suburban yards; it is hardy, grows in almost any soil, and endures city smoke. Dense green foliage that turns glossy red in fall. The blue berries are eaten by several kinds of songbirds, and thickets of this shrub make good nesting cover.

KEY LETTER OR NUMBER ON MAP	HOW MANY PLANTED	COMMON NAME	FOOD[a] RATING	SCIENTIFIC NAME	TYPE[b] OF PLANT	HEIGHT WHEN MATURE (*feet*)
15	1	Amur honeysuckle	..	*Lonicera maacki*	Tall shrub	15'

REMARKS

Very hardy, possibly as adaptable to poor, dry soils and cold weather as Tatarian honeysuckle, *Lonicera tatarica*. A nursery as far north as Manitoba, Canada, raises Amur honeysuckle. We have seen migrating thrushes, robins, catbirds, and brown thrashers eating the red berries of this shrub in late October, when few other shrubs in our neighborhood have juicy fruits on them. We prefer the Amur honeysuckle to Tatarian honeysuckle, because its fruits are ripe at a time of fruit scarcity for small birds in our area.

16	1	Japanese dogwood	4	*Cornus kousa*	Small tree	20'

REMARKS

Birds eat its red, raspberrylike fruit, and its beautiful white flower bracts appear after flowering dogwood has finished blooming. It is not supposed to be hardy, or able to stand the winters, north of southern New England, Pennsylvania, Ohio, southern Indiana, southern Illinois, and Missouri.

17	1	Dwarf Japanese yew	..	*Taxus cuspidata densa*	Shrub evergreen	4'

REMARKS

The Japanese yews are fine dark-green ornamentals that are hardy in most of the northeastern states and will grow in many different kinds of soils. They are raised in most American nurseries and are hardier than the English yew, *Taxus baccata* and its varieties.

18	26	Japanese barberry	..	*Berberis thunbergi*	Medium shrub	7'

REMARKS

One of the most widely used hedge plants, and noted for its ability to grow in dry soils. Its dense, thorny growth, bright red fruits, which hang on all winter, and scarlet leaves in autumn, make it desirable in most gardens. It is a favorite nesting bush for songsparrows, at least in the Northeast Region. At least seven kinds of birds eat its red fruits.

KEY LETTER OR NUMBER ON MAP	HOW MANY PLANTED	COMMON NAME	FOOD [a] RATING	SCIENTIFIC NAME	TYPE [b] OF PLANT	HEIGHT WHEN MATURE (*feet*)
19	12	Blackberries	2	*Rubus* (genus name)	Medium shrub	6'–9'
19	12	Raspberries	2	*Rubus* (genus name)	Medium shrub	6'–9'

REMARKS

Some nurseries specialize in growing these and blueberry plants. Although some varieties grow over a great area, it is best to write to your state college of agriculture, *before you buy your plants*, and ask them what varieties they recommend for your locality. Also ask them for a bulletin that will tell you how to plant and care for them.

20	12	Highbush blueberries	11	*Vaccinium* (genus name)	Tall shrub	12'

REMARKS

We like varieties Weymouth and June for early fruit; Ivanhoe and Stanley for midseason; Atlantic, Jersey, and Coville for late berries. Consult your state agricultural college before you buy your plants.

21	5	Japanese yew	..	*Taxus cuspidata*	Evergreen tree-shrub	15'–20'

REMARKS

Some nurserymen call this tall, upright yew, variety "capitata." Dark-green ornamental background for other plants, and good winter cover for birds. Be sure to plant both male and female plants if you want the attractive pink-red fruit.

22	4	Trumpet creeper	..	*Campsis radicans*	Vigorous vine	20'–30'

REMARKS

Excellent hummingbird food plant—has scarlet, and orange, trumpet-shaped flowers in midsummer. A hybrid, *Campsis tagliabuana*, variety "Madame Galen," has larger, showier flowers and is said to be equally attractive to hummingbirds.

23	8	European cranberry-bush	..	*Viburnum opulus*	Tall shrub	12'

REMARKS

Red fruit persists, sometimes until spring. Eaten by pine grosbeaks and other wintering birds. This plant seems to be hardy across the northern United States to the Mountain Desert region and beyond to the Pacific region.

KEY LETTER OR NUMBER ON MAP	HOW MANY PLANTED	COMMON NAME	FOOD[a] RATING	SCIENTIFIC NAME	TYPE[b] OF PLANT	HEIGHT WHEN MATURE (*feet*)
24	40	Virginia creeper	10	*Parthenocissus quinquefolia*	Vine	10'–20'

REMARKS
Beautiful ornamental leaves in fives, turn scarlet in fall; blue fruit very attractive to many kinds of birds. This vine is healthy, but never grows so vigorously that it will be running wild in your garden as some vines might do.

25	1	Sargent crabapple	..	*Malus sargenti*	Small tree	8'

REMARKS
The smallest of the crabapples; no larger than a shrub, gets as wide as tall. Resistant to the cedar-apple rust—a fungus disease that attacks red cedars and apple trees. Beautiful in flower and in fruits.

26	20	Black haw	..	*Viburnum prunifolium*	Small tree	15'

REMARKS
This makes a luxuriant hedge and single plants make good specimens. Good for "screen planting" to give you privacy or to blot out an ugly view. Provides fruit and nesting places for songbirds.

27	8	Small-leaved cotoneaster	..	*Cotoneaster microphylla*	Low shrub	3'

REMARKS
Handsome, shiny-leaved, low plant, particularly good for embankments or in rock gardens. Provides red fruit throughout the winter available to birds. In California, people see birds frequently eating the red berries of the cotoneasters. In England, in the winter of 1949–1950, bird scientists found Bohemian waxwings eating immense quantities of the fruit of cotoneasters. Some of these birds ate far more than their own weight of the berries each day.

WHEN OUR TREES, SHRUBS, AND VINES ARE IN FLOWER AND THE AUTUMN COLORS OF THEIR LEAVES

The list does not include the red cedar, Russian mulberry, yews, and pines because their flowers are inconspicuous. The blooming period given is for southern New York and southern New England generally. Some of the plants on our list, when grown farther north, would bloom weeks later. Those grown farther south would bloom weeks earlier. For specific information about the blooming periods of trees, shrubs, and vines, refer to *Trees for American Gardens* and to *Shrubs and Vines for American Gardens*. Both books are written by Dr. Donald Wyman and published by The Macmillan Company, New York.

KEY LETTER OR KEY NO. ON MAP	TIME OF BLOOM	NAME OF PLANT	FLOWERS	AUTUMN COLOR OF LEAVES
		APRIL		
E	Early April	American elm, *Ulmus americana*	Not showy	Usually yellow-brown
F	Mid-April	Box elder, *Acer negundo*	Not showy	Usually dull green to brown
9	Mid-April	Gray birch, *Betula populifolia*	Not showy	Bright yellow
7	Late April	Serviceberry (shadbush), *Amelanchier laevis*	Showy white flowers	Yellow to red
		MAY		
2	Early May	Fire cherry (pin cherry), *Prunus pensylvanica*	Small white flowers	Red
18	Mid-May	Japanese barberry, *Berberis thunbergi*	Not showy	Scarlet
5	Mid-May	Flowering dogwood (white), *Cornus florida*	Showy white flower bracts	Scarlet
5	Mid-May	Flowering dogwood (pink), *Cornus florida* variety rubra	Showy pink flower bracts	Scarlet
25	Mid-May	Sargent crabapple, *Malus sargenti*	Showy pure white fragrant flowers	Green

KEY LETTER OR KEY NO. ON MAP	TIME OF BLOOM	NAME OF PLANT	FLOWERS	AUTUMN COLOR OF LEAVES
		MAY (*continued*)		
C	Mid-May	White oak, *Quercus alba*	Not showy	Purple red, violet, and sometimes rusty green-gold
26	Late May	Black haw, *Viburnum prunifolium*	White, in flat clusters	Shining red
10	Late May	Seibold viburnum, *Viburnum seiboldi*	Cream-white, in flat clusters	Red
8	Late May	Maries doublefile viburnum, *Viburnum tomentosum mariesi*	Cream-white, in flat clusters	Dull red
15	Late May	Amur honeysuckle, *Lonicera maacki*	White to yellow-ish fragrant flowers	Green
20	Late May	Highbush blueberry, *Vaccinium corymbosum*	White, or pinkish flowers	Scarlet
		JUNE		
16	Early June	Japanese dogwood, *Cornus kousa*	Showy white to pink flower bracts	Scarlet
14	Early June	Arrowwood, *Viburnum dentatum*	Cream-white, in flat clusters	Glossy red
13	Early June	Linden viburnum, *Viburnum dilatatum*	Showy cream-white flowers	Green to russet-red
23	Early June	European cranberry-bush, *Viburnum opulus*	White, in flat clusters	Red

KEY LETTER OR KEY NO. ON MAP	TIME OF BLOOM	NAME OF PLANT	FLOWERS	AUTUMN COLOR OF LEAVES
		JUNE (*continued*)		
3	Mid-June	Washington hawthorn, *Crataegus phaenopyrum*	Showy, white, in many-flowered clusters	Scarlet to orange
27	Mid-June	Small-leaved cotoneaster, *Cotoneaster microphylla*	Small and white, not showy	Evergreen, shining
11	Mid-June	Gray dogwood, *Cornus racemosa*	Cream-white, in flat clusters	Purple
4	Late June	Common elderberry, *Sambucus canadensis* variety *maxima*	Large, showy white flower clusters, a foot in diameter	Green to dull brown
		JULY		
12	Early July	Orange-fruited viburnum, *Viburnum setigerum aurantiacum*	White, in flat clusters	Green to russet-red
22	Mid-July	Trumpet creeper, *Campsis radicans*	Handsome orange-red trumpet-shaped "hummingbird" flowers	Purplish brown

THE MONTHS WHEN OUR PLANTS[a] OFFER FOOD TO BIRDS

Unusually large flocks of birds may suddenly descend on these plants and strip them of their fruits long before the bearing periods of the plants have ended. Some individual plants may drop their fruits early, while others of their own kind continue to hold them. These circumstances will help to explain why some of the plants listed may not *always* bear their fruits during the seasons shown for them here. Generally they will.

Listed below are the times of the year during which our plants ordinarily hold their fruits in our Long Island, New York, area of the Northeast region. During some years, our plants may have large crops; in other years, small ones.

WINTER (Dec., Jan., and Feb.)	Kind of Fruit and Its Color	SPRING (March, April, and May)	Kind of Fruit and Its Color
Red cedar[b]	Blue berries	Red cedar[b]	Blue berries
Linden viburnum	Red berries	Linden viburnum	Red berries
European cranberry-bush	Red berries	European cranberry-bush	Red berries
Japanese barberry	Red berries	Japanese barberry	Red berries
Washington hawthorn	Small red applelike fruits	Washington hawthorn	Small red applelike fruits
Sargent crabapple	Small dark-red apples	Sargent crabapple	Small dark-red apples
Small-leaved cotoneaster	Red berries	Small-leaved cotoneaster	Red berries
Box elder (a maple)	Seeds	Box elder (a maple)	Seeds

THE CRITICAL TIMES—WINTER AND SPRING

The value of the above plants is their ability to hold their fruits and seeds on their branches for a long time. Here, above the snow, they are available to birds during periods when they may need them the most. These fruits and seeds we call "emergency foods." Birds do not usually eat them until other foods are scarce, or covered by snow. Perhaps a certain amount of weathering of some of these fruits, like Japanese barberry, is necessary before they are palatable to birds. At any rate, they do not seem to turn to them until they are forced to. Then the fruits of Linden viburnum, European cranberry-bush, and others, which have hung on the trees and shrubs for months, quickly become a feast for the birds. Plants of this kind may help many of the birds wintering in your garden to survive.

[a] This list includes only the woody plants (trees, shrubs, and vines) in our yard. The herbaceous flowers (annuals and perennials) that offer seeds to seed-eating birds, and nectar to hummingbirds, but die back each fall or wither to the ground, are listed in the Appendix.

[b] You will note that red cedar and Linden viburnum are listed as having berries on them during all four seasons of the year. This is true, except in the latter part of spring, when many of the old berries drop off, and in early summer, when a new crop of berries is forming.

THE MONTHS WHEN OUR PLANTS[a] OFFER FOOD TO BIRDS
(*Continued*)

WINTER (Dec., Jan., and Feb.)	Kind of Fruit and Its Color	SPRING (March, April, and May)	Kind of Fruit and Its Color
Gray birch	Seeds	American elm	Buds, flowers, and seeds
Amur honeysuckle	Red berries		
Black haw	Blue-black berries		
Virginia creeper	Blue-black berries		
Winter: total of 12 kinds		*Spring:* total of 9 kinds	

SUMMER (June, July, and August)	Kind of Fruit and Its Color	FALL (Sept., Oct., and Nov.)	Kind of Fruit and Its Color
Red cedar[b]	Blue berries	Red cedar[b]	Blue berries
Linden viburnum	Red berries	Linden viburnum	Red berries
Russian mulberry	White to dark-red berries	European cranberry bush	Red berries
Serviceberry (shadbush)	Small red applelike fruit	Japanese barberry	Red berries
Raspberries and blackberries	Black berries and red berries	Washington hawthorn	Small dark-red fruit
Blueberries	Blue berries	Sargent crabapple	Small dark-red apples
Fire, or pin, cherry	Small red cherries	Small-leaved cotoneaster	Red berries
Doublefile viburnum	Red berries	Box elder (a maple)	Seeds

SUMMER (June, July, and August)	Kind of Fruit and Its Color	FALL (Sept., Oct., and Nov.)	Kind of Fruit and Its Color
Seibold's viburnum	Red berries	Gray birch	Seeds
White pine	Seeds	Amur honeysuckle	Red berries
Gray dogwood	White berries	Black haw	Blue-black berries
Japanese dogwood	Red raspberrylike fruit	Virginia creeper	Blue-black berries
Trumpet creeper[c]	Flower nectar for hummingbirds	Fire, or pin, cherry	Small red cherries
Common elderberry	Blue to purple-black berries	Gray dogwood	White berries
Arrowwood	Blue berries	Japanese yews	Red berries
Japanese yews	Red berries	White pine	Seeds
Virginia creeper	Blue-black berries	Red pine	Seeds
		White oak	Acorns
		Flowering dogwood	Red berries
		Orange-fruited viburnum	Orange berries
Summer: total of 17 kinds		*Fall:* total of 20 kinds	

[c] This is a hummingbird, woody food plant.

How Scientists Discovered What Songbirds Eat

In government laboratories in Washington, D. C., beginning in 1883, men began examining the contents of birds' stomachs. Their researches were mainly to discover what services the birds were doing for mankind by eating certain insects, rats, mice, and other creatures that feed upon farm crops. Along with the insect foods of birds, they discovered the kinds of fruits and seeds that birds eat. Professor F. E. L. Beal, one of those early investigators, personally examined the contents of more than 37,000 birds' stomachs. W. L. McAtee, a younger bird food-habits expert, not only took over much of Professor Beal's work in the Biological Survey, but wrote many government bulletins [1] about the food habits of birds, and how to attract them.

Plants Birds Need the Year Around

We looked on our choice of plants for the birds in our yard somewhat in the way we would provide for our own needs. We knew that the greatest use birds get out of trees, shrubs, and vines are for: (1) food, (2) shelter from cold and snow and from summer storms, and (3) nesting places. (If you will refer for a moment to the tables "The Struggle to Survive" and "How You Can Help the Birds" in the appendix, you will see how important woody plants are in the lives of many songbirds.)

If we could provide the three basic needs for songbirds —year-round food, winter shelter, and summer nesting

[1] Some of these government publications are still available at a small cost from the Superintendent of Documents, U. S. Government Printing Office, Washington 25, D. C.

More recently, the results of sixty-five years of U. S. government research in wild animal food habits have been compiled by several government scientists in a book, *American Wildlife and Plants*, published by the McGraw Hill Book Company, New York. This book is so complete that it is likely that people will refer to it for years to come, whenever they want to learn what plant and insect foods are eaten most by songbirds and by other kinds of wild animals throughout the United States.

My lists of trees, shrubs, and vines to attract birds, in the appendix, are based on the regional food habits of songbirds given in *American Wildlife and Plants*.

places—we had no doubt that they would come to our yard. We were also sure that when our planting had a good start, we would have birds in our garden every day of the year.

We had only one other consideration before we selected our list of plants. We would also try to choose those that would provide colorful fruits, flowers, leaves, and interesting outlines against the sky, even in winter when the leaves and fruits of some of them are gone. This wasn't difficult because most trees and shrubs have some special attraction at some particular time of the year.

If you are too busy to make your own planting plan, I suggest that you consult a landscape architect, who, for a fee, will draw a planting plan for you. Be sure to make it clear that you want him to choose plants for your yard from the list of those preferred as food by the birds of your region. These lists are given, by regions, in the appendix to be found at the back of this book. Most of these plants, whether they are native or introduced from other countries, are excellent ornamentals, besides their food, cover, and nesting values to songbirds. Your landscape architect should be able to draw a beautiful planting plan for your garden. He should also be most capable of recommending the species or *kinds* of trees, shrubs, and vines on your regional plant lists in the appendix that will grow best in your local area.

Or you might consult your county agricultural agent[2] about what you would like to do. If he does not feel capable of advising you, he may be able to suggest other sources of help. Your state college of agriculture will have free bulletins or leaflets that will describe some of the trees, shrubs, and vines that grow in your state. Soil conservationists and federal and state foresters may be willing to tell you what species of trees and shrubs on your regional list will grow best in your community. Perhaps your local

Sources of Help

[2] There is a county agricultural agent in each rural county seat of the United States.

nurseryman may be willing to help you to plan and plant your garden to attract birds.

Deciding
Where to Plant

Before we started our new songbird planting plan, we spent a lot of time as we do now, from spring until fall, on the terrace just in back of our house. It was always pleasant sitting there. On clear days, we had sunshine until noon, and when the sun got over into the west, our house shaded us from the afternoon heat. Sitting in comfortable chairs on the terrace, or lying in the swing, we could look out over our flower beds and lawn clear to our back property-line fence. It was a pretty sight, and if we kept this view open, we could even improve upon it with our bird plantings.

To keep our view from being obstructed, we decided not to plant any trees or shrubs between the terrace and our back lawn, but to concentrate them along the sides of our property and back fence. I was particularly anxious to plant the back line anyway. Just over the line, we faced the backs of two cement-block garages in a neighbor's yard. They weren't pretty to look at, and our back line planting would hide them from our sight.

But first, how far in upon the lawn from our property lines did we want to plant? To give songbirds room to nest and nesting privacy, we knew that they needed a depth (or width) of at least 6 feet of shrubbery from fence line to lawn, and a greater width wherever possible. We decided then that the narrowest part of our shrub border, at any place along our property line, would be at least 6 feet wide.

Curving lines in a planting look well and we had to decide upon an inner line in the yard where shrubs and lawn would meet. Like most people, we wanted to see this line *on the ground* before we decided where it was to be permanently. We took several lengths of garden hose and laid them out in the curve that you see outlined by our flagstone walk on the map (page 139). The line marked by the hose (a clothesline would have done just as well) looked graceful, and it allowed a planting depth, or width, from lawn to fences that would enable us to plant a variety of trees and shrubs that birds like. We knew that the more of the different kinds of their preferred plants we could use, the more attractive our yard would be to a greater variety of birds.

To mark permanently our line where the future shrub planting would meet the lawn, we bought two dozen flat pieces of flagstone. These we set at ground level just below the grass, about every six to eight feet apart along the line marked by the hose. Eventually, we would buy enough flagstones to set them about every two feet apart along this line. For the present, these would mark the future boundary between our shrubbery and lawn. They were the beginning of our flagstone walk that someday would circle completely about our back yard, and serve to keep us and our guests from damaging the grass by walking on it too frequently.

The "needle" evergreens [3]—pines, spruces, yews, junipers, hemlocks, etc.—are the backbone of any planting for songbirds in the northern states and in many parts of the South where winter cold spells may occasionally be severe. The evergreens help songbirds by providing them with protective shelter throughout the year. Of the two hundred trees and shrubs in our yard, about 8 per cent, or eighteen of these, are "needle" evergreens. After you have made your preliminary planting plan on paper, add up the total number of your plants and see how many of them are pines, spruces, yews, etc. If they are from 8 to 12 per cent of your total number of plants, you may feel assured that you have planned adequate planting shelter for the birds in your yard.

Most evergreens, except the dwarf varieties, grow into

Putting the Plants on Your Map

[3] There are also broad-leaved evergreens—the rhododendrons, laurels, American holly, etc.—which do not have needles, but retain their "broad" leaves throughout the year. These also make effective cover for songbirds, but the "needle" evergreens are generally better for this purpose.

tall trees in time. Assign them places in the *back* of your planting, in *corners* of your yard, and in places along the *sides* of your property. There they will make an effective green wall, or a contrasting background for your flowering and fruiting trees and shrubs.

We put some of our cedars along our north and east property lines (see *A* on the map of our planting plan, page 139). They are directly back of our white-flowering dogwoods and white-blossoming serviceberry at 5 and 7. We used pines at *B* as a green background for the white trunk of a birch tree at 9. By planting food-producing trees—dogwoods, serviceberry, and birch—in front of and close to the evergreens to get an ornamental effect, we provided food for birds near the safety of cover. The evergreens, with their densely needled branches, are a refuge where songbirds may escape from small hawks or shrikes that occasionally try to catch them while they are engrossed in feeding.

To make the cover almost immediately useful to birds, without the necessity of having to wait five to ten years for the trees to spread out, we spaced our cedars (and white pines, too) close enough to each other to provide thick cover the first year or two after we had planted them. We did this while quite aware that perhaps in ten or fifteen years we might have to transplant some of the evergreens. By that time they would have broadened, with their branches intermingled and possibly their growth slowed a bit. By planting them close together, we nevertheless achieved our purpose of providing "quick" cover for birds during those first years immediately after planting.

How Far Apart Should You Space Trees and Shrubs?

We planted our tree evergreens and most of our small flowering trees much closer together than a landscape gardener or a nurseryman would recommend. Our dogwoods, serviceberry, fire cherry, and mulberry we spaced about 8 to 10 feet apart. This is approximately one-third the ultimate height of about 30 feet to which most of these trees grow. The majority of small trees and tall shrubs are usually planted a distance apart about equal to *one-half* to two-thirds their maximum height. For example, flowering dogwood trees—which may eventually grow 30 feet tall or more—should be spaced at least 15 to 20 feet apart, instead of 8 to 10 feet apart, as we spaced them. You may prefer to plant yours wider apart than we did, and you will probably have a better-looking planting than ours, after fifteen or twenty years have passed.

If you don't like the idea of having openings that will show up in your wider-spaced planting, you might, before you plant, consider buying larger dogwoods—say 12 to 15 feet tall—instead of the 8- to 10-foot sizes that we chose. These will have wider-spreading branches because of their larger size, which will help to fill in the spaces between them. If your budget won't allow you to buy the larger and more expensive sizes and you still want the wide spacing between your trees, you might consider buying some inexpensive low shrubs—perhaps coralberry or snowberry, for example—and plant these between the trees. These will provide fruits that birds eat until eventually your trees will "shade these out," but in the meantime, they have served their purpose of filling up the open spaces and providing food.

If you don't want to use shrubs to fill in, you can plant a low-growing, permanent ground cover of partridgeberry, bearberry or wintergreen.[4] Each of these has red fruits eaten by birds. If they are difficult to find in nurseries, you can buy English ivy, *Hedera helix*, or its varieties, Japanese spurge, *Pachysandra terminalis*, or some other trailing or low-growing plant. (Don't use Japanese honeysuckle, *Lonicera japonica*, or its varieties. This is a vigorous, climbing vine that will overrun your small trees if it is planted under them.)

All of these small broad-leaved evergreens will keep out the weeds by covering the bare ground, and are attractive to look at all year. Eventually, we chose pachysandra for

Cedar Waxwing

Red Cedar

Mulberry

Pokeberry

[4] These attractive native plants, partridgeberry, *Mitchella repens;* bearberry, *Arctostaphylos uva-ursi;* and wintergreen, *Gaultheria procumbens;* are sold by some nurseries, particularly those that specialize in native wildflowers.

a ground cover under our flowering trees and shrubs. Many nurseries sell it, and it gives a neat, luxuriant finish to our plantings that is especially needed on the inside border, next to the lawn, which is in view of anyone walking about in our yard.

When spacing your shrubs on your planting plan, you can put them closer together, in proportion to their height, than trees. If you are planting a thicket of shrubs to attract birds, as we did with gray dogwood at 11 on the map and with arrowwood at 14, you can set your shrubs about 2 feet apart. When you plant vines at the bases of walls, arbors, and trellises, you might set them close together, as with shrubs, if you want quick results in getting a thick cover.

Large Trees in Your Yard

You may have wondered whether or not your yard is large enough to accommodate a large tree. No matter what tree you buy, or how long it may take it to reach its full height—some oaks and other slow-growing trees may take at least a hundred to two hundred years—you should consider its *ultimate* height in proportion to the size of your yard and house.

Our yard 60 feet wide and 140 feet deep is probably larger than many suburban lots of today. Our house is two floors and an attic high. The white oak tree, near the center of our back yard, and now about 70 feet tall, is neither too big for the property, nor too much out of proportion to the house. If our house were a modern, one-story-high, ranch type, we might consider our oak to be too tall. The oak grew there long before the house was built. Had we planted it, we would have put it in a back corner of the yard, or somewhere along the north property line, where it wouldn't cast a large shadow in summer over the center of the yard, as it does now.

Most modern houses are only one floor high, or perhaps a floor and one-half above the ground. A tree that doesn't get too tall is far better for a low house than one that, someday, will dwarf it.

If you want a fine shade tree for a small yard—a tree that

will endure city smoke, dry, poor soils, and attract birds—
try the sugar hackberry, *Celtis laevigata* (pronounced
SELL-tiss leave-ih-GAY-tah). It grows, after many years,
to 75 or 80 feet tall, and has a dark red or purple fruit that
looks like a berry. These are ripe in September and
October and sometimes stay on the tree through the winter.
About forty-seven different kinds of birds eat these fruits,
including cardinals, cedar waxwings, flickers, mockingbirds, robins, and olive-backed thrushes. The sugar hackberry grows from southern New England west through
Pennsylvania and Ohio to Indiana, south to Texas, and east
to Florida. It looks like an elm and is a good substitute
for it. Another hackberry, *Celtis occidentalis* (pronounced
SELL-tiss ock-sih-den-TAY-liss), is hardy north into
Canada and is much planted for windbreaks in the Plains
and Prairie region of the United States. Unfortunately it
is susceptible to the "witches broom disease" which doesn't
seriously harm it, but forms rather unsightly clusters of
twigs on the tree. If you don't mind this defect, this hackberry is hardier than the sugar hackberry and is slightly
more attractive to birds.

Another, smaller, tree that also endures city smoke and
poor, dry soils, and attracts birds, is the Amur cork tree,
Phellodendron amurense (pronounced Fel-low-DEN-dron
ah-moor-EN-see). In Central Park, New York city, I have
seen flocks of migrating robins, catbirds, and thrushes sit
in one of these trees day after day through October and
November, eating the black, grapelike fruits as long as they
were available. The tree grows to about 45 feet tall, is
wide and spreading, with massive branches and rough bark.
The sexes are separate so you must plant both a male and
a female tree, if you want fruits for birds. The Amur cork
tree is not a large tree, and a property the size of ours would
easily accommodate two of them, if we had no other large
trees in our yard.

If we were using this tree in our garden, we would plant
the male tree on our terrace, near the house, and the female
tree, which bears the black, juicy fruits, in the back of the
yard. There, in late fall when the fruits are ripe, they would

stain no sidewalks when they fell to the ground. This hardy tree will grow from eastern Canada west to Montana in the United States, and southward.

If you have a small yard, you should also consider planting a blue beech, *Carpinus caroliniana* (pronounced Car-PIE-nus car-ol-inna-AY-nah). This small native tree grows to about 35 feet tall and has leaves resembling those of an elm. Its hard nutlets, hanging from the tree in small leaf-like clusters, attract cardinals, myrtle warblers, and other birds, which like the seeds. In Central Park, New York city, where these trees grow commonly, I have watched gray squirrels in autumn feed on the little clusters of seeds day after day until they have eaten them all from the trees. This is one of the hardiest trees in North America and grows from far up in the colder parts of Canada south to Texas and Florida.

In the South, particularly in Florida, where it is known as Christmas-berry tree, people plant the handsome, 40-foot-tall Brazil pepper tree on their lawns and along the city and town streets. In California another species, the California pepper tree, is much planted as a highway or street tree; however, it must not be planted near orange groves because it attracts the black scale, an insect which also attacks citrus trees. In California, bluebirds, mocking-birds, phainopeplas, robins, and other birds eat the abundant red berries that grow in clusters on this tree in the fall.

The Pacific madrone, or madroña (pronounced ma-DRONE-yah), *Arbutus menziesi*, and the strawberry tree, *Arbutus unedo*, are two handsome broad-leaved evergreens with brilliant red to orange berries that birds eat. Both of these are interesting and attractive shade trees for small yards in the Pacific region.

When you decide on the kind of shade tree or trees that you want in your garden—whether a tall oak, elm, or maple or a dogwood, cherry, or other small tree—mark it on your map of your yard near the back or along one of its sides. After the tree is planted, it will look better there and won't shade the center of your yard, which is usually more attractive if kept an open lawn.

After you have chosen your species of trees, shrubs, and vines, visit your nearest nursery to see if he has in stock the plants you want. If you go there in spring or fall, the nurseryman's busiest time, don't expect him to give you the personal attention that he may be able to give you at other times of the year. We like to visit our local nursery in summer when leaves, flowers, or fruit are on plants and we can "browse around," as some people do in a book-shop, without feeling that we are in the way. Our nursery-man knows us so well that he tries to let us know we are always welcome, even though we may only be "window shopping."

It is best to get well-acquainted with your plants before you buy them—to know how they look at different times of the year, their ultimate height, rate of growth, and time of flowering or of fruiting. We don't know of any way to get better acquainted with plants than to visit a nursery, unless you have friends who have planted the kinds of trees and shrubs you are interested in, or know someone who owns, or superintends, a large estate. If you live near an arboretum, or botanical garden, one of those wonderful places where trees, shrubs, and other plants are grown espe-cially for people to see and for scientists to study, you are fortunate. Go there as often as you possibly can, and you will be pleased at how soon and how much you will learn about plants.

Since the first edition of *Songbirds in Your Garden* was published, many of my friends and other readers of this book have written to ask why I did not include pokeberry, or pokeweed, as a recommended birdfood plant for the garden. Its purple-black berries on red stems are eaten by fifty-two kinds of birds.

In listing ornamental plants that attract birds, I did not include pokeberry because of its homeliness. Many people consider it an ungainly weed in the garden; but, if allowed

Virtues of the Homely Pokeberry [5]

[5] Variously called pokeberry, pokeweed, poke, scoke, garget, redweed, and pigeonberry, the botanical name of this plant is *Phytolacca ameri-cana*.

to grow in an inconspicuous place, such as a corner where it is not easily seen, it will add much to your garden's attractiveness to birds. It grows naturally in sunny, moist places, along the edges of woods, fields, roadsides, streams, and fence corners, from Maine to Florida, west to Texas and north through the plains and prairie states of Oklahoma, Missouri, Kansas, Iowa, and Nebraska to parts of Minnesota and Wisconsin.

I don't know of any nursery that sells the plant because it is considered a weed, but it usually is planted by the birds themselves. After eating its berries they drop its black seeds wherever they happen to travel. Mourning doves are especially fond of pokeberries; they are also favored by bluebirds, catbirds, woodpeckers, robins, mockingbirds, thrushes, vireos, cardinals, cedar waxwings, and many other garden birds.

For the ten years that we lived on Long Island, a pokeberry grew up freshly each spring from its big root in a sunny corner in the back of our garden (it is a perennial herb that dies back to the ground each fall). One year, in its prime, our eleven-foot, leafy green plant grew a crop of berries that I estimated at ten thousand. The crop ripened in August. Within a week, our garden birds had eaten every one of the berries from their favorite bush.

9

Making Sounds to Attract Birds

My wife says that she has known for a long time why I spend hours in our garden, watching those fascinating details that make up a bird's life and a bird's world. She thinks I have more than my proper share of curiosity, like those romanticists who never see a hill in the distance without wanting to climb it to see what lies on its farther side. She is right, but what she didn't know, until I was able to prove it to her satisfaction one day, is that birds at times may be almost as curious about people as we are about birds.

One sunny morning in October a few years ago we were working in our yard, raking up russet and golden leaves from the grass under our tall white oak tree. We had sat down to rest on a bench on our terrace when my wife suddenly caught my sleeve. She pointed toward the birdbath.

"What is it?" she whispered.

A small bird, which had dropped down to our birdbath for a drink of water, had fluttered up into a large spruce tree in our next-door neighbor's yard.

I picked up the binoculars that we always keep close by when we are working in the garden. We have these at hand to watch any of the birds that are too far away for us to see them clearly with our unaided eyes. I looked at the spruce tree carefully through the powerful binoculars, but

I couldn't see the bird, nor a movement in the tree that would tell us that it was still there.

We got up from the bench and walked toward the tree. We stopped a few yards from our property-line fence and looked up into the tree just beyond. Still we saw no bird. Not a sound came from the densely needled branches of the spruce.

I raised my right hand to my mouth, and pressed my lips against the back of my hand. By holding one corner of my mouth slightly away from my hand and by sucking air vigorously, I made a series of fine, high-pitched squeaks that sounded like a bird in distress.

Almost instantly a small bird fluttered out from the far side of the spruce tree, circled around toward us, and looped down to alight on the fence only twenty feet away. Focusing quickly on the bird, for it might stay there only a moment, I saw that it looked larger now, as all birds do when seen through a binocular that has a lot of magnifying power. The distance between us seemed shortened, too, as if it were only an arm's length away.

The little olive-green bird shifted its position quickly, hopping about on the fence and turning its head from side to side. First it fixed its bright glance on us with one eye, then with the other. It seemed excited, and it puffed out its throat several times, as if it were calling, but I heard no sound.

That bird, for us, was a record-breaker. After studying it closely, I knew that it was an orange-crowned warbler, the *first* and the *only one* we have ever seen in our yard. This is a rare species in our area, and we wouldn't have seen it had not my wife discovered it. On the other hand, we wouldn't have identified it had I not used the "squeak," as ornithologists call it, to arouse the bird's curiosity and draw it into view.

What Birds Are Attracted by Squeaking Sounds?

I can't remember who first taught me how to squeak to attract birds, but it must have been one of the older ornithologists of a group who took me on birding trips many years ago. Most ornithologists make this thin, high-pitched sound when they want to lure birds from tall grass, thickets, marshes, woodland undergrowth, and other places where birds are hidden from view. I have been using the squeak for years and find it particularly useful in late summer and fall.

In the spring it is much easier to see birds when the leaves on trees and shrubs aren't fully grown, and birds are conspicuous because they are singing almost constantly. But in late summer and autumn, they are inclined to be silent. This is the time of the year when strange birds, on their way south to winter in the tropics, can be in the shrubbery of your yard or neighborhood and you may never even suspect they are there.

In our garden, by squeaking on the back of my hand, I have brought close to us blue jays, chickadees, white-breasted nuthatches, catbirds, scarlet tanagers, brown thrashers, towhees, song sparrows, white-throated sparrows, red-eyed vireos, golden-crowned kinglets, and many other birds.

One summer day I made a series of squeaking notes near a catbird that nested in one of our shrubs. I knew that she was nesting there but paid no attention to her at the time because I was trying to "squeak up" a small bird that I wanted to see which had concealed itself in one of our yews. The catbird, flying from our vegetable garden with a cutworm in her beak to feed her youngsters, heard my squeaking sounds. Instantly she turned in the air and, with an enraged cry, flew down at my head. I ducked or I think she might have struck me. Then I stood looking up at her in astonishment as she perched on a limb overhead, scolding me.

The bird had never acted aggressive toward me before and hadn't even protested when my wife and I had walked by within a few feet of her nest while she fed her family. But I had given a call—a squeak—that sounded to her, I suppose, suspiciously like that of one of her youngsters in distress. After that day, and up until her young ones left the nest, she scolded me whenever I came near. Obviously, she now looked on me as an enemy. I was not to be trusted.

I learned to squeak birds by sucking on the back of my hand, but an easy and equally effective method of attracting small birds is to use the back of one of your thumbs or the back of your index or middle finger. Press your lips on the top of one of the joints of your thumb or fingers and suck in air. This makes an easily produced, whining squeak that sounds like the call of a young bird or the squeak of a mouse. In fact the sound is so mouselike that you can attract the small screech owl, at dusk or after dark, by making these squeaking notes. A few years ago one flew down in our yard and brushed against my hat as it passed. Apparently it had mistaken my squeaking for that of a mouse on which these little owls feed.

Another method of squeaking is to press your lips against your open palm while holding the fingers of your hand straight to allow the sound to escape. Suck in as if kissing your open palm. This is easy to do and makes a louder but *lower-pitched* sound that is more attractive to the medium-sized birds—jays, flickers, robins, and others.

Some ornithologists don't use their hands at all to produce these sounds but make a combined whistling and hissing sound by using their lips, tongue, and teeth. This is most effective in attracting the small, golden-crowned kinglet and the brown creeper, probably because the hissing-whistling sounds resemble their own high-pitched, lisping call notes.

For your squeaking to have its greatest effect upon birds —that is, to lure them closest to you—you should be at least partly hidden in a thicket of shrubs or under the down-sweeping branches of a tree where birds won't be able to see you as clearly as if you stood out in the open. Make yourself comfortable by sitting on the ground or on a stool or chair, and sit quietly without making motions. After squeaking a few times, pause to listen for answering birds, then repeat the squeaking to draw them as near to you as they will come.

Some birds—chickadees, titmice, and kinglets—will come to squeaking with remarkable boldness. Edward A. Preble, Assistant Editor of *Nature Magazine* and a former government biologist, while squeaking birds had a tufted titmouse fly to his hand, cling there, and peck his finger quite sharply. W. E. Clyde Todd, Curator of Birds, Carnegie Museum, Pittsburgh, told me that on one of his scientific trips to Labrador he coaxed, by "squeaking," a pair of boreal chickadees to come closer and closer to him. Finally they perched, side by side, on the barrel of the gun that he carried under one arm. Other birds—the shy thrushes, for example—won't come anywhere near you in response to your squeaking.

The curiosity in the birds—their emotional response that squeaking seems to arouse—varies, too. On some days all the squeak notes that I can utter do not draw one bird near, yet on the following day by squeaking I may easily attract swarms of small birds, especially migrating warblers in the fall of the year.

Manufactured Bird Calls, or "Squeakers"

I have tried to teach my wife how to squeak birds, but she can't seem to master it. Besides, as she points out, she doesn't like to wear her lipstick on the back of her hands or on her fingers. When she despaired over her inability to learn how to squeak, even *without* lipstick, I tried to comfort her by telling her of half a dozen American ornithologists I know who have never been able to learn these methods either.

For these people, and for children too, there are manufactured bird calls, or bird callers, which are easy to use and are effective in attracting the attention of birds. The Audubon Bird Call, made by Roger Eddy of Newington, Conn., is a combination of a pewter plug and a rounded wooden receptacle. It is only two inches long and you can carry one easily in your pocket.

To make sounds with the Audubon Bird Call, you hold

the wooden part of the caller in the fingers of your left hand. Then, with your right hand, you grasp the small, round grip of the pewter plug between your thumb and index finger and turn it backward and forward as you would turn a key in a lock. This produces a squeaking or "creaking wheel" sound which arouses the curiosity of birds. Remember—to be most effective—you must be partly hidden from the bird, or birds, you are trying to lure, and you must stand or sit quietly if you want them to come close to you.

If you have children you have undoubtedly seen the little rubber "squeaking" mice that they like, which are sold in many of the chain stores. I have used one of these and find it effective in exciting the curiosity of birds because of the sharp squeak you can make with it. Hold the rubber mouse in your palm, with its belly against your middle fingers and your thumb on its back. Press down quickly with your thumb, and release the pressure as quickly in a series of rapid motions.

Attracting Birds by Imitating Their Calls   Some birds can be attracted more readily by imitating their songs or call notes than by "squeaking." Each spring I can tremendously excite the male northern oriole of a pair that nests in our yard simply by whistling a fair imitation of his song. This brings him down into a tree or shrub very close over my head, where he whistles at me in what I believe is defiance. Apparently he thinks I am another male oriole that has invaded his territory. He may believe that if he comes near me and keeps whistling that he will drive away this strange unoriolelike creature that "sings" his oriole song.

Theodora Stanwell-Fletcher, author of that delightful book, *Driftwood Valley*, told me that she is more successful in attracting birds by imitating their calls or songs than by squeaking. She often starts rose-breasted grosbeaks and fox sparrows singing, and she believes that she has caused both hermit and wood thrushes to start singing by imitating their songs. She lives near a woodland in which screech owls and horned owls dwell. By imitating their calls she has brought them from the woods into the trees in her yard.

In autumn I have entertained guests by taking them into our garden and imitating the whistled songs of the white-throated sparrows that spend the winter with us. When the white-throats first hear me, three or four of them flutter from the ground up into our shrubbery and sit there whistling back to me their plaintive little song. This becomes a sort of game which makes me wonder if, perhaps, they aren't enjoying it too. As long as I will stand there and whistle that sad, little song, they will reply, even though it is late in the day and it may be growing dark.

It was a glorious afternoon in early autumn. I stood knee-deep in the grass of a hillside in western Pennsylvania. Below me a patchwork of farms spread the length of a valley that lay snuggled between two wooded ridges. All that summer I had heard the whistled call *Bob-white! bob-white!* of quail that lived on the farms in the valley below and upon the slopes of the surrounding hills.

Calling a Covey of Quail

As I glanced down the hillside, over the yellow grass, I saw a quick movement. A brown form scuttled across an opening, followed by another, and then another, until I had counted ten plump, round-backed quail. Soft conversational notes drifted up from them as they moved about. I decided to try an experiment.

Dropping quietly to the ground, I stretched out on my back, then raised slowly on my elbows high enough to see over the tawny grass tops. Softly I whistled, *Wurr-a-lee! Wurr-a-lee! Wurr-a-lee!*

All was silent for a moment, except a crow that called from across the valley. Then, faintly, I heard several notes that sounded like a reply. Once again I whistled, *Wurr-a-lee! Wurr-a-lee! Wurr-a-lee!*

For a moment all was silent again, then, clearly, hesitantly, the call came back to me like an echo out of the past. One of the quail in the flock had answered and its call took me swiftly back to the close of a day of hunting many years ago. A twelve-year-old boy then, I had accompanied a group of older men on a quail and rabbit hunt. As the purple shadows of dusk had fallen over the fields, and the guns had stopped roaring for the day, that pathetic call had come out of the darkness—the darkness of long ago. It was the rally call of the bob-white quail, by which the members of a covey that are not shot bring together at dusk those that are still alive. When they find each other, they draw up in a small, tight circle to roost on the ground for the night, each bird facing outward, ready to warn of danger in the darkness; each ready to fly for its life.

Softly I whistled again, and a reply, hesitant and sweet, came from so near that it startled me. I heard a slight rustling sound, and then several little brown birds ran out of the grass at my feet. Another suddenly appeared at my left side, not eighteen inches away! I dared not move my head, and I hardly dared to breathe for fear of frightening the bright-eyed birds that, like bantam chickens, were now gathering all about me. Without turning I could see them cocking their heads, first on one side and then on the other, looking up curiously at the long figure that lay before them in the grass.

Suddenly I realized, with almost a sense of shock, that they did not know me for a man—their enemy—but only as an inert mass from which a call had come that they understood. I felt ashamed for having fooled them, and I pitied the hesitancy in their actions, their puzzlement, and the struggle that seemed to be going on in them to understand.

Very faintly I whistled the rally call again, and a quail at my feet suddenly reached forward and thumped its bill smartly against the bottom of one of my boots. Its action was so comical, so much like a reproof, that I laughed out loud. In an instant, every bird turned and ran back into the grass.

Slowly I got up, and when I stood fully erect, some of the quail that hadn't run very far saw me. Perhaps they recognized me *now* as an enemy, for a group of them burst into the air with a thunderous roar of their short, rounded wings. Single, scattered birds, farther out in the grass, flew up in quick succession to join them. I watched them speed away until the last bird had disappeared far down the slope.

The memory of that experience still gives me a warm surge of pride to this day. I had discovered that I could speak the language of these birds, and speak it so well that I could call them, unerringly—and trustfully—to my side.

If you live in the northern United States or in Canada where the winters are severe, with snow covering the ground for months at a time, besides songbirds, you may want to help some of the wild game birds to survive. In some parts of the northern states, up to 80 per cent of the ring-necked pheasants may die in winter, especially where no grain crops are raised, and, occasionally, a severe winter has killed off most of the bobwhite quail in New England, especially in the northern part. Game birds are tough and resourceful. But when bitter winds pile great drifts along hedges and woodland borders, covering the weed patches and waste grain, followed by sleet storms that hard-crust the snow and coat every tree and berry-producing shrub with glittering ice, ground-dwelling quail and pheasants may freeze to death, unless they find a dependable source of food.

Early in my career, when I was a field biologist with the Soil Conservation Service, I gave many illustrated lectures about our soil, water, and wildlife conservation work. Winter speaking tours took me from Pennsylvania through upstate New York and into New England. Wherever I spoke, before farmers' groups, 4-H clubs, schools, garden clubs, Boy Scouts, and Rod and Gun Clubs, I found an instant and enormous interest among people in our winter feeding program we had been teaching farmers and suburban dwellers in the North.

Within the farm woodlands or along their thicketed borders, we got farmers to leave a few corn shocks, opened, to give quail and pheasants ready access to grain the farmers scattered there. Others built permanent lean-to or roofed over shelters of sturdy logs and covered with branches of pine, spruce, or other evergreens. Under the shelters they placed wooden hopper-type feeders. The roofed shelters screened the grain spread on the ground from falling snow or rain, but the self-supplying grain in the hopper feeders remained dry, and when refilled once a week, offered quail and pheasants a constant food supply. A hopper feeder about a foot square and three feet high held enough grain for a week or two, and the average feeding station needed several quarts of grain or considerably more each week, depending on the number of birds visiting the station and the severity of the weather. Farmers started their winter feeding programs in October to get the wild game birds accustomed to the location of the feeding station.

To help farmers maintain these feeding stations, Boy Scouts and their leaders from nearby towns and members of the Rod and Gun Clubs traveled to them. Often they went there on snowshoes or on skis to sweep away any snow that blew under the shelters and to replenish with food the ground under them and the hopper feeders. Grain was often donated by kindhearted townspeople and local feed stores.

If you live anywhere that snowfall in winter is heavy and prolonged, you may want to establish one of these feeding shelters in an open corner of your property. You can be almost certain that it will be visited by game birds if your yard or garden borders open fields or a woodland and hedgerows, the places where quail and pheasants winter. Scatter whole corn, buckwheat, wheat, or bird-seed mixtures and scratch grain, including *the very important* grit (see pages 27–29) under your feeding shelter, and you may attract regularly groups of ring-necked pheasants and quail, from fall until spring.

A farmer I knew in western Pennsylvania took great pride in a covey of fifteen bobwhites that came regularly each winter day to his yard to feed. They came at almost exactly 4 o'clock each afternoon. One day when I visited him, we stood and watched through a window as his bobwhites came, running over the snow with little rushes and bursts of speed, to his feeding shelter. They had traveled there under the protection of a hedge that extended from a hillside above the farm to the dooryard below. After feeding, the bobwhites turned and moved slowly back up the hill, staying under the hedge that not only gave them protection from the weather each day, but sheltered them at night as they roosted there on the ground.

Sometimes, roosting on the ground in winter poses a special hazard for quail. All one winter, Mr. Lindley Collins of Marshfield, Massachusetts, fed a dozen bobwhites in his yard. A snowstorm came, followed by a freezing rain. For ten days the quail did not come to feed. Mr. Collins thought the covey might be imprisoned under the snow, and having followed them to their roosting place, he knew where they slept. He went there at once and broke a hole in the crusted snow. The next day the covey came to Mr. Collins to be fed. Later, he discovered that the quail had come out from under the snow through the hole he had broken in the hard surface. Because he knew intimately this covey's habits, Mr. Collins had saved their lives.

10

How to Build a Bluebird Trail [1]

I HAD KNOWN THAT our eastern bluebird, symbol of happiness and eternal spring, had been declining in numbers for seventy-five years; records kept by American ornithologists and bird watchers had proved that. But I was not prepared for the shocking news that came after the winter of 1957–58. During that season of unusually cold weather in the South—called by bird watchers the year of disaster—bluebirds, robins, hermit thrushes, phoebes, and other songbirds that winter there had starved or were frozen to death by the thousands.

Bluebirds were hardest hit. Most birds can stand unbelievable cold if they are well fed. But with the ground and trees coated with ice or snow through much of the winter, the bluebirds' foods of wild berries and insects were unavailable to them. People found their frozen bodies scattered over the ground from Ohio east to Virginia, and from Tennessee through the Carolinas to Florida, the eastern bluebird's main wintering areas. An estimated one-third to one-half of the entire eastern bluebird population

[1] Reprinted by permission of *Woman's Day Magazine*, copyright © 1965 by Fawcett Publications, Inc. Parts of this chapter are also reprinted courtesy of *Home Garden Magazine*, formerly *Flower Grower*, from my article "A Helping Hand to the Bluebird," June 1964 issue—The Author.

was destroyed. Perhaps most of the survivors were those that had learned to come to bird feeders for their favored dried currants, raisins, and chopped peanuts. At Chapel Hill, North Carolina, I had found I could help them in winter by giving them a doughy paste which they loved; I mixed bacon drippings or suet with peanut butter, corn meal, and flour and stuck it in the rough bark of trees or put it in my suspended bird-feeding sticks.

I knew that feeding bluebirds in winter could help them, but it could not overcome the widespread diminishing effect on their numbers due to the six harsh winters which followed the disastrous winter of 1957–58. Unusual winter cold in the South continued to kill bluebirds until their population reached its lowest point in history during the spring of 1963. People who loved them and who watched them return in thinning numbers in the spring were aghast. How long could the bluebird, so vulnerable in winter, survive? I decided to help them in the most effective way they could be helped; along with others, who were doing something about their plight, I would build a bluebird trail.

Bluebirds do not nest in the open in a bush or a tree as many birds do. They carry nesting materials of soft grasses and fragrant pine needles into the abandoned nest holes of woodpeckers, or into the dark hollows of trees and old wooden fences. But most of these favored places are gone. Farmers have replaced the old orchard trees with younger, neatly tended trees without hollows; most fences are no longer wooden but are made of steel posts and wire.

Suffering from an acute housing shortage, bluebirds have been further deprived of nesting places by the more aggressive European starling and house sparrow—introduced into North America in the latter half of the nineteenth century—which also nest in cavities. If anyone was to help the bluebird, he would not only have to build bluebird houses for the garden but also to make many boxes available to bluebirds in the parts of the countryside where most of them live. And the boxes would have to be designed and hung in a way that would discourage pre-emption of them by starlings and sparrows.

I first heard of bluebird trails from my friend and adviser, T. E. Musselman of Quincy, Illinois. He had coined the term in 1934 for the twenty-five bluebird nesting boxes he had set up along country fence posts in Adams County, Illinois, a place in which bluebirds had almost disappeared. In February 1935 he added more houses until 102 were placed along forty-three miles of country roads. Eighty-eight of the boxes, or 86 per cent, were quickly occupied by bluebirds. In the published report of this conservation project, Dr. Musselman wrote that "for the first time in twenty years, bluebirds are a common sight along the roads of Adams County, Illinois, and I believe that any other enthusiast can duplicate this." He called his series of bluebird nest boxes a "bluebird trail," and is credited with originating both the name and the idea.

One evening I went before the Orange County Boy Scout Council, a group of businessmen, doctors, lawyers, writers, and others in Chapel Hill who serve the local Boy Scouts and Cub Scouts by overseeing their projects. I needed at least thirty bluebird houses to start a bluebird trail, and I thought the youngsters could help. And what better project could one offer children? It would not only help bluebirds, but it would give the youngsters an opportunity when traveling the bluebird trail to learn about birds and their ways.

The Council agreed and the Boy Scouts and Cub Scouts built sixty bluebird nesting boxes from a sample bluebird house I had given them. Under my instruction, they wired or nailed them to fence posts along farm-country roadsides. The boxes were set about 4 feet above the ground, each one facing the road, away from pastures where grazing cattle might rub against the boxes and break them. We placed the boxes about 400 feet apart. Setting them closer together would result in too much fighting for their possession (bluebirds are strongly territorial and will drive out other bluebirds from their chosen nesting areas).

The memory of the first bluebird house we hung one April day on a fence post at the edge of a farm field will linger in the mind of every boy who was there. One of the boys, "for luck" he said, had scratched with his knife "Home Sweet Home" on the front panel or door of the box. We had nailed the box to the post; it was low enough so that a house sparrow would hesitate to nest in it, and it had a 1½-inch-round entrance hole which was too small for a starling to enter.

As we walked away and stood at the edge of the road to admire our work, a handsome male bluebird flew to the entrance hole and clung there, looking inside. He warbled gently to his mate. When she answered and flew to him from a tree, we saw that she was a paler blue and a softer brown than he. She alighted at the entrance hole, looked in the box, then shivered her wings ecstatically. We got in our car and drove on, fearful of frightening her and wondering if she would accept the new brown-painted home we had offered her.

On the way back from our three-mile trip down the road to hang the remaining bluebird houses, we stopped near the first nesting box. The boys shouted at what they saw. The female bluebird, with some brown pine needles in her bill, was entering the box. Five days later, she had completed the nest; two days later, she had laid her first pale blue egg. After that, we discovered that she laid an egg each day for five days, usually in the morning between seven and eight o'clock.

When our bluebird had laid her five eggs, she began to incubate them, spending long hours inside the box with her warm breast pressed close to the eggs. Rarely did she come outside, but the male came regularly to the entrance hole with a grasshopper, a beetle, or a soft caterpillar to feed her. Each time that he arrived, we saw her head appear at the doorway to take food from his bill. Then she disappeared to settle down again on her nest.

Two of the boys went with me once a week to inspect the bluebird trail. After fourteen days the eggs had hatched in the first nesting box, and, within another two weeks, the five young bluebirds had flown. By the middle of June, thirty of our bluebird houses had bluebirds nesting in them. Others of the houses had nesting chickadees, wrens, titmice, or nuthatches in them, especially those boxes we had placed on fence posts near woods. These smaller birds were welcome too and so were the big-eyed flying squirrels and the small deer mice that built their nests in two of the empty nesting boxes.

By summer's end, our pairs of bluebirds had each raised two or three broods, but not without tragedy. Several broods disappeared when they were very small, possibly eaten by a snake or a raccoon. A farm cat caught one young bluebird just after it had flown from the box. But from our regular visits along the trail, we knew that our sturdily built boxes had sent more than two hundred young bluebirds successfully into the world.

The next spring we added more bluebird boxes to the trail. By August—the end of the nesting season—under their parents' care, more than three hundred young bluebirds flew from our seventy-five nesting boxes. With the passing of the next two winters, bluebirds in our part of North Carolina were almost as common as they had been before the cold winters of the previous decade.

From time to time I had received similarly encouraging reports from a retired doctor, and several each from educators, insurance men, engineers, construction workers, and housewives who have built bluebird trails. Stiles Thomas of Allendale, New Jersey, began his first bluebird trail in 1955 when he and other members of the Fyke Nature Association put 69 bluebird nest boxes on country fenceposts and poles. Within five years they had placed 107 boxes, of which the most successful were those attached to fenceposts and utility poles, rather than to trees.

W. G. (Bill) Duncan of Louisville, Kentucky, not only developed his own bluebird trail, but also supplied people throughout the United States and Canada with bluebird houses of his own successful design. He also originated a "Bluebird Letter," whose stimulating messages went out to hundreds of correspondents.

William Highhouse of Warren, Pennsylvania, encouraged by Bill Duncan, began a bluebird trail in his county in 1957. Within five years he had placed 100 bluebird nest boxes, about three to a mile, along rural roads. From these, eastern bluebirds raised more than a thousand young of which almost eight hundred were from the first (usually more successful) nesting season. His bluebird trail became a full-time hobby.

Inspired by the work of Bill Duncan, Dick Irwin of Anchorage, Kentucky, put up 161 bluebird boxes on fence-posts over seven square miles of Kentucky roadsides beginning in the spring of 1961. In 1962, his sturdily built nest boxes had seventy-two pairs of bluebirds nesting in them; they produced two hundred young.

His nest boxes are the most practical I have ever seen. The boxes are 4½ by 4½ by 9½ inches, with a 1½-inch entrance hole in a front panel, which, for regular inspection of nesting, swings open on two nails driven into the sides of the box. (No hinges are needed.) They are tightly built, warm and dry inside, with a ventilating space just under the roof (see illustration, p. 185).

Dick said that his bluebird boxes, if kept painted (he painted them white, which reflects light and keeps them cooler) will last fifteen to twenty years. He sent me six to get me started and these began the Dick Irwin Bluebird Trail of Chapel Hill, North Carolina—the trail which I had started with the Boy Scouts and Cub Scouts and which had been dedicated to him.

From my own experience with bluebird trails, and from information I have gathered from those who have long had them, here are some good rules to follow:

1. Choose as a trail leader a parent, Scout Troop leader, or other responsible person. Start a bluebird trail at any time between February 1 and July 1; however, it is best to have boxes up early for first nestings, which may be as early as March. Some bluebirds have second and third nestings through May, June, and into July. The nesting range of the eastern bluebird is from Newfoundland south to Florida and Bermuda, west to the Rocky Mountains, and from Saskatchewan south to Texas.

2. It is best to start modestly with twelve to fifteen bluebird nest boxes. Placed four to a mile, these will stretch

three or four miles out of town. You can add more, or start a new trail each year.

3. Paint the boxes (white, gray, brown, or green) before you put them up, and paint them on the outside only.

4. Choose a quiet, secondary road where there are lots of fenceposts and open fields, and occasional woods along the way. This is typical bluebird country—they like open fields adjacent to country roads and one can often see them perched on utility wires by the roadside. Some bluebird trailers prefer roads that make a circle and will bring them back to the town from which they started. Others do not mind backtracking. You may start your trail in your garden, or in the garden of a friend, and extend outward, unless of course you live in a city.

5. Ask permission of landowners to put up bluebird boxes on their fenceposts. Nail or screw each bluebird house to the side of the fencepost that faces the road. Besides nails or screws, carry some wire with which to fasten the bluebird houses to metal fenceposts.

6. Set the boxes no more than 4 feet above the ground. house sparrows are less likely to occupy a low-placed nestbox; bluebirds will accept them. I have seen bluebirds nesting in the hollows of wooden fenceposts no more than 3 feet above the ground, but about 4 to 5 feet is a good height—about one's eye level with the entrance hole of the box as this allows easy inspection of the nesting progress when opening the swing-front panel of the box. *Do not* put up boxes on fenceposts near farmhouses as house sparrows usually congregate there and will occupy them to the exclusion of bluebirds.

7. Some authorities put up no more than four nest boxes per mile but I have found, as have others, that pairs of bluebirds do not always have territorial squabbles if the boxes are closer together. In your yard you may place up to three bluebird houses, but put them on different sides of the house. This prevents each nesting pair from seeing the others at their nestboxes and reduces fighting. The boxes on our bluebird trail at Chapel Hill were put on fenceposts about 400 to 500 feet apart. We had about 80 per cent occupancy

by bluebirds our first year and have had comparable nesting occupancy ever since. This is equal to or better than average.

8. Boxes may also be attached to isolated trees, trees at the border of open woods, and trees of small or medium size, as bluebirds do not seem to like boxes on large trees—perhaps they fear the squirrels that often race up and down a large tree in their hunt for nuts and acorns. Boxes may also be attached to utility (electric power and telephone) poles but without company permission, these might be torn down by maintenance linemen.

9. Bear in mind that not only bluebirds but chickadees, nuthatches, titmice, wrens, and other desirable hole-nesting birds will also nest in your bluebird houses. These are good tenants just as useful in their insect-eating habits as bluebirds. When you tell farmers and other landowners about your purpose—that you are trying to help birds which in turn help them—I doubt if anyone will refuse you permission to put up boxes on his land.

10. Inspect your bluebird trail at least once a week. Early on Sunday morning may be a good time. Much of the fun and rewards of the trail are in these periodic inspections. The trail leader should open the nest boxes—tap on the box first to allow the bluebird on the nest to get out before you open the box. My friends, especially the young ones, are amused when I tap on the box, or knock on the side panel and ask, "Is there anybody home?" The swing-front panel of the Dick Irwin Bluebird House is ideal for quick and easy inspection. Open the set-screw at the bottom of the front panel with a screw driver. After examining the contents for nest-building progress, number of eggs, or growth of the young, make notes for later reference, then swing the panel back in place and screw it shut to prevent an easy opening of the box by people who might not be as interested in the welfare of bluebirds as you are. By taking notes on eggs and young, you will learn how long it takes for the nest to be built, eggs to hatch, and young to grow large enough to leave the nest.

11. Maintenance of bluebird trails (repair or replace-

ment of boxes damaged by accident or vandals) is important. A small white card tacked to the front of the box below the entrance hole, telling what the box is, and its purpose, may help prevent the destruction of the box by thoughtless people. We tacked the following message on the front of each bluebird box of the bluebird trail at Chapel Hill.

THE DICK IRWIN BLUEBIRD TRAIL

Please do not disturb

This box was designed by Dick Irwin of Anchorage, Kentucky, to help give bluebirds a place to nest. One spring day, while many bluebirds were building their nests in his boxes along roads in Kentucky, Dick Irwin died at age 64. This trail is dedicated to his memory.

Not a single one of our boxes has ever been destroyed.

Materials: ⅛-in. hardboard for top; ¾-in. white pine for other parts; 1½-in. galv. nails; ¾-in. No. 6 brass flat-head screws for top; 1⅝-in. galv. screw for front.

11

Some Problems and
How to Meet Them

FOR SEVERAL GOOD REASONS, we remember the first winter we fed birds in the garden of our home in suburban New York city. Squirrels gave us our first "problem"—big, sleek gray squirrels that practically overrun the suburbs and public parks of New York, Boston, Philadelphia, and other large cities in the eastern United States, and have little natural habitat from which to feed.

In the country, squirrels had seldom visited my feeding trays because the nearest woodland was almost a quarter of a mile away. As any squirrel will tell you—if he could make himself understood—it is risky for him to travel far without the protection of a tree up which he can run to escape from hawks, owls, dogs, cats, and those men and boys who take up a rifle or shotgun to hunt squirrels in the fall of the year.

In the tree- and shrub-planted parks and suburbs of a large city, some of these hazards for squirrels don't exist, or they are reduced to a minimum. It is against the law to hunt within city limits, and the large hawks and owls that ordinarily feed on squirrels and help to keep down their populations seldom live within or close to large cities.

Without these checks on their numbers, gray squirrels have multiplied and become so fearless that they run about in our suburban neighborhood just like domesticated animals.

We like to see squirrels in our yard. During the winter we feed them ears of corn and peanuts, which squirrels are so fond of. Squirrels are beautiful, graceful animals, and they are, to us, just as interesting to watch as are the birds. It was in the beginning, when the squirrels kept birds away from the feeders, that they became a problem.

After we had put up our feeding stations, gray squirrels got into them easily by climbing the wooden posts that support them and by running down the wire with which we suspended one feeder from the limb of a tree in our yard.

When they got in the bird feeders, they sometimes sat there eating for an hour or more. We didn't much mind how much they ate, but meanwhile songbirds, which are afraid of squirrels and won't come to the feeders while they are in them, stayed away. We wanted the squirrels in our yard, but we also wanted the birds. What could we do about it?

Metal Bands and Metal Cones to "Squirrel-Proof" the Feeders

First, we nailed a strip of thin, sheet metal[1] completely around each of the wooden posts that support our feeders. When the squirrels tried to get to them by running up the posts, they couldn't climb over the smooth metal surfaces. That stopped them only temporarily, for the squirrels soon showed us that they had other ways of reaching the feeders.

Squirrels will climb the sides of frame buildings and fences or climb out on the overhanging branches of trees and shrubs to leap down on the feeder from above. We soon found that we had to set every one of our feeding-station posts at least 8 to 10 feet away from any object

[1] Most bird-feeders sold by dealers in bird-attracting supplies are "squirrel-proof." Write for illustrated catalogs. See list that appears in Appendix.

which a squirrel could climb upon to get at a point above, or nearly above, the feeder. In the course of trying to protect our feeders from our furry friends we also discovered that it is best to set feeders on posts at least 54 inches or, preferably, 60 inches above the ground. This keeps them out of the reach of some of our more agile squirrels that seem to have "springs" in their feet.

To prevent squirrels from climbing down the wire to reach the feeder that we suspended from a tree limb, we had a tinsmith make a circular metal cone, about 30 inches in diameter. We slipped this down on the wire to a point about 18 inches above the feeder. The squirrels that ventured down the wire to the metal cone suddenly found themselves sliding down its steep sides until they pitched off it to the ground. After trying a few times and failing to reach the feeder, they gave up and returned to those big yellow ears of corn which we heap in their wire basket feeder that hangs on the trunk of our white oak tree.

The squirrels also gave us a problem with our feeding-sticks, which we had filled with peanut butter to attract chickadees and nuthatches. When the squirrels discovered them, they climbed down the wires to the feeding sticks to see what they were, and ate the peanut butter. We didn't mind them eating the peanut butter, but they also gnawed away pieces of wood from around the edges of the feeding stick holes, which had become saturated with the peanut oil. If the squirrels continued to do this, they would destroy the feeding sticks in a short time. We had to do something to prevent it.

Protecting Feeding-Sticks from Squirrels

Instead of having metal cones made to put on the wires above the feeding sticks, we simply stopped filling the holes in them with peanut butter and substituted suet. We had noticed that our squirrels had never eaten the suet that we occasionally tied to the limbs of trees for the birds. The peanut butter, which our birds like so well, we now put in small, open compartments in those feeders that the squirrels couldn't reach. From that time on, after they discovered we had put suet in the feeding sticks, the squirrels no longer bothered them.

*Keeping
Squirrels off
the Window
Shelf Feeder*
Our first window shelf feeder was a plain board or tray that I fastened to the sill of one of our first-floor windows. The sill is only about 3 feet above the ground and squirrels easily leaped up or ran up the side of the house.

To outwit them, we bought some heavy "fox wire" screening, because poultry wire is too pliable, and squirrels can bend and enlarge its openings. The fox wire had mesh openings about 1½ inches high and about 2 inches long. We enclosed our window shelf feeder with a piece of this, and bent it to form a rectangle about 18 inches high and 12×12 inches square at its ends. We tacked the bottom of this wire frame to the edges of the feeding shelf, and nailed a narrow strip of wood over the edges of the wire where they met the sides of the house. Chickadees, nuthatches, juncos, purple finches, goldfinches, tree sparrows, white-throated sparrows, and song sparrows passed easily through the openings of the wire mesh, but it kept out the larger squirrels, pigeons, starlings, blue jays, and grackles. Our chickadees flew directly through the openings, without touching the wire, but most birds alighted on the horizontal strands when coming into or leaving the shelf feeder.

If you don't want to build your window shelf feeder, some of the dealers in bird-attracting supplies sell glass-enclosed ones. We use one that has a long, narrow opening near the outside bottom of the feeder, which keeps out squirrels and pigeons but allows smaller birds to enter.

How to Keep Squirrels from Gnawing Bird Nesting Boxes

Gray squirrels like to get inside some of the bird nesting boxes, just as the birds do. There they will build a warm, leafy nest to sleep in, or perhaps to raise a litter of young ones in. In much the same way, squirrels in the forest enlarge the entrance holes to woodpecker nesting cavities in the dead stubs of trees. Our suburban squirrels, in gaining entrance to our man-made bird boxes, are following an old, established squirrel custom. If your bird boxes are on trees where squirrels can gnaw them, this is easily prevented by nailing a metal ring, or a piece of sheet metal an inch or two wide around the outside of the entrance hole to the bird nesting box. The strip also may be run into the bird box and nailed on the inside of the front panel so that the entrance hole inside and out is covered with the metal. This will discourage squirrels from gnawing at the edges of the hole to enlarge it. Make certain that the metal is smooth and that it has no sharp projecting edges which can injure a bird going in and out of the nest box.

Should You Discriminate Between Your Bird Guests?

Some people object to feeding the larger and more aggressive birds, claiming that they frighten away smaller ones. In all the years we have fed birds we have never seen the jays, starlings, and grackles in our garden keep the smaller birds from the feeders for very long. If you have only one feeding station you will notice that, as soon as the larger birds leave it, the smaller sparrows and juncos will fly to it and feed there until the larger birds return. We scatter some grain and pieces of bread on the ground at several places in the yard, which distributes the birds about, and allows most of them to eat peaceably in our yard, all at the same time. Many of our smaller birds come to our glassed-in, window shelf feeder, where they feed undisturbed because the opening is too narrow to admit a blue jay, grackle, or starling.

How the Blue Jay Serves Other Birds

One fall day several years ago my wife and I went out on our terrace in the back yard and sat down to watch our birds. I had filled the feeders with our wild bird seed mixture and had scattered some on the ground under the shrubs along our north property-line fence for the flock of white-throated sparrows that had come to spend the winter with us. The white-throats like to scratch about among the fallen leaves under the shrubs, and they seem to prefer eating grain there to eating it in the feeders.

We sat watching half a dozen of them hopping about, picking up the seeds and cracking them in their bills, only pausing now and then to look about them and call *s-s-s-s-s-s-s-t-t-t!* in that lisping way in which they seem to talk among themselves. Two blue jays sat on the edge of our open feeder. This is fastened on top of a post set in the lawn about 15 feet from where the white-throats were feeding. The jays were eating sunflower seeds, and bolting them down one after another. The yard seemed peaceful.

Suddenly one of the jays straightened and raised its feathered crest. It looked toward the shrubbery under which the white-throats were feeding, then flew quietly toward them. It alighted in the top of the tallest shrub above the white-throats, looked down toward the ground, and screamed, *Y-a-a-a-n-n-h-h! Y-a-a-a-n-n-h-h! Y-a-a-a-n-n-h-h!*

The white-throats flew up into the branches of our oak tree and began calling excitedly. I got up and walked quietly toward the place where they had been feeding. A black cat jumped out from under the down-sweeping branches of one of our pine trees and ran out of our yard. It had been stalking the sparrows, and had been almost upon them when the blue jay's warning cry had sent them flying to safety.

These little dramas of life or death for the birds are

played in our yard every day. Invariably it is the blue jay that first warns the other birds of danger—of a cat or a threatening hawk or a shrike—even before the sharp-eyed, wary starlings have discovered it. We call our blue jays our "watchdogs for the birds," for we know that they have saved the lives of many of them with their loud, timely warnings.

Each of our birdhouses has either one of its sides or the top of the box hinged. This enables us to open them and clean out the old nesting material at least once a year. If we didn't, the birds might not use them the following year. Besides, other animals smaller than the birds, may get in the nesting boxes in the fall or winter, before the birds return to nest in the spring. During several winters we have had some of the big-eyed, white-footed mice that usually live in a nearby woodland move into one of our bird boxes. These are gentle little wild folk that remind us of the pixies of the fairy tales we read when we were children. They are harmless to birds, but a pair of wrens or bluebirds may not nest in the box if they find it already occupied by mice.

Once, when I lived in the country, a pair of flying squirrels made a nest in one of our flicker boxes. These small squirrels are so beautiful and were so interesting to us that we did not disturb them or the nest box until we found that they had deserted it. Then we cleaned it out thoroughly to prepare for the next family of flickers that later moved in.

We clean out our bird boxes about March 15, which is just before the songbird nesting season begins in our New York city area. If we find a family of white-footed mice in one of them, we don't feel so badly about evicting them at that time because winter is usually past. Some people clean out their birdhouses in the fall, after the nesting season is over, but we delay ours until spring for a most important reason. The young of many hole-nesting birds are parasitized by an insect which in its young, or "grub," form may either directly or indirectly kill them.

*Housecleaning
Your Bird
Nesting Boxes*

*The Blow Fly
"Enemy" or
Nestling Birds*

It is to help control this insect that we clean our birdhouses in the spring. Here's why.

Shortly after the hatching of young bluebirds, tree swallows, chickadees, crested flycatchers, and other birds which will nest in bird boxes, a blow fly, or blue bottle fly, may call on the young birds. The fly will lay its eggs on them and the tiny grubs, which hatch from the fly's eggs, attach themselves to the young birds and begin sucking their blood. In the summer of 1951 three young house wrens in one of our garden broods died from the attacks of these grubs.

Fortunately for the young birds the grubs have an insect parasite which destroys them and thus helps the birds. It is a tiny chalcid fly (pronounced KAL-sid) which lays its eggs on the blow fly grubs. When the young of the chalcid fly hatch, they eat the grub that is sucking blood from the birds. Many of these chalcid flies sleep through the winter in the bird nest material within the bird box. If you destroy this material in the fall, especially if you burn it, you will destroy the valuable chalcid flies. That is why we wait until early spring to dump the nest material out on the ground in some inconspicuous place where the chalcid flies can emerge to go on with their good work.[2] Remember—do *not* burn the old nest material. Simply sweep it out on the ground just before the nesting season begins.

Disinfecting and Repairing Birdhouses   When you clean out your birdhouses, just before the nesting season, this is an excellent time to repair or replace sides, tops, or bottoms that may be cracked, broken, or rotted from long use. If you think the outside of the bird box

[2] A bird scientist in New England has discovered an even more effective way to get rid of the blow flies and, yet, save the chalcid flies, both of which may spend the winter in the same bird nesting material. After each brood of young birds has flown, he empties the nest material out of the bird boxes into a metal container and covers this with a piece of fine-mesh window screening. When the blow flies hatch from the pupal cases in which they have transformed from grubs to adults, they are too large to escape through the fine-wire mesh, and so they die. When the smaller chalcid flies emerge, they can escape through the wire screening and are free to continue their work of parasitizing the blow fly grubs that attack young birds.

needs to be treated again with a wood preservative or repainted, this is a good time to do it. After cleaning the inside of the box thoroughly, spray with creolin (1 part creolin to 10 parts water) obtainable at most drugstores. This will destroy bird lice or other insects that may remain hidden in the cracks and corners.

One summer day some years ago, a man in Nebraska who had a pair of wrens nesting in a bird box in his yard discovered one of them dead just inside the entrance hole. It was a female and, as he found out later, she had been stung to death by a wasp. Two days later the male got another mate and brought her to the nest box. She, too, was stung by a wasp as she entered the box and died just within the doorway. A colony of paper-making wasps[3] had got established in the nest box, perhaps after the wrens had built their nest, and had killed two of the birds before the man discovered them. We had heard of many bird boxes in which wasps and birds had nested at the same time, but had never known a wasp to kill a bird until we learned of the Nebraska man's experience.

Wasps in Birdhouses

The *Polistes* wasps, although able to sting painfully, are not as aggressive and as fiery as the white-faced hornets that nest in big, gray paper nests. These nests are shaped like footballs, and the hornets build them suspended from the branches of trees and shrubs. The *Polistes* will allow you to approach them in their open nests quite close, if you move quietly and don't make sudden motions that anger them. Usually these wasps do not attack birds. In our few experiences with them in our bird nesting boxes, they got into them early in spring, before nesting had started. This made it much easier to get rid of them.

[3] These wasps are called by scientists *Polistes*. They live in colonies and each colony builds a flat, open cluster of cells that the queen begins when she awakens from hibernation in the spring. These paper cells that make up the "nest" look like the comb of a honeybee and are the nurseries or chambers for the young wasps of the growing colony. The *Polistes* wasps build these nests suspended from the inside roofs of open sheds, inside bird boxes, and in other places that are sheltered.

In the beginning, we had used an aerosol bomb to destroy the wasps. After dark, when they were gathered quietly on the nest, we plugged the entrance hole with a cloth to prevent the wasps from getting out of the bird box. Then we shot a spray of an insecticide from the bomb [4] into the box for about ten to fifteen seconds. The next morning when we opened the birdhouse, we found that every wasp within had been killed by the deadly liquid. Although we never found a dead bird in the nest box later, when it was occupied by a pair of wrens, I was uneasy about the possible lasting lethal effects on them or their nestlings.

One August day I wrote to the U.S. Fish and Wildlife Service, Washington, D.C., and asked if there were any other means of evicting wasps from birdhouses without using an insecticide such as DDT. The Service wrote that they had made a series of experiments on the effects of spraying DDT inside the nest boxes of birds, or directly on the nests, eggs, or young. They found that DDT had no observable effect on the adult birds, but that it might have some effect on the survival of the nestlings. Instead of using DDT, they advised Sevin, a carbamate with which they had been experimenting. It gave excellent control of insects within the nest boxes, and was relatively nontoxic to birds; however, it can be extremely toxic to bees. They suggested that, used within bird boxes, the compound would not threaten bees, which do not live inside of bird nesting boxes as wasps do, and would be useful for insect control within the birdhouses early in the year, before the birds' nesting season has begun. The Service does not advise using Sevin during the time that the young are in the nest. The boxes become warm inside during the day and the insecticide might subject the nestlings to some respiratory intoxication; however, it had not been observed in their studies.

In evicting wasps from bluebird houses along my bluebird trail in North Carolina (see the chapter "How to Build a Bluebird Trail") I do not use an insecticide but

[4] Aerosol bombs are sold to destroy many kinds of household insect pests. Hardware stores and others that sell gardening equipment usually have them.

open the front of the bird box and then assault the wasps and their nest with a blunt stick. However, in this method there is a risk of getting stung. After the nest is destroyed, the wasps will remain out of the nest box temporarily but will try to renest in it again. They must be evicted repeatedly until a pair of birds is in possession, when there is far less likelihood of the wasps nesting in the box.

Although we have never experienced it, friends of ours who live in the country once had a flicker come to their house on a fall day and start drilling a hole in one of its outside walls. What was the bird's purpose, they asked, and what could they do to stop him?

In autumn, flickers and other woodpeckers will drill holes in the dead stubs of trees where they hollow out a place to sleep during the cold winter nights. Once in a while, if there are no dead stubs of trees about, they will drill into the sides of barns and other buildings to gain a sleeping place for the winter.

As with the flicker that had drilled holes in the barn, to solve the problem, we advised our friends to put up at least one flicker nesting box in a tree that stood near their house. Then, if it didn't abandon its hole-making for the flicker box, they should frighten it away by firing a gun into the air. Although they had to fire the gun several times before the flicker would abandon the idea of roosting in their attic for the winter, the bird finally left.

There is a happy sequel to the story. The following spring, a pair of these birds nested in the box they had put up, and during the following winter a flicker roosted in the box each night. Whether one of these was the same flicker that had tried so hard to break into their house they never knew. But they have a much kindlier feeling toward flickers now that they understand them and have them for their nearest neighbors.

Almost every spring, one of the robins that nests in or near our yard discovers his image in one of our basement windows and starts to fight it. Robins are strongly territorial, and each male will chase away other male robins that come within the invisible boundaries of the part of our yard that he has declared to be his own. If we don't try to stop our robin, he may jump at his reflection in the window, sparring with it like a bantam rooster for a week or more. A robin nesting in the yard of one of our neighbors fought all one day with his image that he saw reflected from the shining metal disk on one of the rear wheels of their car. To prevent the bird from exhausting himself, they kept their car in the garage the next day.

We stopped our robin from its wearing battle with our basement window by putting a fine-mesh window screen in front of it. Apparently this broke the image, for the bird stopped fighting its imaginary rival.

Preventing Birds from Flying into Picture Windows

We don't have a picture window in our house, but a woman in North Carolina wrote me about one in her home which accounted for the deaths of at least a dozen hummingbirds before she found a way to prevent it. The birds, seeing the reflected trees, shrubs, and grass in the window, apparently saw them as a further extension of the garden. When they tried to fly into it, they struck the plate glass window and were killed.

The woman bought some of the sheerest nylon marquisette she could get—enough to cover completely an area six feet long by five feet high, or the size of the picture window. The plate glass of her window was set back about two inches from the outside face of the house and window frame. She had the nylon stretched tight across the window opening and held in place by a narrow strip of molding tacked around the outside edge of the window frame. In this position the nylon screen prevents her hummingbirds from flying into the window yet does not obstruct her view when looking out because the nylon is sheer. She renews this inexpensive material about every two or three years.

Birds, like ourselves, are creatures of habit. They get accustomed to flying in certain directions to and from their nests. Sometimes they follow aerial "paths," as we follow our trail of flagstones when we walk along the edges of our garden.

In the spring of 1982, because he left his garage doors open, one of our next-door neighbors lost one of the pair of catbirds that nested in his yard. Ordinarily he keeps them closed. On this day he had backed his car a little way down the driveway and had propped the doors wide open. The catbird, accustomed to flying along one side of the garage and then turning sharply to fly across the front of it to reach its nest, struck one of the doors and was killed.

A man I know near Philadelphia, who has been attracting birds and banding them for twenty-five years, lost a male cardinal in the same way. Early in his bird-attracting and bird-banding career he had a pair of cardinals nesting in his yard. He had banded both birds. By their band numbers he knew them to be the same mated pair that had lived in his garden for five years. One day he, too, left open one of his garage doors, which were usually closed. The cardinal, flying swiftly along one of its regular aerial routes, turned the corner of the garage and struck the opened door before it could check its speed or swerve to avoid it.

Robins, phoebes, or barn swallows may build their nests on the rafters and inside ledges of your garage if you leave the doors open for a few days in spring or early summer. If you want the birds to nest in your garage, you should leave the doors open all through the nesting season so they can get in and out to feed their young ones or to incubate their eggs. Hungry young birds, shut off from their parents, may starve to death within a day if deprived of food. If you don't want birds to nest in your garage, be sure to keep the doors closed in spring and early summer to prevent a nesting tragedy.

Vines to Cover Your Fireplace Chimney

One of our neighbors likes birds and is greatly interested in them. Yet he admitted to me one day that he had made a mistake when he planted an English ivy vine at the base of his fireplace chimney. Within twenty-five years, the vine had covered the outside brickwork from ground level to chimney top with a luxuriant growth of dark-green leaves. The vine was beautiful and added greatly to the attractiveness of his home, but he said, "It had become too noisy with roosting birds."

House sparrows and starlings swarmed into the vine to sleep, especially during the winter, because of the warmth of the chimney, and the evergreen leaves that protected them from wind, rain, and snow. Our neighbor, who is a light sleeper, said that early in the morning the chatter of birds, which like to linger on cold days in their warm shelter against the chimney, kept him awake.

No matter how much you may be interested in birds, it would be well for you to consider our neighbor's problem. If you, too, are a light sleeper, it might not be wise to risk losing your ardor for the birds by inviting them to sleep just outside your window. We have an ivy vine on the outside of our chimney, and we don't mind the early morning chatter of the birds because we, too, are usually early risers. If you like to sleep late, you might plant your vine at the base of a large tree [5] or a tree stump, somewhere in your yard away from the house. There the birds will have their roost and you will get your proper rest—an arrangement that our neighbor says, rather ruefully, he wishes he had made.

Cats and Birds

I don't know of any problem in bird-attracting that is more perplexing to some people than the one of cats and birds. I have known a number of families who hesitated

[5] Not many vines in the United States, except Japanese honeysuckle and grape, are vigorous enough to kill trees.

about starting to attract birds because they owned a cat. They were in honest doubt about the wisdom of drawing birds to their yard while they had a pet whose natural instincts are to hunt and kill. I know people who have cats and stoutly maintain that they *never* kill birds; others who have them are equally sure that they do; and some of the people who don't own cats and attract birds are positive that cats kill little else but birds.

Our position on this vexing question is, we hope, a sensible one. We are very fond of cats, and have had several of them during the years we have been attracting birds. We don't believe that cats, in general, can ever be taught *not* to hunt birds, but if you keep your cat where it will not be able to reach them, your garden birds should be safe from it. We kept our cat within a screened porch most of the time during summer. When someone in the family took it out for exercise, they put it on a long leash. Although this prevented our cat from catching birds, it did not stop our neighbors' cats from occasionally catching them.

We don't own a cat now but, having had one, we appreciate the affection that people may have for them. A cat stalking one of your favorite chickadees or cardinals may arouse your fury, but you should remember that the cat may be someone's pet—perhaps a child's—and any harm you bring it may cause a neighborhood quarrel and possibly a lasting regret over any hasty action on your part.

What to Do About Your Neighbor's Cat

Our neighbors have cooperated wonderfully in helping us with the cat problem. They have "belled" their cats—put a small bell on the cat's collar, which tinkles with its every movement when it tries to stalk birds. This helps, but they have also told me to chase their cats and to frighten them off in any way that we think will teach their pets to stay out of our yard. By repeatedly chasing them away, whenever we see them, we have not had to use violence and the neighborhood cats have learned to avoid our yard, at least during the day.

A "cat proof" fence, 6 feet high and made of strong woven wire, with 1½-inch mesh openings, will keep cats, dogs, and almost all other creatures out of your yard. The fence should overhang 2 feet at its top *toward the outside*, to prevent any animal from climbing over it. These fences are expensive; but, if you can afford one, they will give your songbirds complete protection against all animals, except predatory birds [6]—the small hawks, owls, and shrikes that sometimes kill and eat songbirds.

My wife and I shall never forget one cold February day a few years ago when we counted 346 songbirds feeding in our back yard. Red-winged blackbirds, grackles, cowbirds, house sparrows, and starlings fairly swarmed over several of the open feeders; downy woodpeckers, nuthatches, and chickadees were eating suet from our feeding sticks; and a mourning dove, a flock of juncos, and white-throated, fox, tree, and song sparrows pecked at the ground under shrubs where we had spread seeds for them. Four blue jays flew in and away from the feeders, carrying peanuts up into our white oak tree where they sat holding them under their feet and hammering them open with their beaks. The calling of the red-wings, cowbirds, grackles, and starlings made a bedlam of creaking, whistling bird sounds that our neighbors could hear a block away.

We were watching the birds out of the window when we heard a jay scream a warning. Instantly the birds in our yard fell silent and flattened themselves on the feeders, on the ground, against trees, or wherever they happened to be.

Then, with the suddenness of a stroke of lightning, a small brown hawk swooped down out of the air and darted at the birds in one of the feeders. Just before it reached them, songbirds exploded upward all over the yard with a roar of wings that must have been as startling to the hawk as it was to us. The hawk, disconcerted by the birds that were in the air all about him, seemed to bound straight up into the air, turned sideward, and shot down again toward the feeder. That moment of indecision by the hawk was all that the songbirds had needed. Not one remained

[6] Birds also are animals, although many people think that only dogs, cats, raccoons, and other four-footed creatures that wear fur should be so classified. Man, too, is an animal.

in sight. All had dived into shelter—into spruce trees, yews, and pines.

The American kestrel—for that is what it was—alighted atop a brush pile that we had built in our garden about fifteen feet away from the most exposed open feeder. I looked at the bird through my binoculars and saw him in all his magnificent wildness, his reddish brown feathers puffed out, his tail pumping up and down, his black eyes blazing eagerly as he looked about. For several moments he sat there, then sprang upward into the air and with a piercing cry flew rapidly away.

I almost felt sorry for the hawk, for his seeming disappointment at missing a meal on that cold day, had I not remembered what great little mousers these American kestrels are. In the grassy fields of our suburban neighborhood the hawk would not need to hunt long in order to catch a field mouse—a happy substitute for one of our garden birds.

For two minutes after the hawk had flown away, not a bird came out of hiding, except our bold little chickadees, which seem to have little fear of hawks. I walked out to the brush pile I had built for the birds for just this kind of emergency. I kicked it lightly and 14 birds—juncos, white-throated sparrows, fox sparrows, and English sparrows—flew out. The brush pile had undoubtedly saved the life of at least one of them on this day, as it has on other days since.

How to Build a Brush Pile

Some of our friends have been surprised to learn that there is a right and a wrong way to build a brush pile for birds. We prepare for ours in advance by saving the limbs of trees and the branches of shrubs that we prune in the spring and fall. These we pile in a far corner of the yard, under a leafy tree or shrub where they can't be seen during summer. Some of the heavier limbs are from trees that we may not cut once in four or five years. It is these that we use for the sturdy "foundation" of the brush pile, and they will last for several years.

About November 1 we build the brush pile on the bare ground of our vegetable garden. We put down the heavy tree branches first, crisscrossing them until we have a tangled pile about 6 feet square and about 30 to 40 inches high. On top of these and in among the heavy branches we put lighter limbs until we have built the pile to about 5 feet above the ground. To finish it, or "top it off," we lay on small branches of evergreen trees—hemlock, spruce, balsam fir, and yew. If the weather is mild, we don't put this final layer or "roof" on until after Christmas, when our discarded Christmas tree and those of our neighbors' give us plenty of material. These evergreen boughs protect the inside of the brush pile from snow and rain and make it a warm, dry, safe retreat that the birds spend much time in during cold weather. We often spread feed around the base of the brush pile for them when there is snow on the ground.

About April 1, or at any time before birds start nesting, we dismantle our brush pile. We burn the lighter branches, but save the heavy ones for the new one that we build the following fall.

Shrikes
Around
Feeding
Stations

Besides attracting small hawks in winter, the songbirds at your feeders will attract shrikes—another kind of predatory bird. Shrikes are usually gray, black, and white,[7] about the size of a robin or a little smaller. They will catch and eat songbirds when they can't find mice or the grasshoppers and crickets that make up a large part of their food in summer.

Although small birds are sometimes killed by shrikes at the feeders, they can escape (1) by flying straight up into the air, keeping above the shrike; (2) by out-dodging it; (3) by darting into thick cover; (4) by remaining perfectly still when a shrike appears.

A shrike chased a brown creeper into the yard of friends of ours and the creeper escaped by alighting on the bark of a tree and remaining motionless. The shrike, which had

[7] Females and immatures are a dull *brown*, black, and white. Shrikes sometimes kill robins, mockingbirds, blue jays, and other medium-sized birds, but they more often take the smaller starlings, house sparrows, juncos, goldfinches, crossbills, siskins, bush-tits, and others of the four-to eight-inch sizes.

been flying closely after it, flew up into the tree and looked down at the bark intently for fully five minutes. The motionless creeper blended so well with the bark of the tree that, apparently, the shrike didn't see it and finally flew away. A minute later, when the creeper was sure that the shrike had gone, it moved up the tree, spiraling its way up the trunk as if nothing had happened.

In all the years that we have been feeding birds, we have never had a hawk or shrike that we couldn't get rid of by frightening it off or by live-trapping,[8] if it became too persistent. We have never killed a hawk or shrike that has been attracted to our garden by our birds. When one comes to our yard and stays, we stop putting grain in our feeders where the birds would be exposed to attacks by hawks or shrikes. We scatter the grain, instead, under the shrubs and evergreen trees where our songbirds can feed close to protective cover.

What Should You Do About Hawks and Shrikes in Your Garden?

We believe that if we are to attract birds and remain on good terms with all nature and with all birds, we must not allow ourselves to become prejudiced against any of the wild creatures that come to our garden. We do everything possible to protect our birds against the hawks or shrikes that attempt to kill them. But in doing so we remember that *we* are responsible for attracting the large population of birds that has, in turn, attracted the hawks and shrikes.

When you feed birds in your garden, this phenomenon —that one bird, a hawk or a shrike, must kill another bird to keep life in its own body—may be the hardest for you

[8] People who operate bird-banding stations for the U. S. Fish and Wildlife Service sometimes catch small hawks and shrikes in their bird-banding traps. These wire traps are usually set by banders in their back yards to catch songbirds, which they band and then release in order to trace their migrations and length of life. Hawks or shrikes sometimes enter these traps to catch the songbird that may be hopping about, unharmed, within it, eating the grain with which the trap is baited to lure the songbird inside. After the bird-bander removes the hawk or shrike from the trap, he usually bands it, carries it at least ten miles away, and releases it. Hawks or shrikes released that far away seldom return to the bird-bander's yard.

to accept. If you don't accept it, your enjoyment of birds for what they are—free, wild, uninhibited creatures—will be less and your breadth of view narrowed.

I shall not ask you to harden your feelings against the death of birds in your garden, even if that were possible for you. I *shall* ask you to look on predatory birds as creatures which are living as nature has directed them to live, and to realize that the action of the hawk, which strikes down a sparrow at your feeder, is no different from that of the sparrow itself, which only a moment before killed a beetle to satisfy its own hunger.

To live is to die, and one creature in your garden lives only until that day that it must give up its life to another—for another. Like the tides that roll upon an ocean beach, the lives of birds in your back yard will ebb and flow. But life—a rich, fascinating, varied life—will always be with you while your trees, shrubs, food, and water are there to say *Come and live with us!* to the songbirds in your garden.

Appendix

THE STRUGGLE TO SURVIVE–
THE BIRD'S YEAR

This is a table of the natural changes during each season that affect the lives of birds throughout the year. It applies specifically to birds and seasonal changes in the northern half of the United States, across the continent, and south to wherever winter brings freezing weather, ice, or snow. Winter in the South, even where it is mild, can be critical for birds if they are short of natural food.

What Winter Means to the Birds

In many parts of the United States, there are now spells of bitterly cold weather. Snow and ice often cover seeds and berries that have fallen to the ground. Many insects have either been killed by the cold or have retired under the ground, or have hidden inside trees and in other places where they sleep through the winter.

Leaves have fallen from most plants and there is a general scarcity of protective cover where birds can roost at night and find shelter from cold winds, rain, and snow.

What Spring Means to the Birds

Times are getting better for birds. Snow and ice are disappearing in March and April, uncovering seeds and fallen fruits of the previous year. Insects are hatching from eggs or awakening from winter sleep as the days grow warmer. New leaves are opening and, day by day, offer more protective and nesting cover for birds.

Early spring snowstorms, late, cold, spring weather, prolonged spring rains make this period still a critical one for many kinds of birds.

What Summer Means to the Birds

These are probably the most "prosperous" times of the whole year for birds. Most of them are raising their families. Berries and insects to feed their youngsters and themselves are abundant. Cover—the leafy shelter of trees, shrubs, and vines—is the most luxuriant of any time of the year.

Summer may still be a critical time for some birds, if they have no places to nest. If they do have nesting places and still must travel far to get fresh berries to feed their young ones or for drinking and bathing water, they may be exposed to extra dangers. Food and water close by will eliminate or lessen these hazards.

What Fall Means to the Birds

Food and cover are gradually declining. Berries are being eaten up by birds or are falling to the ground. Leaves are falling and shelter for birds is shrinking. Insects are dying from frosts or hibernating in the ground and in other places inaccessible to many birds. Weather is getting colder and the days are getting shorter, which means that birds have less time to hunt for food than during the long summer days.

HOW YOU CAN HELP THE BIRDS

Practically all wild animals can be "helped," or their populations increased, by improving their living conditions. Songbirds can be attracted in greater numbers and variety to your garden by providing those things that birds need which may be lacking in your yard. Increasing songbird foods, shelters, and nesting places will be remarkably effective. This table applies to the same areas as the preceding table.

WHAT THE BIRDS NEED IN WINTER

Food: Fleshy fruits of barberries, hollies, cedars, mountain ashes, crabapples, and hawthorns that persist on the plants into spring. These are valuable emergency foods. Also seeds of maples, ashes, birches, alders and seeds of pines, spruces, hemlocks, and other evergreens. Acorns of oak trees.

Your feeding stations will help (see chapter 2).

Shelter: Pines, hemlocks, spruces, yews, and firs where birds can roost at night or escape from cold winds and storms in daytime.

Birdhouses and roosting boxes will help (see chapter 3).

Water: Most streams and ponds are now periodically frozen over. Keep water in your birdbath thawed and supply it with fresh water daily (see chapter 5).

WHAT THE BIRDS NEED IN SPRING

Food: Fleshy fruits of barberries, hollies, cedars, mountain ashes, crabapples, and hawthorns that persist on the plants into spring. These are valuable emergency foods. Also seeds of maples, ashes, birches, alders and seeds of pines, spruces, hemlocks, and other evergreens. Acorns of oak trees.

Your feeding stations will help (see chapter 2).

Shelter: Pines, yews, spruces, etc., still valuable protection against spring cold and storms.

Plant trees, shrubs, and vines in your yard now. Spring is the best time to plant your evergreens (pines, hemlocks, etc.); also excellent time to plant other trees, shrubs, and vines.

Water: Keep birdbath water thawed in early spring and supply fresh water daily.

Nesting Places: Put up bird boxes now—the earlier the better (see chapter 3).

What the Birds Need in Summer

Nesting Places: Pines, spruces, yews, barberry hedges, grapevine thickets, hawthorns, hollow trees. *You can help by putting up bird boxes,* and your spring-planted trees, shrubs, and vines will help.

Water: Perhaps more important now, especially in hot, dry weather, than at any other time of the year. *You might better keep birdbaths filled with fresh water than to operate feeding stations during the summer.*

Food: Fleshy fruits of cherries, mulberries, serviceberries, blackberries, raspberries, blueberries, elderberries especially needed now by many nesting birds. *You can help by having some of these plants in your yard.*

What the Birds Need in Fall

Food: Fleshy fruits and seeds that persist on plants above snows of early winter. *This is a good time to plant many kinds of trees, shrubs, and vines,* excepting the "needle-evergreens" (pines, yews, etc.), which seem to do better if planted in spring, rather than in fall.

Shelter: Pines, spruces, and other evergreens becoming increasingly important to birds for shelter against cold and storms of early winter. *Bird nesting boxes and roosting boxes will help.* Now is the best time to put them up because the bird nesting boxes, if weathered, may be more acceptable to birds next spring.

Water: Keep birdbaths thawed when the water in them freezes. *Fill them with fresh water daily* (see chapter 5).

SOME BIRDS OF THE UNITED STATES AND CERTAIN PLANTS ON THE FOLLOWING LISTS THAT ESPECIALLY ATTRACT THEM

KIND OF BIRD	PLANT GROUP FOOD–RATING NUMBERS [a]
Bluebirds	2, 3, 4, 6, 7a, 8, 10a, 10b, 11, 13, 20, 24; also bayberries, hackberries, Russian olives, California pepper tree
Cardinal	2, 3, 4, 6, 8, 10b, 11, 13, 17, 21; also hackberries and Russian olives
Catbird	2, 3, 4, 6, 7a, 8, 10a, 10b, 11, 13, 20, 21, 24; also bayberries, hackberries, persimmons, Russian olives, buffaloberries, buckthorns
Chickadees	1, 5, 7b, 9, 10a, 11, 15, 16, 18, 20, 23; also bayberries and sweet gum
Crossbills	1, 7a, 9, 18, 23
Duck, wood	5, 14, 16, 21, 22a, 22b
Finch, purple	4, 7a, 7b, 10b, 12, 16, 17, 22b, 27b; also sweet gum
Flickers (see woodpeckers)	
Flycatcher, crested	3, 4, 8, 10a
Goldfinches	7b, 16, 17, 19; also sweet gum

[a] Look at the food-rating numbers for the Northeast Region to identify the plants that each kind of bird prefers. Certain plants, the fruits or seeds of which birds favor highly in some regions, may be eaten so infrequently in the Northeast that they are not listed under this region. The probable reason for this is not any change in a bird's taste, but that some of these plants and their fruits are more abundant in some regions than in others. Plants that are favored outside of the Northeast are given by name instead of by number.

KIND OF BIRD	PLANT GROUP FOOD-RATING NUMBERS
Grosbeaks	1, 2, 3, 4, 5, 7a, 7b, 8, 9, 10b, 13, 14, 16, 20, 22a, 22b, 25, 26; also hackberries, Russian olives, manzanitas, buffaloberries, snowberries
Jays	1, 2, 5, 6, 7a, 10b, 11, 13, 14, 20, 22a; also bayberries and manzanitas
Juncos	1; also sweet gum and Russian olives
Kingbirds	3, 4, 6, 8, 11, 13
Mockingbirds	2, 4, 6, 7a, 8, 10a, 10b, 12, 13, 20, 21, 24; also hackberries, palmettos, persimmons, manzanitas, California pepper tree
Nuthatches	1, 5, 7b, 9, 10a, 13, 14, 22a, 23
Orioles	2, 8, 11, 13, 20
Phainopepla	3, 6, 8, 13; also buckthorns and California pepper tree
Phoebes	2, 10b, 11, 13; also hackberries
Quails	1, 5, 7a, 10b; also hackberries, prickly pears, wild roses, Russian olives, manzanitas, mesquite, buffaloberries
Redpolls	15, 19
Robin	2, 3, 4, 6, 7a, 8, 10a, 10b, 11, 12, 20, 21, 24; also hackberries, palmettos, persimmons, Russian olives, buckthorns, California pepper tree
Siskin, pine	1, 9, 15, 18, 19
Solitaire	3, 7a, 10b, 26; also hackberries and wild roses
Sparrow, fox	2, 6, 10a, 15, 21, 26; also hackberries and manzanitas
Sparrow, song	2, 3, 13
Sparrow, tree	11, 15

Sparrow,
white-throated   2, 3, 6, 11, 13, 21; also sweet gum

Starling   3, 4, 8, 10*b*, 12, 13; also bayberries and Russian olives

Swallow, tree   4, 7*a*, 10*a*; also bayberries

Tanagers   2, 3, 4, 6, 8, 11, 12, 13, 20; also bayberries and Russian olives

Thrashers   1, 2, 3, 4, 5, 6, 8, 10*a*, 10*b*, 11, 12, 13, 20, 24; also hackberries, prickly pears, buffaloberries, buckthorns

Thrushes   2, 3, 4, 6, 7*a*, 8, 10*a*, 10*b*, 11, 12, 13, 20, 21, 24, 25; also hackberries, wild roses, buckthorns, snowberries, Pacific madrone, California pepper tree

Titmice   1, 2, 5, 6, 10*a*, 14; also hackberries

Towhees   1, 2, 3, 5, 11, 13, 20, 24, 27*b*; also hackberries, sweet gum, Russian olives

Vireos   2, 3, 4, 6, 8, 10*a*, 10*b*, 13, 24; also bayberries, wild roses, snowberries

Warblers   1, 2, 4, 6, 7*a*, 8, 10*b*, 13; also bayberries, persimmons, California pepper tree

Waxwing, cedar   2, 3, 4, 6, 7*a*, 8, 9, 12, 13, 20, 21, 24, 25, 26; also hackberries, persimmons, Russian olives, buffaloberries, California pepper tree

Woodpeckers   1, 2, 3, 4, 5, 6, 8, 9, 10*a*, 10*b*, 12, 13, 14, 20, 21, 22*a*, 24, 26, 27*a*; also bayberries, hackberries, palmettos, prickly pears, buckthorns, California pepper tree

Wren, cactus   10*b*, 13; also prickly pears

Wren, Carolina   1; also bayberries and sweet gum

NORTHEAST REGION

(Connecticut, Delaware, Indiana, Kentucky, Maine, Maryland, Massachusetts, Michigan, Minnesota, New Hampshire, New Jersey, New York, Ohio, Pennsylvania, Rhode Island, Vermont, Virginia, West Virginia, Wisconsin)

SOME RECOMMENDED TREES, SHRUBS, AND VINES FOR PLANTINGS TO ATTRACT BIRDS

NOTE: Scientific plant names follow *Hortus Second*, by L. H. Bailey and Ethel Zoe Bailey (The Macmillan Company, New York), except that the second name (the species name) always begins with a small letter.

SONGBIRD FOOD RATING	SPECIES OF PLANTS
1	PINES: Jack pine, *Pinus banksiana;* Japanese black pine, *Pinus thunbergi;* Korean pine, *Pinus koraiensis;* red pine, *Pinus resinosa;* pitch pine, *Pinus rigida;* white pine, *Pinus strobus.*
2	BLACKBERRIES: Cultivated varieties Eldorado, Snyder, Taylor, and Erie. (Write to your state college of agriculture for the names of the varieties of both the blackberries and raspberries that they recommend for your area.)
3	WILD CHERRIES: Sour cherry,[a] *Prunus cerasus;* fire or pin cherry, *Prunus pensylvanica;* wild black, or rum, cherry, *Prunus serotina;* chokecherry, *Prunus virginiana.*
4	DOGWOODS: Siberian dogwood, *Cornus alba*

[a] This small, very hardy cherry tree is not a "wild" cherry but was introduced into this country many years ago. Its native home is West Asia and southeastern Europe, but it is now naturalized in the northeastern United States. It is one of the few fruit trees suitable for shady places and its fruits are especially attractive to songbirds.

	variety *sibirica;* pagoda dogwood, *Cornus alternifolia;* rough-leaved dogwood, *Cornus asperifolia;* flowering dogwood, *Cornus florida;* Japanese dogwood, *Cornus kousa;* gray dogwood, *Cornus racemosa.*
5	OAKS: White oak, *Quercus alba;* red oak, *Quercus borealis;* scarlet oak, *Quercus coccinea;* bur or mossy-cup oak, *Quercus macrocarpa;* chestnut oak, *Quercus montana;* pin oak, *Quercus palustris.*
6	WILD GRAPES: Summer grape, *Vitis aestivalis;* frost grape, *Vitis vulpina;* fox grape, *Vitis labrusca;* riverbank grape, *Vitis riparia;* also cultivated grapes.
7a	CEDARS [b] OR JUNIPERS: Eastern red cedar, *Juniperus virginiana* and its varieties *canaerti* and *tripartita.*
7b	MAPLES: Amur maple, *Acer ginnala;* box elder,[o] *Acer negundo;* red maple, *Acer rubra;* sugar maple, *Acer saccharum.*
8	MULBERRIES: [d] White mulberry, *Morus alba;* Russian mulberry, *Morus alba* variety *tatarica;* red mulberry, *Morus rubra;* and cultivated mulberry varieties New American, Thorburn, and Trowbridge.
9	SPRUCES, *Picea.*

[b] The male and female flowers on many cedars or junipers, instead of being on the same tree or combined in *one* flower, as the flower sexes of many plants are, grow on separate trees. The female cedar tree, which bears the fruit, usually produces a crop only when pollen from the male tree reaches its flowers. Plant at least one male cedar tree (a staminate plant) in your yard, along with the female (pistillate) trees that produce the blue fruits, or cedar "berries."

[o] The male and female flowers of the box elder are on separate trees. Be sure to tell your nurseryman you want your tree or trees to produce the keys, or seeds, for birds.

[d] The flower sexes of some of the different kinds of mulberry trees and most of the hollies, also are on separate plants, and some have both the male and female flowers on the same tree. Make certain that your nurseryman understands that you want a tree, or trees, that will bear fruit.

10*a*	Virginia creeper, *Parthenocissus quinquefolia*.
10*b*	Sumacs, *Rhus*.
11	Blueberries: High-bush blueberry, *Vaccinium corymbosum;* low-bush blueberry, *Vaccinium angustifolium*. *Cultivated varieties:* (early) Cabot, June, Weymouth; (mid-season) Rancocas, Concord, Pioneer, and Stanley; (late) Atlantic, Burlington, Jersey, Pemberton, Rubel, and Wareham. Write to your state college of agriculture for the names of the varieties they recommend for your area.
12	Black gum, *Nyssa sylvatica*.
13	Elderberries: American elder, *Sambucus canadensis;* red elder, *Sambucus pubens*.
14	Beech, *Fagus*.
15	Birches: Sweet or black birch, *Betula lenta;* paper birch, *Betula papyrifera;* gray birch, *Betula populifolia*.
16	Elms, *Ulmus*.
17	Tulip tree, *Liriodendron*.
18	Hemlocks, *Tsuga*.
19	Alders, *Alnus*.
20	Serviceberries: Downy serviceberry, *Amelanchier canadensis;* apple serviceberry, *Amelanchier grandiflora;* Allegany serviceberry, *Amelanchier laevis;* thicket serviceberry, *Amelanchier oblongifolia;* dwarf juneberry, *Amelanchier stolonifera*.
21	Greenbriers, *Smilax*.
22*a*	Hickories, *Carya*.
22*b*	Ashes, *Fraxinus*.
23	Firs, *Abies*.
24	Hollies:[d] Inkberry, *Ilex glabra;* American holly, *Ilex opaca;* long-stalk holly, *Ilex pedunculosa;* winterberry, *Ilex verticillata*.
25	Mountain ashes, *Sorbus*.
26	Hawthorns: Cockspur thorn, *Crataegus crusgalli;* Lavalle hawthorn, *Crataegus lavallei;* Washington hawthorn, *Crataegus phaenopyrum*.

SONGBIRD	
FOOD RATING	SPECIES OF PLANTS
27a	HAZELNUTS, *Corylus.*
27b	ASPENS, *Populus.*

SOME HELPFUL LEAFLETS, CIRCULARS, AND BULLETINS *

GENERAL: *Growing Erect and Trailing Blackberries,* Farmer's Bulletin 1995, 15 cents; *Raspberry Culture,* Farmer's Bulletin 887, 15 cents; *Blueberry Growing,* Farmer's Bulletin 1951, 20 cents; *Useful and Ornamental Gourds,* Farmer's Bulletin 1849, 10 cents; *Palm Trees in the United States,* Agricultural Information Bulletin 22, 15 cents; *Attracting Birds,* Conservation Bulletin 1, 5 cents; *Homes for Birds* (Birdhouses), Conservation Bulletin 14, 10 cents. These publications are for sale by the Superintendent of Documents, U. S. Government Printing Office, Washington 25, D.C.

INDIANA: *Ornamental Evergreens: Their Planting and Care,* by R. B. Hull, Extension Bulletin 320, Purdue University, Lafayette, Indiana.

MICHIGAN: *Landscaping the Home Grounds,* by C. P. Halligan, Extension Bulletin 199, and *Hardy Shrubs for Landscape Planting in Michigan,* by C. P. Halligan, Extension Bulletin 152, Michigan State College, East Lansing, Michigan.

MINNESOTA: *Evergreens,* by L. C. Snyder, *et al,* Extension Bulletin 258, and *Woody Plants for Minnesota,* by L. C. Snyder and Marvin Smith, Extension Bulletin 267, University of Minnesota, University Farm, St. Paul 1, Minnesota.

NEW YORK: *Woody Plants for Shady Places,* by R. W. Curtis and J. F. Cornman, Cornell Extension Bulletin 465, and *Shade Trees for the Home Lawn,* by Donald J. Bushey, Cornell Extension Bulletin 724, New York State College of Agriculture, Ithaca, New York.

* The prices of these recommended government publications may no longer be as listed, and some titles may no longer be available. Write to the U.S. Government Printing Office, Washington, D.C. 204203.

Beautifying the Home Grounds, by Victor H. Ries, Extension Service Bulletin 73, Ohio State University, Columbus, Ohio.

SOUTHEAST REGION

(Alabama, Arkansas, Florida, Georgia, Louisiana, Mississippi, North Carolina, southeastern Oklahoma, South Carolina, Tennessee, eastern Texas)

SOME RECOMMENDED TREES, SHRUBS, AND VINES FOR PLANTINGS TO ATTRACT BIRDS

NOTE: Scientific plant names follow *Hortus Second,* by L. H. Bailey and Ethel Zoe Bailey (The Macmillan Company, New York), except that the second name (the species name) always begins with a small letter.

SONGBIRD FOOD RATING	SPECIES OF PLANTS
1	PINES: Slash pine, *Pinus caribaea;* shortleaf pine, *Pinus echinata;* longleaf pine, *Pinus palustris;* loblolly pine, *Pinus taeda.*
2	OAKS: Laurel oak, *Quercus laurifolia;* blackjack oak, *Quercus marilandica;* water oak, *Quercus nigra;* willow oak, *Quercus phellos;* live oak, *Quercus virginiana.*
3	BLACKBERRIES: Cultivated varieties: Nanticoke, Rathbun, Agawan, Dorchester, Early King, Lawton. Better write to your state college of agriculture for names of varieties of both the blackberries and raspberries they recommend for your area.
4	WILD GRAPES: Summer grape, *Vitis aestivalis;* frost grape, *Vitis vulpina;* muscadine grape, *Vitis rotundifolia;* currant grape, *Vitis simpsoni;* and cultivated varieties.
5	VIRGINIA CREEPER, *Parthenocissus quinquefolia.*
6	POISON IVIES. (Although songbirds are fond of the white, berrylike fruits of these plants, they are not recommended for planting.)
7	WILD CHERRIES: Wild black cherry, *Prunus serotina;* chokecherry, *Prunus virginiana;* also cultivated cherries.

8	HOLLIES: [a] Dahoon holly, *Ilex cassine;* possum-haw, *Ilex decidua;* American holly, *Ilex opaca;* winterberry, *Ilex verticillata;* yaupon, *Ilex vomitoria.*
9	GREENBRIERS, *Smilax.*
10	WAXMYRTLES OR BAYBERRIES: [a] Waxmyrtle, *Myrica cerifera;* bayberry, *Myrica pensylvanica;* dwarf waxmyrtle, *Myrica pumila.*
11	BLUEBERRIES: Cultivated varieties: (early) Wolcott and Murphy; (mid-season) Rancocas; (late) Jersey. Write to your state college of agriculture for names of varieties they recommend for your area.
11	DOGWOODS: Siberian dogwood, *Cornus alba sibirica;* pagoda dogwood, *Cornus alternifolia;* rough-leaved dogwood, *Cornus asperifolia;* flowering dogwood, *Cornus florida;* gray dogwood, *Cornus racemosa.*
12	MULBERRIES: [b] Black mulberry, *Morus nigra* and cultivated variety Black Persian; red mulberry, *Morus rubra* and cultivated varieties Hicks and Stubbs; Texas mulberry, *Morus microphylla.*
13	BLACK GUM, *Nyssa.*
14	BEECH, *Fagus.*
15	ELDERBERRIES: American elder, *Sambucus canadensis* and its varieties.
16	CEDARS [c] OR JUNIPERS: Eastern red cedar, *Jun-*

[a] The flower sexes of some of the hollies and most, if not all, of the waxmyrtles and bayberries are on separate plants. Be sure to plant both male and female plants to make certain that the female (pistillate) plants produce the fruits which attract birds.

[b] The flower sexes of some of the mulberry trees are on separate plants, and some of them have both the male and female flowers on the same tree. Be sure to tell your nurseryman that you want a tree, or trees, that will bear fruit.

[c] The male and female flowers on many cedars or junipers, instead of being on the same tree or combined in *one* flower, as the flower sexes of many plants are, grow on separate trees. The female cedar tree, which bears the fruit, usually produces a crop only when pollen from the male tree reaches its flowers. Plant at least one male cedar tree (a staminate plant) in your yard, along with the female (pistillate) trees that produce the berrylike, blue fruits.

iperus virginiana and its varieties *canaerti*, and *tripartita*.

17*a*   MAPLES, *Acer.*
17*b*   TULIP TREE, *Liriodendron.*
18   HICKORIES, *Carya.*
19   ASHES, *Fraxinus.*
20   HACKBERRIES: Sugar or southern hackberry, *Celtis laevigata*; and common hackberry, *Celtis occidentalis.*
21   PALMETTOS, *Sabal.*
22*a*   PERSIMMON, *Diospyros.*
22*b*   SWEET GUM, *Liquidambar.*

SOME HELPFUL LEAFLETS, CIRCULARS, AND BULLETINS

GENERAL: *Growing Erect and Trailing Blackberries,* Farmer's Bulletin 1995, 15 cents; *Raspberry Culture,* Farmer's Bulletin 887, 15 cents; *Blueberry Growing,* Farmer's Bulletin 1951, 20 cents; *Useful and Ornamental Gourds,* Farmer's Bulletin 1849, 10 cents; *Palm Trees in the United States,* Agricultural Information Bulletin 22, 15 cents; *Attracting Birds,* Conservation Bulletin 1, 5 cents; *Homes for Birds* (Birdhouses), Conservation Bulletin 14, 10 cents. These publications are for sale by the Superintendent of Documents, U. S. Government Printing Office, Washington 25, D.C.

ARKANSAS: *Planting Materials for Arkansas Landscape Designs,* by L. H. Burton, Miscell. Publication No. 37, and *Arbor Day,* by L. H. Burton. Write to University of Arkansas, Extension Service, Fayetteville, Arkansas, for these leaflets.

FLORIDA: *Propagation of Ornamental Plants,* by John V. Watkins, Extension Service Bulletin 150; *Native and Exotic Palms of Florida,* by Harold Mowry, Extension Service Bulletin 152; *Ornamental Hedges for Florida,* by Harold Mowry and R. D. Dickey, Extension Service Bulletin 443; *Ground Covers for Florida Gardens,* by J. M. Crevasse, Jr., Extension Service Bulletin 473. Write to

University of Florida, Agricultural Experiment Station, Gainesville, Florida, for these bulletins.

LOUISIANA: *Louisiana Trees and Shrubs*, by Clair A. Brown, Bulletin No. 1, Louisiana Forestry Commission, Baton Rouge, Louisiana.

MISSISSIPPI: *An Illustrated Guide to Identification and Landscape Uses of Mississippi Native Shrubs*, by F. S. Batson, Extension Service Bulletin 369; *An Illustrated Guide to the Care of Ornamental Trees and Shrubs*, by F. S. Batson and R. O. Monosmith, Extension Service Bulletin 354; *An Illustrated Guide to Landscaping Mississippi Homes*, by R. O. Monosmith and F. S. Batson, Extension Service Bulletin 340. Write to Mississippi Agricultural Experiment Station, State College, Mississippi, for these bulletins.

NORTH CAROLINA: *Planting for the Future*, by John H. Harris, Extension Circular 305, North Carolina State College of Agriculture, State College Station, Raleigh, North Carolina.

TENNESSEE: *Better Home Grounds: Growing and Transplanting Trees and Shrubs*, by W. C. Pelton, Extension Service Publication 196, University of Tennessee, Knoxville, Tennessee.

TEXAS: *Catalogue of the Flora of Texas*, by V. L. Cory and H. B. Parks, Extension Service Bulletin 550, Texas Agricultural Experiment Station, College Station, Texas.

PLAINS AND PRAIRIE REGION

(Eastern Colorado, Illinois, Iowa, Kansas, eastern Montana, Missouri, Nebraska, North Dakota, Oklahoma, South Dakota, central and western Texas, eastern Wyoming)

Some Recommended Trees, Shrubs, and Vines for Plantings to Attract Birds

NOTE: Scientific plant names follow *Hortus Second*, by L. H. Bailey and Ethel Zoe Bailey (The Macmillan Company, New York), except that the second name (the species name) always begins with a small letter.

SONGBIRD FOOD RATING	SPECIES OF PLANTS
1	HACKBERRIES: Common hackberry, *Celtis occidentalis;* sugar hackberry, or sugarberry, *Celtis laevigata.*
2	GRAPES: Long's grape, *Vitis longi;* riverbank grape, *Vitis riparia;* also domestic or cultivated grapes. Write to your state college of agriculture for the names of varieties they recommend for your area.
3	WILD CHERRIES: Sour cherry,[a] *Prunus cerasus;* western chokecherry, *Prunus virginiana* variety *demissa;* fire or pin cherry, *Prunus pensylvanica;* wild black cherry, *Prunus serotina.*
4	POISON IVIES. (Although songbirds are fond of the white, berrylike fruits of these plants, they are not recommended for planting.)
5	DOGWOODS: Siberian dogwood, *Cornus alba*

[a] This small, very hardy cherry tree is not a "wild" cherry, but was introduced into this country many years ago. Its native home is West Asia and southeastern Europe, but it is now naturalized in some parts of the Prairie and Plains region. It is one of the few fruit trees suitable for shady places and its cherries are especially attractive to songbirds.

	variety *sibirica;* pagoda dogwood, *Cornus alternifolia;* rough-leaved dogwood, *Cornus asperifolia;* round-leaved dogwood, *Cornus rugosa;* gray dogwood, *Cornus racemosa.*
6	HOLLIES: [b] Possum-haw, *Ilex decidua;* inkberry, *Ilex glabra;* long-stalk holly, *Ilex pedunculosa;* winterberry, *Ilex verticillata.*
7	PRICKLY PEARS, *Opuntia.*
8	ALDERS, *Alnus.*
9	MULBERRIES: [b] White mulberry, *Morus alba* and its cultivated varieties; also Russian mulberry, *Morus alba* variety *tatarica.*
10	SERVICEBERRIES OR SASKATOONS: Alder-leaved serviceberry, *Amelanchier alnifolia;* downy serviceberry, *Amelanchier canadensis;* apple serviceberry, *Amelanchier grandiflora;* Allegany serviceberry, *Amelanchier laevis;* thicket serviceberry, *Amelanchier oblongifolia.*
11	PINES: Lodgepole pine, *Pinus contorta* variety *latifolia;* limber pine, *Pinus flexilis;* western yellow pine or ponderosa pine, *Pinus ponderosa.*
12	OAKS: Shingle oak, *Quercus imbricaria;* bur oak, *Quercus macrocarpa;* black jack oak, *Quercus marilandica;* post oak, *Quercus stellata.*
13	BLACKBERRIES: Write to your state college of agriculture for the names of cultivated varieties of blackberries and raspberries they recommend for your area.
14	SUMACS, *Rhus.*
15	WILD ROSES, *Rosa.*
16	CEDARS: [c] Creeping juniper, *Juniperus horizontalis;* Rocky Mountain red cedar, *Juniperus scopulorum,* and its horticultural varieties; also eastern red cedar, *Juniperus virginiana* and its varieties *canaerti, keteleeri,* and *tripartita.*

[b] The flower sexes of some of the hollies and mulberries are on separate plants. Tell your nurseryman that you want plants that will bear fruit.

[c] The male and female flowers on many cedars or junipers, in-

Some Helpful Leaflets, Circulars, and Bulletins

GENERAL: *Ornamental Hedges for the Central Great Plains*, Farmer's Bulletin 2019, 10 cents; *Ornamental Shrubs for the Southern Great Plains*, Farmer's Bulletin 2025, 20 cents; *Growing Erect and Trailing Blackberries*, Farmer's Bulletin 1995, 15 cents; *Raspberry Culture*, Farmer's Bulletin 887, 15 cents; *Blueberry Growing*, Farmer's Bulletin 1951, 20 cents; *Useful and Ornamental Gourds*, Farmer's Bulletin 1849, 10 cents; *Palm Trees in the United States*, Agricultural Information Bulletin 22, 15 cents; *Attracting Birds*, Conservation Bulletin 1, 5 cents; *Homes for Birds* (Birdhouses), Conservation Bulletin 14, 10 cents. These publications are for sale by the Superintendent of Documents, U. S. Government Printing Office, Washington 25, D.C.

COLORADO: *Trees for Colorado Farms*, Bulletin 395-A, Colorado A. and M. College, Fort Collins, Colorado.

ILLINOIS: *Selected Trees and Shrubs for Landscaping About the Illinois Home Grounds*, a mimeographed Extension Service Bulletin, and *Sunflowers as a Seed and Oil Crop for Illinois*, Circular 681. Write to Agricultural Experiment Station, University of Illinois, Urbana, for these.

IOWA: *Iowa Landscape Plants*, pamphlet issued by the Extension Service, Iowa State College of Agriculture, State College, Ames, Iowa.

KANSAS: *Native Woody Plants of Kansas for Landscaping the Home Grounds*, mimeographed leaflet, Kansas State College, Manhattan, Kansas.

MISSOURI: *Selection and Care of Ornamental Shrubs*, by Louise Woodruff and Julia M. Rocheford, Extension Service Circular 567, University of Missouri, Columbia, Missouri.

---

stead of being on the same tree or combined in *one* flower on the tree, as the flower sexes of many plants are, grow on separate trees. The female cedar tree, which bears the fruit, usually produces a crop only when pollen from the male tree reaches its flowers. Plant at least one male cedar tree (a staminate plant) in your yard, along with the female (pistillate) trees that produce the blue fruits.

MONTANA: *Woody Plant Materials for Montana*, and *Evergreen and Deciduous Trees, Shrubs, and Vines for Landscape Use*, mimeographed leaflets by Extension Service, Montana State College of Agriculture, Bozeman, Montana.

NEBRASKA: *Twelve Broadleaf Trees for Nebraska*, Extension Service Circular 1727; *Developing Attractive Farmsteads in Nebraska*, Extension Service Circular 1271; *Tree Identification Manual*, Extension Service Circular 1703. Write to University of Nebraska at Lincoln for these publications.

NORTH DAKOTA: *Trees and Shrubs for Eastern North Dakota Windbreaks*, Extension Service Circular A-122; *Trees and Shrubs for Western North Dakota Windbreaks*, Extension Service Circular A-123; *Shrubs and Trees to Attract Birds*, Circular A-156; *Pruning Trees and Shrubs*, Special Circular A-63. Write to the North Dakota Agricultural College at Fargo for these publications.

OKLAHOMA: *Woody Plant Materials for Oklahoma*, mimeographed leaflet; *Woody Plant Material*, Circular 546; *Landscaping Home Grounds*, Circular 456; *Home Grounds Beautification*, Circular 544. Write to Oklahoma A. and M. College at Stillwater for these publications.

SOUTH DAKOTA: *The Shade, Windbreak, and Timber Trees of South Dakota*, Bulletin 246; *Evergreens of South Dakota*, Bulletin 254; *The Ornamental Trees of South Dakota*, Bulletin 260. Write to the South Dakota State College of Agriculture at Brookings for these publications.

TEXAS: *Catalogue of the Flora of Texas*, Extension Service Bulletin 550; *Ornamentals for Southwest Texas*, Extension Service Bulletin 695. Write to the Texas Agricultural Experiment Station at College Station for these publications.

WYOMING: *Landscape Your Farm or Ranch*, Circular 104, Agricultural Extension Service, University of Wyoming, Laramie, Wyoming.

MOUNTAIN AND DESERT REGION

(Arizona, western Colorado, Idaho, western Montana, Nevada, New Mexico, eastern Oregon, western Texas, Utah, eastern Washington, western Wyoming)

SOME RECOMMENDED·TREES, SHRUBS, AND VINES FOR PLANTINGS TO ATTRACT BIRDS

NOTE: Scientific plant names follow *Hortus Second*, by L. H. Bailey and Ethel Zoe Bailey (The Macmillan Company, New York), except that the second name (the species name) always begins with a small letter.

SONGBIRD FOOD RATING	SPECIES OF PLANTS
1	PINES: Mexican pinon, *Pinus cembroides;* pinyon, also called nut pine, *Pinus cembroides* variety *edulis;* limber pine, also called Rocky Mountain white pine, *Pinus flexilis;* shore pine, *Pinus contorta;* lodgepole pine, *Pinus contorta* variety *latifolia;* western yellow pine, *Pinus ponderosa.*
2	SERVICEBERRIES OR SASKATOONS: Alder-leaved serviceberry, *Amelanchier alnifolia;* Baker serviceberry, *Amelanchier bakeri;* Cusick serviceberry, *Amelanchier cusicki;* Utah serviceberry, *Amelanchier utahensis.*
3	HACKBERRIES: Douglas hackberry, *Celtis douglasi;* common hackberry, *Celtis occidentalis;* thick-leaved hackberry, *Celtis reticulata.*
4	CEDARS [a] OR JUNIPERS: Cherrystone juniper, *Jun-*

[a] The male and female flowers on many cedars, or junipers, instead of being on the same tree or combined in *one* flower on the tree, as the flower sexes of many plants are, grow on separate trees. The female cedar tree, which bears the fruit, usually produces a crop only when pollen from the male tree reaches its flowers. Plant at least one male cedar tree (a staminate plant) in your yard, along with the female (pistillate) trees that produce the blue fruits.

iperus monosperma; western juniper, *Juniperus occidentalis;* Rocky Mountain red cedar, *Juniperus scopulorum;* Utah juniper, *Juniperus utahensis.*

5   RUSSIAN OLIVES: Russian-olive, *Elaeagnus angustifolia;* cherry elaeagnus, *elaeagnus multiflora;* and autumn elaeagnus, *elaeagnus umbellata.*

6   ALDERS: White alder, *Alnus rhombifolia;* mountain or thinleaf alder, *Alnus tenuifolia.*

7   GOOSEBERRIES, *Ribes.* (Not recommended for planting because both gooseberry and currant plants are intermediate hosts for white pine blister rust, a deadly fungus that kills five-needled, or white, pine trees.)

8   OAKS: Canyon live oak, *Quercus chrysolepis;* Emory oak, *Quercus emoryi;* Gambel oak, *Quercus gambeli;* gray oak, *Quercus grisea;* Rocky Mountain white oak, *Quercus utahensis.*

9   MANZANITAS: Great-berried manzanita, *Arctostaphylos glauca;* greenleaf manzanita, *Arctostaphylos patula;* pointleaf manzanita, *Arctostaphylos pungens;* bearberry, *Arctostaphylos uva-ursi.*

10   BLACKBERRIES: Write to your state college of agriculture for the names of cultivated varieties of blackberries and raspberries that will grow in your region or state.

11   MESQUITE: Mesquite, *Prosopis glandulosa.*

12   GRAPES: Canyon grape, *Vitis arizonica;* California grape, *Vitis californica;* also cultivated grapes. Write to your state college of agriculture for the names of varieties they recommend for your area.

13   PRICKLY PEARS, *Opuntia.*

14   WILD CHERRIES: Bitter cherry, *Prunus emarginata;* fire or pin cherry, *Prunus pensylvanica;* western chokecherry, *Prunus virginiana,* variety *demissa.*

15   BIRCHES: Red or water birch, *Betula fontinalis.*

16   FIRS: White fir, *Abies concolor;* Alpine fir,

Abies lasiocarpa; corkbark fir, *Abies lasio-carpa,* variety *arizonica.*

17 SPRUCES: Engelmann spruce, *Picea engelmanni;* white spruce, *Picea glauca;* Alberta spruce, *Picea glauca,* variety *albertiana;* blue spruce, *Picea pungens* and its varieties.

18 BUFFALOBERRIES: [b] Silver buffaloberry, *Shepherdia argentea;* Canadian buffaloberry, *Shepherdia canadensis.*

SOME HELPFUL LEAFLETS, CIRCULARS, AND BULLETINS

GENERAL: *Russian Olive for Wildlife and Good Land Use,* by A. E. Borell, U. S. Department of Agriculture Leaflet 292, 5 cents; *Southwestern Trees: A Guide to the Native Species of New Mexico and Arizona,* U. S. Department of Agriculture Handbook No. 9, 30 cents; *Growing Erect and Trailing Blackberries,* Farmer's Bulletin 1995, 15 cents; *Raspberry Culture,* Farmer's Bulletin 887, 15 cents; *Blueberry Growing,* Farmer's Bulletin 1951, 20 cents; *Useful and Ornamental Gourds,* Farmer's Bulletin 1849, 10 cents; *Palm Trees in the United States,* Agricultural Information Bulletin 22, 15 cents; *Attracting Birds,* Conservation Bulletin 1, 5 cents; *Homes for Birds* (Birdhouses), Conservation Bulletin 14, 10 cents. These publications are for sale by the Superintendent of Documents, U. S. Government Printing Office, Washington 25, D.C.

COLORADO: *Trees for Colorado Farms,* Bulletin 395-A, Colorado A. and M. College, Fort Collins, Colorado.

IDAHO: *Shrubs and Trees Noted for Their Attractive Flowers or Fruits,* mimeographed leaflet, University of Idaho, Moscow, Idaho.

MONTANA: *Woody Plant Materials for Montana,* and *Ever-*

[b] The flower sexes of the buffaloberries, or *Shepherdia,* are on separate plants. Be sure to use a few male (staminate) plants along with the female (pistillate) plants if you want the fruits which attract birds.

greens and Deciduous Trees, Shrubs, and Vines for Landscape Use, mimeographed leaflets by the Extension Service, Montana State College of Agriculture, Bozeman, Montana.

NEW MEXICO: *Ornamentals for New Mexico*, by L. C. Gibbs, Circular 224; *Shrubs for Northeastern New Mexico*, Bulletin 358, New Mexico College of Agriculture and Mechanic Arts, State College, New Mexico.

WYOMING: *Landscape Your Farm or Ranch*, Circular 104, Agricultural Extension Service, University of Wyoming, Laramie, Wyoming.

PACIFIC REGION

(California, western Oregon, western Washington)

Some Recommended Trees, Shrubs, and Vines for Plantings to Attract Birds

NOTE: Scientific plant names follow *Hortus Second*, by L. H. Bailey and Ethel Zoe Bailey (The Macmillan Company, New York), except that the second name (the species name) always begins with a small letter.

SONGBIRD FOOD RATING	SPECIES OF PLANTS
1	PINES: Shore pine, *Pinus contorta;* Coulter pine, *Pinus coulteri;* Jeffrey pine, *Pinus jeffreyi;* sugar pine, *Pinus lambertiana;* western white pine, *Pinus monticola;* western yellow pine or ponderosa pine, *Pinus ponderosa;* digger pine, *Pinus sabiniana.*
2	OAKS: Coast live oak, *Quercus agrifolia;* canyon live oak or golden-cup oak, *Quercus chrysolepis;* California blue oak, *Quercus douglasi;* Oregon white oak, *Quercus garryana;* California black oak, *Quercus kelloggi;* valley white oak, *Quercus lobata.*

3	POISON OAK, *Rhus diversiloba*. (Not recommended for planting.)
4	ELDERBERRIES: Blueberry elder, *Sambucus caerulea;* redberry elder, *Sambucus callicarpa;* black elder, *Sambucus melanocarpa*.
5	BLACKBERRIES: Write to your state college of agriculture for the names of varieties of blackberries, dewberries, loganberries, etc., that will grow in your area.
6	BUCKTHORNS: [a] Alder-leaved buckthorn, *Rhamnus alnifolia;* California buckthorn or coffee berry, *Rhamnus californica;* hollyleaf buckthorn or red berry, *Rhamnus crocea;* cascara buckthorn, *Rhamnus purshiana*.
7	WILD CHERRIES: Bitter cherry, *Prunus emarginata;* hollyleaf cherry, *Prunus ilicifolia;* Catalina cherry, *Prunus lyoni;* western chokecherry, *Prunus virginiana* variety *demissa*.
8	DOGWOODS: Creek dogwood, *Cornus californica;* brown dogwood, *Cornus glabrata;* Pacific dogwood, *Cornus nuttalli;* western dogwood, *Cornus occidentalis*.
9	SNOWBERRIES: Snowberry, *Symphoricarpus albus;* mountain snowberry, *Symphoricarpus oreophilus;* round-leaved snowberry, *Symphoricarpus rotundifolius*.
10	ALDERS: White alder, *Alnus rhombifolia;* red alder, *Alnus rubra;* Sitka alder, *Alnus sinuata;* mountain or thin-leaved alder, *Alnus tenuifolia*.
11	MISTLETOES, *Phoradendron* and *Arceuthobium*. (Green plants parasitic on trees, not recommended to establish. The dwarf mistletoes are harmful to evergreens, especially in the West.)

[a] Some of the buckthorns, particularly hollyleaf, *Rhamnus crocea*, and cascara, *Rhamnus purshiana*, are secondary hosts for the crown rust of oats. It is best not to plant these two species near where oats are grown.

12	CEDARS [b] OR JUNIPERS: California juniper, *Juniperus californica;* western juniper, *Juniperus occidentalis;* Rocky Mountain red cedar, *Juniperus scopulorum.*
13	MANZANITAS: Parry manzanita, *Arctostaphylos manzanita;* greenleaf manzanita, *Arctostaphylos patula;* pointleaf manzanita, *Arctostaphylos pungens;* Stanford manzanita, *Arctostaphylos stanfordiana;* woolly manzanita, *Arctostaphylos tomentosa;* bearberry, *Arctostaphylos uva-ursi.*
14	GOOSEBERRIES, *Ribes.* (Not recommended for planting because both gooseberry and currant plants are intermediate hosts for white pine blister rust, a deadly fungus that kills five-needled, or white, pine trees.)
15	PACIFIC MADRONE, *Arbutus menziesii.*
16	SERVICEBERRIES: Alder-leaved serviceberry, *Amelanchier alnifolia;* western serviceberry, *Amelanchier florida.*
17	PRICKLY PEARS, *Opuntia.*
18	BIRCHES: Red or water birch, *Betula fontinalis.*
19	FIRS: White fir, *Abies concolor;* lowland white fir or giant fir, *Abies grandis;* Alpine fir, *Abies lasiocarpa;* California red fir, *Abies magnifica;* noble fir, *Abies nobilis.*
20	SPRUCES: Engelmann spruce, *Picea engelmanni;* Alberta spruce, *Picea glauca* variety *albertiana;* Sitka spruce, *Picea sitchensis.*

[b] The male and female flowers of many cedars or junipers, instead of being on the same tree or combined in *one* flower on the tree, as the flower sexes of many plants are, grow on separate trees. The female cedar tree, which bears the fruit, usually produces a crop only when pollen from the male tree reaches its flowers. Plant at least one male cedar tree (staminate) in your yard, along with the female (pistillate) trees that produce the blue fruits.

Some Helpful Leaflets, Circulars, and Bulletins

GENERAL: *Growing Erect and Trailing Blackberries,* Farmer's Bulletin 1995, 15 cents; *Raspberry Culture,* Farmer's Bulletin 887, 15 cents; *Blueberry Growing,* Farmer's Bulletin 1951, 20 cents; *Useful and Ornamental Gourds,* Farmer's Bulletin 1849, 10 cents; *Palm Trees in the United States,* Agricultural Information Bulletin 22, 15 cents; *Attracting Birds,* Conservation Bulletin 1, 5 cents; *Homes for Birds* (Birdhouses), Conservation Bulletin 14, 10 cents. These publications are for sale by the Superintendent of Documents, U. S. Government Printing Office, Washington 25, D.C.

CALIFORNIA: *Shrubs for Coast Counties in California; Trees for Southern California; Trees for the Sacramento and San Joaquin Valleys of California; Trees for California Coastal Districts;* and *Ornamental Gourds and Gourdlike Fruits.* For these mimeographed publications write to Extension Service, University of California College of Agriculture, Berkeley 4, California.

OREGON: *Trees to Know in Oregon,* by Charles R. Ross, Extension Bulletin 697; *Culture of Trailing Berries in Oregon,* Station Bulletin 441; *Raspberry Culture in Oregon,* Station Bulletin 443; *Growing Small Fruits in Eastern Home Gardens,* Extension Bulletin 617. Write to Oregon State College at Corvallis for these publications.

WHAT TO FEED BIRDS

Kinds of foods and some of the birds attracted to each
(Birds are listed alphabetically for ease of reference.)

BEEF SUET:

Blackbird, red-winged
Bluebird, eastern
Bushtit
Catbird, gray
Chickadee, black-capped
Chickadee, Carolina
Chickadee, Chestnut-backed
Creeper, brown
Crossbill, white-winged
Flicker, yellow-shafted
  (common)
Goldfinch, American
Grackles
Grosbeak, rose-breasted
Jay, blue
Jay, gray
Juncos
Kinglet, golden-crowned
Kinglet, ruby-crowned
Mockingbird
Nutcracker, Clark's
Nuthatch, red-breasted
Nuthatch, white-breasted
Oriole, Baltimore (northern)
Ovenbird
Owl, screech
Robin, American

Sapsucker, yellow-bellied
Shrike, northern
Siskin, pine
Sparrow, fox
Sparrow, tree
Sparrow, white-throated
Starling
Thrasher, brown
Thrasher, curve-billed
Thrush, hermit
Thrush, Swainson's
Thrush, wood
Titmouse, tufted
Towhee, rufuous-sided
Warbler, myrtle (yellow-
  rumped)
Warbler, orange-crowned
Warbler, pine
Woodpecker, downy
Woodpecker, hairy
Woodpecker, pileated
Woodpecker, red-bellied
Wren, Bewick's
Wren, cactus
Wren, Carolina
Wren, house
Wren, winter

WHITE BREAD:

Blackbird, red-winged
Bluebirds

Bunting, painted
Cardinal

Catbird, gray
Chickadees
Cowbird, brown-headed
Creeper, brown
Finch, house
Grackles
Jays
Juncos
Longspur, Lapland
Mockingbird
Nuthatch, white-breasted
Pheasants
Quail
Redpolls
Robin, American
Shrikes
Sparrow, black-throated
  (desert)
Sparrow, chipping
Sparrow, field
Sparrow, fox

Sparrow, song
Sparrow, tree
Sparrow, white-crowned
Sparrow, white-throated
Starling
Tanager, scarlet
Tanager, summer
Thrasher, Bendire's
Thrasher, brown
Thrasher, curve-billed
Thrush, hermit
Thrush, Swainson's
Thrush, wood
Titmouse, tufted
Towhee, rufous-sided
Warbler, yellow-throated
Wren, Bewick's
Wren, cactus
Wren, house
Wren, winter

CORN BREAD:

Blackbird, red-winged
Bluebirds
Cardinal
Catbird, gray
Cowbird, brown-headed
Jay, blue
Juncos
Kinglet, ruby-crowned
Mockingbird
Nuthatch, white-breasted

Robin, American
Sparrow, chipping
Sparrow, field
Sparrow, white-crowned
Thrasher, brown
Titmouse, tufted
Woodpecker, downy
Wren, Bewick's
Wren, Carolina
Wren, house

SUNFLOWER SEEDS:

Blackbird, rusty
Brambling
Bunting, painted
Cardinal
Chickadees

Cowbird, brown-headed
Crossbill, red
Crossbill, white-winged
Dickcissel
Dove, mourning

Finch, house
Finch, purple
Goldfinches
Grackles
Grosbeak, blue
Grosbeak, evening
Grosbeak, rose-breasted
Jay, blue
Jay, scrub
Juncos
Nuthatch, red-breasted
Nuthatch, white-breasted
Quail, bobwhite
Quail, Gambel's
Redpolls
Siskin, pine

Sparrow, chipping
Sparrow, fox
Sparrow, tree
Sparrow, song
Sparrow, white crowned
Sparrow, white-throated
Thrasher, brown
Titmouse, tufted
Towhee, rufous-sided
Waxwing, cedar
Woodpecker, downy
Woodpecker, hairy
Woodpecker, red-bellied
Woodpecker, red-headed
Wren, Carolina

HEMP SEEDS:

Chickadees
Crossbills
Finch, house
Finch, purple
Goldfinches
Grosbeak, pine
Juncos
Nuthatch, white-breasted

Redpolls
Siskin, pine
Sparrow, song
Sparrow, tree
Sparrow, vesper
Sparrow, white-crowned
Sparrow, white-throated

MILLET SEEDS:

Blackbird, red-winged
Blackbird, rusty
Bunting, indigo
Bunting, painted
Dickcissel
Dove, common ground
Dove, mourning
Finch, house
Finch, purple
Goldfinches
Jay, blue
Juncos
Longspur, Lapland

Quail
Redpolls
Siskin, pine
Sparrow, chipping
Sparrow, field
Sparrow, fox
Sparrow, house
Sparrow, song
Sparrow, tree
Sparrow, vesper
Sparrow, white-crowned
Sparrow, white-throated
Thrasher, brown

WHOLE CORN:

Cardinal
Chickadees
Dove, mourning
Dove, rock (domestic pigeon)
Grackles
Grosbeak, blue
Grouse, ruffed

Jay, blue
Nuthatch, white-breasted
Pheasants
Quail
Turkey, wild
Woodpecker, red-bellied

WHOLE OATS:

Blackbird, red-winged
Blackbird, yellow-headed
Bunting, snow
Cardinal
Chickadees
Dickcissel
Dove, mourning
Dove, rock

Finch, purple
Flickers
Grouse, ruffed
Juncos
Meadowlarks
Quail
Sparrow, house
Towhees

WILD BIRD SEED MIXTURE (millets, rape, hemp, canary seeds, sunflower seeds, peanut hearts):

Blackbird, red-winged
Bunting, snow
Cardinal
Cowbird, brown-headed
Finch, house
Finch, purple
Goldfinches
Grosbeak, pine
Juncos
Lark, horned

Longspur, Lapland
Redpolls,
Siskin, pine
Sparrow, field
Sparrow, fox
Sparrow, house
Sparrow, song
Sparrow, tree
Sparrow, white-crowned
Sparrow, white-throated

A Suggested Bird Seed Mixture of 100 pounds

Hemp seeds	25 pounds
Millet seeds	25 pounds
Sunflower seeds	25 pounds
Buckwheat	10 pounds
Peanut hearts	10 pounds
Grit (coarse white sand or ground oyster shells	5 pounds

SCRATCH FEED (coarse for larger birds; fine for smaller ones)

Blackbird, red-winged
Blackbird, rusty
Bunting, painted
Bunting, snow
Cowbird, brown-headed
Dickcissel
Dove, ground
Dove, mourning
Finch, house
Finch, purple
Goldfinches
Grackles
Grouse, ruffed
Jay, blue
Juncos
Lark, horned
Longspur, Lapland
Pheasants
Pyrrhuloxia

Quail, bob-white
Quail, Gambel's
Siskin, pine
Sparrow, chipping
Sparrow, field
Sparrow, fox
Sparrow, house
Sparrow, song
Sparrow, tree
Sparrow, white-crowned
Sparrow, white-throated
Starling
Thrasher, Bendire's
Thrasher, brown
Turkey, wild
Woodpecker, downy
Woodpecker, pileated
Woodpecker, red-bellied
Woodpecker, red-headed

PEANUT BUTTER (mixed with suet and corn meal):

Bushtit
Chat, yellow-breasted
Chickadee, black-capped
Chickadee, Carolina
Chickadee, chestnut-backed
Creeper, brown
Finch, house
Flickers
Goldfinches
Jay, blue
Jay, Steller's
Juncos
Kinglets
Nuthatches
Redpolls
Robin, American
Siskin, pine

Sparrow, fox
Sparrow, song
Sparrow, tree
Tanager, western
Thrasher, brown
Thrasher, curve-billed
Thrush, hermit
Thrush, varied
Thrush, wood
Towhee, brown
Warbler, Audubon (yellow-
    rumped)
Warbler, orange-crowned
Warbler, Tennessee
Woodpecker, downy
Woodpecker, hairy
Wren, Carolina

WALNUT MEATS (black or English, crumbled):

Cardinal
Catbird, gray
Chickadees
Finch, house
Goldfinches
Jays
Juncos
Nuthatch, red-breasted
Nuthatch, white-breasted
Siskin, pine
Sparrow, house
Sparrow, song
Sparrow, white-crowned
Thrasher, brown
Titmouse, tufted
Warbler, myrtle (yellow-rumped)
Woodpeckers
Wren, Carolina

DOUGHNUTS (suspended whole from tree branches or crumbled in feeders):

Bluebirds
Bushtit
Chat, yellow-breasted
Chickadee, black-capped
Chickadee, Carolina
Crossbills
Finch, house
Finch, purple
Flicker, red-shafted (common)
Jay, blue
Juncos
Kinglet, ruby-crowned
Mockingbird
Nuthatch, red-breasted
Nuthatch, white-breasted
Robin, American
Sapsucker, yellow-bellied
Sparrow, chipping
Sparrow, golden-crowned
Sparrow, song
Sparrow, white-crowned
Sparrow, white-throated
Tanager, western
Thrasher, brown
Thrush, hermit
Warbler, Audubon's (yellow-rumped)
Warbler, orange-crowned
Wren, Bewick's
Yellowthroat (a warbler)

FRUITS:

Sliced pieces of raw apple: Hairy woodpecker, blue jay, cactus wren, mockingbird, curve-billed thrasher, American robin, hermit thrush, cedar waxwing, yellow-breasted chat, orange-crowned warbler, orioles, house finch, white-crowned sparrow

Baked apple: American robin, bluebirds

Frozen crabapples: American robin, cedar waxwing, purple finch

Grapes (either wild or cultivated; offer in sliced halves in feeders; white seedless are especially attractive to birds): Acorn woodpecker, gray jay, mockingbird, gray catbird, California thrasher, American robin, Swainson's thrush, bluebirds, cedar waxwing, many warblers, Baltimore (northern) oriole, hooded oriole, Scott's oriole, western tanager, black-headed grosbeak, rose-breasted grosbeak, house finch, towhees.

Grape jelly (may be put on feeding tray in special container to keep it from mixing with other bird foods; according to John V. Dennis, it does not freeze in winter): yellow-bellied sapsucker, myrtle (yellow-rumped) warbler, Baltimore (northern) oriole

Bananas (peeled, then may be cut in pieces or put whole on feeding tray): Hairy woodpecker, gray jay, Carolina wren, mockingbird, gray catbird, starling, Tennessee warbler, yellow-breasted chat, western tanager, indigo bunting, house finch

Strawberries: Bobwhite quail, mockingbird, gray catbird, American robin, bluebirds, black-headed grosbeak, rose-breasted grosbeak

Bayberries (cut fruiting branches from bushes, then put berries on feeding shelves or on tray feeders): Chickadees, myrtle (yellow-rumped) warbler

Oranges (cut in halves and impale on sharp twigs of trees or on nails with points up, projecting upward from porch railings or from a special feeding board): Red-bellied woodpecker, mockingbird, gray catbird, brown thrasher, myrtle (yellow-rumped) warbler, Baltimore (northern) oriole, to which especially attractive, scarlet tanager, summer tanager, western tanager, rose-breasted grosbeak

Cherries (canned or fresh): gray catbird, American robin, thrushes, starling, cedar waxwing, tanagers

Cranberries (fresh or canned): gray catbird, American robin, starling, pine grosbeak

Watermelon pulp or rind: mockingbird, warblers, orioles, grosbeaks, house finch

MISCELLANEOUS:

Baking powder biscuits (short and crumbly): American robin, bluebirds

Dog biscuits (ground): Horned lark, blue jay, chickadees, white-breasted nuthatch, starling, grackles, dark-eyed (slate-colored) junco, tree sparrow, Lapland longspur, snow bunting

Corn bread: Eaten dry by red crossbill but usually offered birds in mixture with suet and peanut butter.

Cake, cracker, and cookie crumbs: Blue jay, gray jay, tufted tit-mouse, gray catbird, chipping sparrow, house sparrow

Pie crust (dry): Chickadees, tufted titmouse, house wren, gray catbird, bluebirds, starling, northern (Baltimore) oriole, grackles, scarlet and summer tanagers, dark-eyed (slate-colored) junco

Unbaked dough: Blue jay

Cottage cheese, or pot cheese: Carolina wren, gray catbird, American robin, bluebirds

Fried, mashed, or baked potatoes: Blue jay, common crow, cactus wren, gray catbird, curve-billed thrasher, starling, grackles

Fresh tomatoes (halved and put on open feeder): Gray catbird, Tennessee warbler, pyrrhuloxia, white-crowned sparrow

Egg shells of poultry (finely crushed, may be put on bird feeder or pieces scattered on lawn): Purple martin, blue jay

Barrel cactus seeds (in Southwest): House finch, green-tailed towhee, lark bunting, black-throated (desert) sparrow, white-crowned sparrow

Cantaloupe seeds: Red-breasted nuthatch, white-breasted nut-hatch, house sparrow

Ground pumpkin seeds: Chickadees, white-breasted nuthatch, myrtle (yellow-rumped) warbler, dark-eyed (slate-colored) junco, tree sparrow

Broken squash seeds: Chickadees, white-breasted nuthatch, dark-eyed (Oregon) junco

Pecan meats (broken or ground): Ground dove, woodpeckers, jays, chickadees, tufted titmouse, Carolina wren, house wren, gray catbird, ruby-crowned kinglet, American robin, blue-birds, hermit thrush, red-winged blackbird, brown-headed cowbird, indigo bunting, purple finch, pine siskin, gold-finches, juncos, field sparrow, white-crowned sparrow

Rice: Bobwhite quail, mourning dove, white-crowned sparrow

Soybeans: Ruffed grouse, quail, pheasants, mourning dove, meadowlark

Rolled oats: Band-tailed pigeon, curve-billed thrasher, pine sis-kin, dark-eyed (Oregon) junco

Chaff (barn floor sweeping): Quail, horned lark, redpolls, savannah sparrow, vesper sparrow, tree sparrow, Lapland longspur, snow bunting

Sugar water: See under Hints and Suggestions

SOME DEALERS IN
BIRD-ATTRACTING SUPPLIES

(Write to them for catalogues; some sell bird
seeds as well as bird houses, feeders, etc.)

Audubon Workshop, 1501 Paddock Drive, Northbrook, Illinois
60062

Crow's Nest Book Shop, Laboratory of Ornithology at Cornell
University, Sapsucker Woods, Ithaca, New York 14850

Droll Yankees, Inc., Mill Road, Foster, Rhode Island 02825

Hyde Bird Feeder Company, 56 Felton Street, Waltham, Massachusetts 02154

Libner Grain Company, 25 Commerce Street, Norwalk, Connecticut 06850

Massachusetts Audubon Society (The Audubon Shop), South
Great Road, Lincoln, Massachusetts 01773

Nature House Inc., Purple Martin Junction, Griggsville, Illinois
62340

Presco Galaxy, 255 Banker Street, Greenpoint, New York 11222

Wild Birds Unlimited, 1430 Broad Ripple Avenue, Indianapolis,
Indiana 46220

SOME SONGBIRDS IN THE WEST THAT
WILL BATHE IN THE GARDEN BIRDBATH

Bunting, Lazuli

Bushtit

Catbird, gray

Finch, house

Finch, purple

Goldfinch, green-backed
  (Lesser)

Goldfinch, Lawrence's

Grosbeak, black-headed

Jay, California (scrub)

Mockingbird

Oriole, Bullock's (northern)

Oriole, hooded

Phainopepla

Robin, American

Sparrow, chipping

Sparrow, golden-crowned
Sparrow, rufous-crowned
Sparrow, song
Sparrow, white-crowned
Tanager, western
Thrush, hermit
Thrush, Swainson's
Towhee, brown
Towhee, rufous-sided
Vireo, Bell's
Vireo, Hutton's
Vireo, solitary

Vireo, warbling
Warbler, Audubon's
 (yellow-rumped)
Warbler, black-throated
 gray
Warbler, Nashville
Warbler, orange-crowned
Warbler, yellow
Warbler, Wilson's
Wren, house
Wren-tit
Yellowthroat

SOME GARDEN FLOWERS THAT ATTRACT
HUMMINGBIRDS

NAME OF PLANT	NAMES OF HUMMINGBIRDS KNOWN TO VISIT THE PLANTS
Abelia grandiflora, GLOSSY ABELIA (shrub)	Ruby-throated hummingbird
Aesculus spp.[a] Tree and shrub HORSE-CHESTNUT, or BUCK-EYES	Ruby-throated and black-chinned hummingbirds
Agave americana, CENTURY PLANT, also other species of *Agave*	Black-chinned, rufous, Costa's, broad-tailed, blue-throated, and Rivoli's hummingbirds
Albizzia julibrissin, SILK-TREE, or "MIMOSA"	Ruby-throated hummingbird
Althea spp., MARSH-MALLOW; HOLLYHOCKS	Ruby-throated, black-chinned, and rufous
Anisacanthus thurberi, TAPE-ROSA (shrub)	Ruby-throated, black-chinned, and broad-tailed
Aquilegia spp., COLUMBINE	Ruby-throated, black-chinned, rufous, blue-throated, calli-

[a] The symbol "spp." means species, or that more than one species of this plant are attractive to hummingbirds.

	ope, and Rivoli's humming-birds
Begonia spp., BEGONIA	Ruby-throated hummingbird
Beloperone californica, CHU-PEROSA, and *Beloperone gut-tata*, SHRIMP PLANT	Black-chinned hummingbird
Buddleia spp., BUTTERFLY-BUSHES (shrubs)	Ruby-throated and black-chinned hummingbirds
Campsis radicans, TRUMPET CREEPER, or TRUMPET VINE	Ruby-throated and black-chinned hummingbirds
Canna generalis, COMMON GARDEN CANNA	Ruby-throated, and black-chinned hummingbirds
Caragana arborescens, SIBERI-AN PEA-TREE	Ruby-throated hummingbird
Cestrum purpureum, PURPLE CESTRUM	Ruby-throated hummingbird
Citrus spp., ORANGE TREE	Ruby-throated, black-chinned, rufous, Anna's, and calliope hummingbirds
Cleome spinosa, SPIDER FLOWER or SPIDER PLANT	Ruby-throated hummingbird
Crataegus spp., HAWTHORN TREE, or THORN-APPLE	Ruby-throated, Anna's, and calliope hummingbirds
Delonix regia, ROYAL POINCI-ANA	Ruby-throated hummingbird
Delphinium spp., LARKSPUR	Ruby-throated, black-chinned, rufous, and broad-tailed hummingbirds
Dianthus spp., PINKS; SWEET WILLIAMS	Ruby-throated hummingbird
Erythrina cristi-galli, COCK-SPUR CORAL-TREE	Anna's hummingbird
Eucalyptus spp., EUCALYPTUS TREES, especially the scarlet-flowering kinds	Anna's hummingbird
Fouquieria splendens, OCO-TILLO, COACH-WHIP, or VINE-CACTUS	Black-chinned, and broad-tailed hummingbirds
Fuchsia spp., FUCHSIA	Ruby-throated hummingbird

NAME OF PLANT	NAMES OF HUMMINGBIRDS KNOWN TO VISIT THE PLANTS
Gilia spp., SCARLET GILIA; SKY-ROCKET; SKUNKWEED; BIRDS-EYES	Ruby-throated, blue-throated, rufous, and broad-tailed hummingbirds
Gladiolus spp., GLADIOLUS, or GLADIOLI	Ruby-throated, and black-chinned hummingbirds
Grevillea robusta, and *Grevillea thelemanniana*, SILK-OAK	Anna's, rufous, and calliope hummingbirds
Hamelia erecta, SCARLET BUSH	Ruby-throated hummingbird
Hemerocallis spp., DAY LILIES	Ruby-throated hummingbird
Heuchera sanguinea, CORAL BELLS	Ruby-throated hummingbird
Hibiscus spp., SHRUB ALTHEA; ROSE MALLOW; CONFEDERATE ROSE; ROSE-OF-CHINA; CRIMSON EYE	Ruby-throated and black-chinned hummingbirds
Impatiens balsamina, GARDEN BALSAM	Ruby-throated hummingbird and black-chinned
Ipomoea spp., MORNING GLORIES	Ruby-throated, and black-chinned hummingbirds
Iris spp., IRIS	Black-chinned hummingbird
Jasminum spp., JASMINE, or JESSAMINE (shrub)	Ruby-throated and black-chinned hummingbirds
Kolkwitzia amabilis, BEAUTY-BUSH (shrub)	Ruby-throated hummingbird
Lantana camara, LANTANA, and other species	Ruby-throated, black-chinned and rufous
Lilium spp., LILIES	Ruby-throated hummingbird
Lonicera japonica, JAPANESE HONEYSUCKLE, and *Lonicera sempervirens*, TRUMPET HONEYSUCKLE	Ruby-throated, black-chinned, broad-tailed, blue-throated, and Rivoli's
Lupinus spp., LUPINES	Ruby-throated, broad-tailed, and rufous
Malvaviscus drummondi, TEXAS MALLOW, or SPANISH APPLE (shrub)	Ruby-throated hummingbird
Melaleuca spp., BOTTLE-BRUSHES	Anna's hummingbird
Monarda spp., HORSE-MINT; OSWEGO TEA; BERGAMOT	Ruby-throated and broad-tailed hummingbirds

NAME OF PLANT	KNOWN TO VISIT THE PLANTS
Nepeta cataria, CATNIP	Ruby-throated hummingbird and black-chinned
Nicotiania glauca, TREE TOBACCO	Anna's and black-chinned
Nicotiana sanderae, FLOWER-ING TOBACCO	Ruby-throated hummingbird
Parkinsonia microphylla, PALO VERDE	Black-chinned hummingbird
Pedicularis spp., WOOD BETONY, or LOUSEWORT	Broad-tailed hummingbird
Pelargonium spp., GERANIUMS	Ruby-throated hummingbird
Penstemon spp., BEARD-TONGUE	Black-chinned, broad-tailed, and rufous
Petunia spp., PETUNIAS	Ruby-throated, black-chinned, and rufous
Phlox spp., PHLOX	Ruby-throated hummingbird
Poinciana gilliesi, BIRD-OF-PARADISE	Black-chinned hummingbird
Quamoclit spp., STAR IPOMOEA; CYPRESS VINE; CARDINAL CLIMBER	Ruby-throated hummingbird
Rhododendron spp., AZALEAS	Ruby-throated hummingbird
Robinia pseudoacacia, BLACK LOCUST (tree)	Ruby-throated hummingbird
Salvia spp., SAGE	Ruby-throated hummingbird, rufous, Costa's, and broad-tailed
Saponaria officinalis, BOUNCING BET, or SOAPWORT	Ruby-throated hummingbird
Scabiosa spp., SCABIOUS, MOURNING BRIDE, or PIN-CUSHION FLOWER	Ruby-throated hummingbird
Tecomaria capensis, CAPE HONEYSUCKLE	Ruby-throated hummingbird
Tritonia spp., MONTBRETIA, or RED-HOT POKER; *Kniphofia*	Ruby-throated hummingbird
Tropaeolum majus, GARDEN NASTURTIUM	Ruby-throated, black-chinned, and broad-tailed humming-birds

Verbena spp., VERBENA	Ruby-throated, black-chinned, and rufous
Vinca major, PERIWINKLE	Black-chinned hummingbird
Vitex agnus-castus, CHASTE-TREE	Ruby-throated hummingbird
Weigela spp., WEIGELA, or WEIGELIA	Ruby-throated hummingbird
Yucca spp., ADAMS-NEEDLE; SPANISH BAYONET; SPANISH DAGGER	Black-chinned, and rufous hummingbird

SOME GARDEN FLOWERS WHOSE SEEDS ATTRACT BIRDS [a]

Amaranthus, Love-lies-bleeding *(Amaranthus caudatus)*, and prince's feather *(Amaranthus hybridus* var. *hypochondriacus)* are especially good.

Asters, especially China aster *(Callistephus chinensis)*, which has full heads of seeds.

Batchelor's buttons, or cornflower, *(Centaurea cyanus)*.

Calendula.

Campanula, or bellflower.

Carduus, especially blessed thistle *(Carduus benedictus)*.

Chrysanthemums.

Columbines *(Aquilegia)*.

Coneflowers *(Rudbeckia)*, or black-eyed susans.

Coreopsis *(Calliopsis)*, or tickseed.

Cosmos.

Dianthus *(sweet williams and pinks)*.

Forget-me-nots *(Myosotis)*.

Four-o-clocks *(Mirabilis)*.

Gaillardias.

Larkspurs, or delphiniums.

[a] These are the seed-eating songbirds, especially those that either normally or occasionally feed on or near the ground. Some of them include doves, quails, blackbirds, buntings, cardinals, cowbirds, finches, grackles, grosbeaks, juncos, larks, native sparrows—the chipping, fox, white-throated, white-crowned, tree, song sparrow, etc.—and towhees and thrashers. If you plant some of the flowers on the above list in your garden and let them go to seed, they will provide summer, fall, and winter foods for birds.

Marigolds *(Tagetes)*.

Petunias.

Poppies, particularly *Eschscholzia californica*, the California poppy.

Portulaca, or purslane. (The flowers of these plants produce especially abundant crops of seeds.)

Phlox, particularly the annual, *Phlox drummondi*.

Scabiosa, mourning bride, or pincushion flower.

Sunflowers *(Helianthus)*.

Tarweed, particularly *Madia elegans*, the common tarweed.

Verbena, especially the common garden verbena, *Verbena hybrida*.

Zinnias.

POTENTIAL LIFE SPAN OF SOME
NORTH AMERICAN BIRDS IN THE WILD

SPECIES, OR KIND OF BIRD	YEARS	SPECIES, OR KIND OF BIRD	YEARS
Blackbird, red-winged	4–14½	Nuthatch, red-breasted	7½
Bluebird, eastern	3–6½	Nuthatch, white-	
Cardinal	4–13½	breasted	5–9¾
Catbird, gray	4–10	Oriole, northern	
Chickadee, black-capped	5–12½	(Baltimore)	6–8(?)
Cowbird, brown-headed	5–13¾	Owl, screech	6–13
Creeper, brown	3–5	Phoebe, eastern	8–9
Crow, common	6–14	**Quail, bobwhite	7–8
Dove, common ground	6	**Quail, California	4–5
Dove, mourning	5–10	Robin, American	4–11½
Dove, rock (domestic		Sparrow, chipping	2–9¾
pigeon)	6–16+	Sparrow, fox	6–9¾
Finch, house	6–10	Sparrow, house	13⅓
Finch, purple	6–12½	Sparrow, song	2½–10⅓
Flicker, common		Sparrow, tree	6–9
(yellow-shafted)	5–12½	Sparrow, white-crowned	7–13⅓
Flycatcher, great crested	6–11	Sparrow, white-	
Goldfinch, American	4–8¾	throated	5½–9½
Grackle, common	4–16	Starling	5–16
Grosbeak, black-headed	5–6	Swallow, barn	6–8¼
Grosbeak, evening	4–13½	Swallow, cliff	4–5
Grosbeak, pine	6–8¾	Swallow, tree	5–9
Grosbeak, rose-breasted	4–9	Tanager, scarlet	3–9
*Hummingbird, blue-		Tanager, summer	6
throated	12(?)	Thrasher, brown	4–12¾
Hummingbird, ruby-		Thrush, wood	3–8¾
throated	5	Titmouse, plain	5–7
Jay, blue	5–15	Titmouse, tufted	3½–12
Jay, gray	9–10	Towhee, brown	7–10
Jay, scrub (Florida)	11	Towhee, rufous-sided	4–12¼
Junco, dark-eyed		Waxwing, cedar	3–7
(slate-colored)	3–10¾	Woodpecker, downy	4–10½
**Kestrel, American		Woodpecker, hairy	7–12¾
(sparrow hawk)	2–4	Woodpecker, red-bellied	6½–20½
Kingbird, eastern	3–8(?)	Wren, Carolina	3–6
Martin, purple	4–8	Wren, house	5–7
Mockingbird	4–12	Wren, winter	5¾

Ages are from official banding records of birds from files of the U.S. Fish and Wildlife Service, Washington, D.C.

* A male, individually identifiable, regularly dominant over other hummingbirds, appeared in a garden in Ramsay Canyon, Arizona, for twelve years.

**Birds often shot that otherwise might live to at least ten years.

(?) A question mark indicates the higher figure is not definitely known from banding records.

Note: Hummingbirds, warblers, and other small birds probably live only a year or two but the medium or large birds that live to three years may survive for up to ten years. Two thirds of the young birds that reach the flying stage die in their first year; about one fourth of the population dies in the second year.

NESTING RECORDS FOR SOME BIRDS OF CITY AND COUNTRY GARDENS IN THE UNITED STATES AND CANADA

SPECIES, OR KIND, AND GENERAL NESTING RANGE	NUMBER OF EGGS LAID IN CLUTCH	DAYS TO HATCH	DAYS YOUNG IN NEST	NUMBER OF BROODS EACH YEAR	NEST AND ITS LOCATION
Bluebird, eastern[a] (eastern N. America, west to Rockies)	3–6[b]	13–16[c]	15–18	2, sometimes 3	Grassy, built in natural cavity of tree, post, woodpecker hole, birdhouse, etc.
Bunting, painted (southern U.S.)	3–5	11–12	12–14	2, 3, sometimes 4	Grassy, or weedy, cup usually built 3–6 ft. up in dense bush, low tree, vines
Bushtit (western U.S.)	5–13	12	14–15	1 to 2(?)	Gourd-shaped pocket of twigs, mosses, etc., suspended from tree, bush, 6–25 ft. up
Cardinal (eastern U.S., west to prairies, also in Southwest)	3–4	12–13	10–11	2 to 4	Bowl-shaped nest of grasses, twigs, rootlets, concealed in forks of twigs, sometimes on branch, 4–5 ft. up in vines, trees, bushes, etc.
Catbird, gray (most of U.S., not West Coast or Southwest)	2–6	12–15	10–15	Often 2	Ragged mass of sticks, weed stems, etc., often in garden shrubs, 3–10 feet up, inner cup lined with pine needles, bark, etc.

a Birds that will nest in birdhouses.

b The clutch, set, or number of eggs laid by each kind of bird varies usually in each species. Number shown here is usual variation.

c The time for wild birds to hatch their eggs usually varies in each species and varies according to how closely the parents incubate. Among songbirds, both the male and female of a pair may share in the hatching of the eggs and feeding of their young. With some species—hummingbirds for example—this responsibility may be solely the female's. If the weather is cool and stormy and insects less abundant or more difficult to find, birds may be forced to spend longer than usual periods off the nest hunting for food. If the eggs become chilled, this may delay hatching. Also, weather that causes a scarcity of insect food, upon which the young are fed, may slow their development and lengthen their time spent in the nest.

d Birds that will nest on a shelf, or bracket, put up for them.

e The English, or house, sparrow, first introduced successfully into the United States at Greenwood Cemetery, Brooklyn, New York, by Nicholas Pike, in the spring of 1853, is not a true sparrow. It is a member of the Old World Weaverbird family, called Ploceidae.

(?) A question mark indicates that this information is not known or that there is not enough to give approximate figures.

SPECIES, OR KIND, AND GENERAL NESTING RANGE	NUMBER OF EGGS LAID IN CLUTCH	DAYS TO HATCH	DAYS YOUNG IN NEST	NUMBER OF BROODS EACH YEAR	NEST AND ITS LOCATION
Chickadee, black-capped[a] (across middle and northern N. America)	6–8	11–13	14–18	2	Pair digs nest hole in rotted birch, pine stub, usually 1–10 feet up, also uses woodpecker holes; nest of plant fibers, wool, etc.
Dove, common ground (southern and southwestern U.S.)	2–3	12–14	(?)	1	Nest in depression on ground, in fields, woods, or few twigs in low bush, tree, 1–21 ft. up
Dove, mourning (nests in all states of U.S.)	2–4	14–15	14–15	2 to 5	Platform sticks in tree crotch, on branch usually 5–25 feet up, also in vines, on stumps, roof gutters, arbors in gardens, etc.
Dove, rock (domestic pigeon)	1–2	17–19	35–37	Several	Flimsy platform, sticks, twigs, grasses, on buildings, cliffs, beams in barns
Finch, house[a] (West, now in eastern U.S.)	2–6	12–16	11–19	2, sometimes 3	Nest of grasses leaves, etc., in holes of poles, trees, birdhouses, in shrubs, vines, etc.
Flicker, common[a] (Atlantic to Pacific, southern Canada)	5–10	11–12	25–28	1 or 2	Digs nesting hole in stub or trunk of dead tree above surrounding bushes; eggs laid on fresh chips at bottom of cavity

Flycatcher, great crested[a] (eastern U.S., southern Canada, west to prairies)	4–8	13–15	15–18	1 possibly 2	In natural cavities of trees, in abandoned woodpecker holes, birdhouses; builds cuplike nest of leaves, mosses (see p. 56)
Goldfinch, American (coast to coast, southern Canada, most of U.S.)	4–6	12–14	10–16	1	Builds thick-walled, cuplike nest of woven plant fibers in hedges, bushes, in fork of hardwood saplings, trees, 1–33 feet up
Grackle, common (in summer most of N. America east of Rockies)	4–7	14	18–20	1	Builds nest of twigs, weeds, rags, etc., in tall evergreens, elms, maples, low bushes of swamps, marshes, in lower part osprey's nest
Grosbeak, black-headed (Rockies to Pacific)	2–5	12–13	12	1	Loose, thin nest of rootlets, twigs, usually in deciduous trees or shrubs along stream, also in gardens, 6–12 ft. up in dense outer foliage
Grosbeak, rose-breasted (northeastern U.S., southern Canada)	3–5	12–13	9–12	1	Loose, cuplike nest of twigs, usually 5–15 ft. up near crotch or fork, in small trees in woods or thickets, in or near gardens

NESTING RECORDS FOR SOME BIRDS OF CITY AND COUNTRY GARDENS IN THE UNITED STATES AND CANADA

SPECIES, OR KIND, AND GENERAL NESTING RANGE	NUMBER OF EGGS LAID IN CLUTCH	DAYS TO HATCH	DAYS YOUNG IN NEST	NUMBER OF BROODS EACH YEAR	NEST AND ITS LOCATION
Hummingbird, Allen's (Pacific coast, Oreg. to southern Calif.)	2	15–17	22	2	Thick-walled cup, 2 inches across, of dried weeds, leaves, plant down, lichens, 1–90 feet from ground, saddled on weed stalks, in vines, shrubs, pine trees, buildings, in shade
Hummingbird, Anna's (northern Calif., south to Baja Calif.)	2	16–19	18–21	2	Tiny, lichen-covered cup in bush or small tree, in semishade, 17 inches to 30 feet up, sometimes on face of cliff, etc.
Hummingbird, black-chinned (southern Canada and Pacific coast, east to Rockies, south to Mexico)	2	16	20–21	2 or 3	Cup of plant down 1½ inches across, 1 inch high, saddled on drooping branch or fork of limb 4 to 8 feet up, often over water or dry creek bed, in gardens
Hummingbird, ruby-throated (southern Canada, south to Fla., west to Great Plains)	2	16	20–22	2 or 3	Cup of mosses, plant down, lichens, about 1 inch across, usually in open woods, saddled on limb or twig of maple, beech, etc., 5–20 feet up

Jay, blue (southern Canada to Gulf States, east of Rockies)	3–6	16–18	17–21	1	Bulky, of twigs, sticks, bark, mosses, leaves, grasses, in crotch or on branch close to trunk of tree, also in bushes, vines, 5–50 feet up
Jay, scrub (in West Calif. to Wash. to Colo., south to Tex., also in Fla.)	2–7	16–19	18	1	Bulky, of sticks, rootlets, in low tree or bush, 2–12 feet above ground
Kestrel, American[a] (from Alaska, Canada, south over most of U.S.)	4–5	29–30	27–33	Usually 1	Prefers old tree-nesting holes of flickers, hollows in cactus, niches in walls of city buildings, cliffs, in birdhouses
Kingbird, eastern (across Canada to Nova Scotia, south to northeastern Calif. to Tex. and Fla.)	3–5	13–16	13–14	1	Usually well out on limb of isolated tree or in low shrubs, on rain gutters of houses; built of twigs, straw, weed stems, feathers, 2–60 feet above ground, bulky nest
Martin, purple[a] (southern Canada, south to Mexico, Atlantic to Pacific)	3–8	16–18	26–31	Usually 1	In colonies, in cavities of trees, in cavities in cliffs, now mostly in birdhouses; nest of grasses, leaves, twigs, feathers, etc.

NESTING RECORDS FOR SOME BIRDS OF CITY AND COUNTRY GARDENS IN THE UNITED STATES AND CANADA

SPECIES, OR KIND, AND GENERAL NESTING RANGE	NUMBER OF EGGS LAID IN CLUTCH	DAYS TO HATCH	DAYS YOUNG IN NEST	NUMBER OF BROODS EACH YEAR	NEST AND ITS LOCATION
Mockingbird (across U.S. from northern Calif. to Atlantic coast, south to Gulf of Mexico)	4–5	12–13	10–12	2 or 3	Of string, leaves, cotton, cloth, grasses, twigs in fork of small tree, bush, 1–50 ft. up; often in vines, cactus, red cedar, spruce, pine, boxwood, privet, in gardens, yards, country
Nuthatch, white-breasted (southern Canada throughout much of U.S. to Mexico)	5–8	12	14	1	Often high in large tree in natural cavity, woodpecker hole, knothole, in oak, elm, etc., also in birdhouse; nest of wool, cowhair, bark, feathers
Oriole, northern (Baltimore), (eastern U.S., west to plains and prairies, southern and western Canada)	4–6	12–14	12–14	1	Gray, swinging pouch, 5–6 inches deep, woven of plant fibers, hairs, will use short pieces of colored yarn put out on lawn or shrubbery; nest usually suspended from drooping branch of elm, maple, 25–30 feet up

Oriole, northern (Bullock's), (commonest oriole over most of West, from Great Plains to Calif.)	3–6	14	14	1	Hybridizes with Baltimore oriole in Great Plains where ranges of these two meet; locally common in shade trees, nest an oval woven bag, 6 inches deep attached to outer twigs of branches of cottonwood, birch, etc., about ranches
Owl, screech[a] (from extreme southern Canada throughout U.S., two color forms, either red or gray)	3–7	21–30	25–30	1	Lays eggs on bottom of natural cavity in trees, usually no nesting materials, also in old nesting holes of flickers, in sycamores, elms, dead pines, oaks, saguaros in deserts, and birdhouses, holes of utility poles, and streamside trees
Pewee, eastern wood (southern Canada, south to Fla., west to Dakotas, Tex.)	2–4	12–13	15–18	1	Thick-walled cup of plant fibers, weed stems, etc.; built on horizontal limb, 15–50 ft. up, in oak, maple, locust, elm, etc., nest about 3 inches diameter, like knot atop branch
Pheasant, ring-necked (southern Canada, across northern U.S., New England to Oreg. and Calif.)	10–12	23–25	Leave nest with female after hatching and before able to fly	1	Usually on ground in depression, lined with bits of grasses, weeds, in fields of grass or grain, sometimes at edge of garden, edge of hedge, roadsides, ditches, etc.

NESTING RECORDS FOR SOME BIRDS OF CITY AND COUNTRY GARDENS IN THE UNITED STATES AND CANADA

SPECIES, OR KIND, AND GENERAL NESTING RANGE	NUMBER OF EGGS LAID IN CLUTCH	DAYS TO HATCH	DAYS YOUNG IN NEST	NUMBER OF BROODS EACH YEAR	NEST AND ITS LOCATION
Phoebe, eastern[d] (southern Canada, east to Atlantic coast, west to Rockies, south to New Mex.)	3–8	14–17	15–16	Usually 2, sometimes 3	Cup of mud and mosses lined with grasses, hairs, etc., in recess of rock ledge, in caves, now builds extensively on beams under bridges, on rafters of barns, porches, sheds, tops of shutters, etc., on nesting shelf built for it
Quail, bobwhite (entire eastern U.S., eastern Canada, west to Wyo. and in Southwest)	14–16	23–24	Young leave nest with parents at hatching	1, but will renest if early nests broken up	Nest in shallow depression on ground, arched over and lined with grasses; in fencerows, edges of gardens, fields, woods, golf courses, swamps
Quail, California (resident along Pacific coast, southern Oreg. to Baja Calif., also, Nev., Utah, etc.)	12–16	21–23	Young leave nest with parents at hatching	1, sometimes 2	Nest in slight hollow in ground, lined with grasses, leaves, under bush, hedge, clumps of grass or weeds in orchard, vineyard, cactus, under brush pile; near house or garden or beside much traveled road or path

Robin, American[d] (over N. America from wilderness Canada, Alaska, south to Gulf coast, southern Calif.)	3–6	12–14	14–16	2 or 3	Built from ground to treetops, in crotch of maples, elms, usually 5–20 feet up; on rail fence, posts, porch gables, often on garden arbor; of weeds, grasses, usually mud-lined
Sparrow, chipping (Alaska and Canada, south throughout most of U.S.)	3–5	11–14	8–12	1 or 2	Often on limb of spruce, pine, or small cedar in garden, also in orchard trees; 1–40 feet up, usually under 6 feet; of grasses, weeds, rootlets, hairs of people, cattle, horses
Sparrow, house[a,e] (across central and southern Canada, most of U.S., except parts of West)	3–7	11–12	15–17	3 or more	Will fill birdhouse with grasses, chicken feathers, cotton, string; nest also in hollows of trees, shutters of houses, under eaves, also builds dome-shaped nest in trees
Sparrow, song[d] (Alaska, south to Mexico, across Canada and U.S., Atlantic to Pacific)	3–6	12–13	10	2, 3, or 4	Most nests on ground early in nesting season, later 2–4 feet up in small conifer, shrub, in cattails (marshes), in pine sapling; nest built of grasses, weeds, bark, animal hairs

NESTING RECORDS FOR SOME BIRDS OF CITY AND COUNTRY GARDENS IN THE UNITED STATES AND CANADA

SPECIES, OR KIND, AND GENERAL NESTING RANGE	NUMBER OF EGGS LAID IN CLUTCH	DAYS TO HATCH	DAYS YOUNG IN NEST	NUMBER OF BROODS EACH YEAR	NEST AND ITS LOCATION
*Starling[a] (southeastern Alaska across southern Canada and most of U.S.)	4–6	12–14	14–21	2, sometimes 3	Nest of grasses, straws, twigs, debris; built in natural cavity in tree, old woodpecker hole, and in birdhouse
Swallow, barn[d] (Alaska and Canada to Mexico, Atlantic to Pacific)	3–5	14–16	21	2	Nests in colonies in farm outbuildings, eaves, under bridges, boat docks, in rock caves, holes, or natural cavities in cutbanks; nest is cup of mud mixed with grasses, feathers, etc.
Swallow, cliff[a] (locally, Alaska Canada, south to Mexico, Pacific to Atlantic)	3–6	15–16	23	1 or 2	Nests in colonies under eaves of houses, barns, churches, and in canyon walls in mountains; nests flask shaped of mud or clay pellets, entrance on side, and nest plastered against vertical surface

Swallow, tree[a] (Alaska, Canada, and Calif. to Va., wherever open water with marsh or meadow)	4–6	13–16	16–24	2	Nest of grasses, straws, lined with chicken feathers; built in natural tree cavities, old woodpecker holes, birdhouses, rural mailboxes, and cavities in eaves or cornices of old buildings
Swallow, violet-green[a] (west of Great Plains, Alaska to Mexico)	4–6	13–14	23	Usually 1, possibly 2	Nest of weed stems, grasses, feathers, some in colonies in holes of dead pines, in deserted woodpecker holes, birdhouses, natural cavities in cliffs
Tanager, scarlet (southern Canada, eastern U.S., west to N. Dak., Okla.)	3–5	13–14	9–11	1 or 2(?)	Shallow saucerlike nest of twigs, rootlets, grasses, out on limb of oak, ash, beech, hemlock, maple, etc., 4–75 feet above ground

* First introduced successfully in N. America when 60 released in Central Park, New York City, in 1890; 40 more in 1891; started to nest immediately with first nest discovered under eaves of American Museum of Natural History, next to Central Park, in summer 1890; by 1952 had extended its range throughout entire U.S. except southern Fla., and throughout southern Canada; on Feb. 4, 1959, sixty-nine years after introduction into Central Park, reported for first time at San Diego, Calif., most southwestern county in the U.S.; is permanent resident in areas where it is found in most of U.S., however, some individuals migrate in N. America as they do in Europe, usually from mid-February to early March in spring, late September, October, and through November in fall.

NESTING RECORDS FOR SOME BIRDS OF CITY AND COUNTRY GARDENS IN THE UNITED STATES AND CANADA

SPECIES, OR KIND, AND GENERAL NESTING RANGE	NUMBER OF EGGS LAID IN CLUTCH	DAYS TO HATCH	DAYS YOUNG IN NEST	NUMBER OF BROODS EACH YEAR	NEST AND ITS LOCATION
Tanager, summer (Del., Md., west to Okla., Neb., south to Fla., west to southern Calif.)	3–5	12(?)	(?)	1 or 2(?)	Nest a loosely built shallow cup of leaves, weed stems, grasses, well out on horizontal limb of dogwood, oak, pine, 10–35 feet up, in oak-pine woods; in Southwest in willow, cotton wood
Thrasher, brown (southern Canada to Gulf of Mexico, Atlantic to base of Rockies)	4–5	12–14	9–13	Usually 2	Sometimes on ground or usually low in bush, or in brush piles, usually 1–5 feet up; large, of twigs, dead leaves, paper, thin bark, grasses, cup lined with rootlets
Thrush, wood (largely eastern U.S., southern Canada, west to N. Dak. south to Tex., northern Fla.)	2–5	13–14	12–13	2	Like robin's but distinguished by dead leaves and mosses, lined with rootlets, often has white paper or cloth outside; 6–50 feet up in crotch or saddled on branch of tree, shrub, or sapling
Titmouse, plain (Rockies to Pacific, Oreg. to Baja Calif.)	3–9	14–16	16–21	1, sometimes 2 (?)	Nest of mosses, grasses, lined with rabbit fur, feathers, in natural cavities of trees, pair also digs own

Species and range					Nest
					cavity, nests in old woodpecker holes, often prefers to nest in birdbox
Titmouse, tufted[a] (eastern and southern U.S., common mainly east of Great Plains)	5–6	13–14	17–18	1, sometimes 2	Nest of wool, mosses, hair, cotton, leaves, in natural cavities of trees, 3–90 feet up, in old woodpecker holes, hollow metal pipes, fence posts, birdhouses
Towhee, brown (western and southwestern U.S., Oreg. to Tex.)	2–6	11	8	2 to 3	Bulky, of twigs, grasses, plant stems, on ground and to 35 feet up in densest part of bush or tree, usually 3–12 feet up
Towhee, rufous-sided (across southern Canada, south in most of U.S. to Mexico)	2–6	12–13	10–12	2	On ground under bush, brush pile, also in vines, trees, bushes; usually 1–5 feet up; nest of grasses, rootlets, twigs, leaves, string, lined with horsehair, cattle hair
Waxwing, cedar (southeastern Alaska, south to northern Calif., across northern U.S. to Atlantic coast, south to Georgia)	3–5	12–16	14–18	Usually 1, sometimes 2	Nest of twigs, grasses, weeds, mosses, lichens, in fork or on horizontal limb of deciduous or coniferous trees, in orchard or in shade tree, sometimes in colonies in clump of pines, 6–50 feet up; may even come to one's hands for string or yarn for nesting material

NESTING RECORDS FOR SOME BIRDS OF CITY AND COUNTRY GARDENS IN THE UNITED STATES AND CANADA

SPECIES, OR KIND, AND GENERAL NESTING RANGE	NUMBER OF EGGS LAID IN CLUTCH	DAYS TO HATCH	DAYS YOUNG IN NEST	NUMBER OF BROODS EACH YEAR	NEST AND ITS LOCATION
Woodpecker, downy[a] (southern Alaska, across Canada, and in suitable places in most of U.S. to Gulf of Mexico and Fla.)	4-5	12	21-24	1 or 2	Usually excavated in dead stubs of trees, round entrance hole 1¼ inches diameter, 5–50 feet above ground, generally in dead snag, sometimes in solid branch; will also nest in birdhouse designed for it
Woodpecker, hairy[a] (in all types of forest, from tree limit in Alaska and Canada, south to Fla. & Gulf coast)	3-6	14	28-30	1	Excavates cavity mostly in living trees, maple, oak, apple, aspen, beech, sometimes in tops of dead trees; entrance hole 1½–2 inches diameter, 5–30 feet or more up, with soft bed of fresh wood chips in bottom; will also nest in birdhouse designed for it

Woodpecker, red-bellied (Minn., east to Ontario, Canada, south to central Tex., east to Gulf coast and Fla.)	3–8	11½	24–26	1 but in South 2 to 3	Usually dug in old stump, decayed top of dead tree (stub, limb) utility poles, fence posts, 2 inches diameter, 5–70 feet up (but usually less than 40 feet), also in old woodpecker holes
Wren, Bewick's[a] (mostly from southern Canada, east to central Pa., Va., south to Ga., S. C., Baja Calif.)	5–7	14	14	2 to 3	In almost any cavity, knotholes, trees, in fence posts, mail boxes, old woodpecker holes, birdboxes; nest materials of mosses, sticks, dead leaves, cotton, hairs, wool, inner cup lined with feathers
Wren, Carolina[a] (Neb., east to southern Ontario, southeastern Mass., south to central Tex., southern Fla.)	4–8	14	12–14	2	Built in cavity of tree, stump, hole in bank, upturned roots of tree, stone wall, in old clothes, rafters, small baskets in buildings; nest materials of grasses, weeds, leaves, mosses, feathers, etc.
Wren, house[a] (from Atlantic to Pacific coasts, Canada to Mexico)	5–8	13–15	12–18	2, sometimes 3	Usually in cavity, old woodpecker holes, holes in trees, stumps, in birdboxes, etc.; nest materials of sticks, twigs, lined with hair, feathers, wool, spiders, cocoons, catkins, etc.

HINTS AND SUGGESTIONS

House wrens will nest in a birdhouse suspended in the air from a tree, but in our experience, all other birds that nest in birdhouses prefer them set firmly on a post or attached to some other solid object. (See also page 56.)

Do *not* put a perch on the outside of a birdhouse. Wrens, woodpeckers, chickadees, and other native birds that nest in man-made birdhouses do not need it. The perch will give English sparrows and starlings a place to cling from which they can harass the rightful occupants, and possibly evict them. (See also page 59.)

To keep English sparrows out of bluebird houses, place the bluebird house on a post *no higher than five feet above the ground.* English sparrows usually will not nest this close to the ground. If the English sparrows persist in nesting in the low-placed bluebird houses, cut a *rectangular* entrance hole in the box, 1½ inches high and only 1¼ *inches wide.* This will allow the slenderer bluebird to get in, but will usually keep out the pudgier sparrow. (See also page 61.)

Many bluebirds will not nest in a box that has old nesting material in it. After each nesting is over and the young birds have left the box, sweep out the old nesting material. Be certain that the nest is abandoned and not a newly built one.

After checking on eggs laid by bluebirds, leave the nest box quickly. Bluebirds lay one egg a day and will not remain in the box incubating until the full set of eggs is laid.

The often reported deaths of nestling bluebirds, tree swallows, and house wrens, still in the bird nesting box and unable to fly, may be caused especially when the bodies of these young birds are heavily parasitized by the blood-sucking grubs (larvae) of the blue bottle fly (see suggested methods of control, pages 193–194). In the spring of 1965 and of 1966, Raymond F. Potter, a bird bander at Enfield, Maine, tested a new method for control of the prevalent larvae of the blue bottle fly in bird boxes. In thirty-four of thirty-seven tree swallow nesting boxes, after the adults had laid their eggs, he dusted both eggs and nest with 1 per cent rotenone (the ordinary garden mix one can buy at almost any seed store). After the young tree swallows hatched and were about ten days old, he again dusted the nests with the 1 per cent rotenone. Meanwhile, for comparison, Potter had not treated three of the tree swallow nesting boxes. Nesting success for each spring (young raised to flying stage or leaving the nest) was 100 per cent in the treated nest boxes but only 69 per cent in the untreated ones. Potter concluded that using rotenone* in bird nesting boxes in spring, not only controlled the larvae of the blue bottle fly, but the larvae of other parasites in birds' nests such as bird fleas and tachinid (biting) flies.

Watch for signs of aspergillosis (as-per-jil-LOW'-sis) in your garden birds. It is a locally acute or chronic fungal infection usually fatal to them (see page 36). Cowbirds, grackles, juncos, house sparrows, and other garden birds may become infected. The disease progresses through stages: at first afflicted birds gasp and wheeze, then they begin to mope or to sit about with their feathers fluffed. Among seed-eating birds, crowded at feeders or at feeding places on the ground, the sick ones may continue to feed and to stand feebly in the bird feeder while doing so. One of the last signs of the disease may be severe diarrhea, after which the individual birds afflicted may fall over and die. Healthy birds become infected when they eat at feeders or on ground contaminated with the sick birds' feces. There seems to be no cure for the infection, and the best way to prevent its spread has been suggested (page 36): Stop feeding for at least a week or two or until the sick birds have died or moved elsewhere, then clean the feeders with Lysol, or another disinfectant, before putting them back into use again.

At times, evening grosbeaks and other northern finches may swarm over the feeders in the garden, and the evening grosbeaks, especially, may usurp them and temporarily exclude

---

* Be careful that rotenone does not get into a pond or stream, for it destroys aquatic life.

from them some of the smaller garden birds. The grosbeaks, however, like to feed high above the ground, and you may lure them away from the main feeders in the garden by attaching an open feeding tray to one of your second story window-sills (see window shelf feeder, page 19). Keep this feeder well supplied with plenty of sunflower seeds, and you will have the pleasure of watching these handsome birds, close-by, through your window and of knowing that they are not hindering the feeding of the smaller chickadees, nuthatches, native sparrows, and other small birds at your garden feeders.

BIRDS THAT STORE FOOD

Many people who feed birds have noted that, at times, white-breasted nuthatches, tufted titmice, and red-bellied and red-headed woodpeckers, instead of eating at the feeder, will snatch up a piece of suet, a sunflower seed, or bread and fly away with it in the bill. If near woods, they will shove the food into bark crevices or into knotholes and the crotches of trees or even into cracks in fence posts and utility poles. Some will tuck food under leaves or into soft ground. Other birds, however, may quickly steal the aboveground stores. John V. Dennis at his feeding station in Virginia noted that in one hour a male white-breasted nuthatch carried away thirty-eight pieces of suet which it pushed into crevices of bark. Most of these stores were discovered a little later and eaten by a brown creeper, chickadees, and other nuthatches. Most birds do not defend their caches but Lewis' and red-headed woodpeckers vigorously chase other birds from their winter stores of acorns and nuts, wedged into the bark or cracks of trees and poles.

Food that birds hide under leaves or store in the ground, however, may not be stolen. Members of the Crow Family are great storers of food. Jays store food everywhere: We have watched the blue jays in our Little Neck garden pick up in their bills acorns and hazel nuts, sunflower seeds, and peanuts in the shells from our main bird feeder and fly with them to the ground under our shrub border. There, using the bill, they thrust them under leaves or into the soft earth. The western Steller's jay similarly buries acorns, and in California, people have seen scrub jays burying pieces of bread, potato chips, grapes, peanuts, apple slices, pretzels, cheese crackers, cookies, hard-boiled eggs, sunflower seeds, and even marbles. Later, the buried sunflower seeds sprouted into ten-foot tall stalks all over hillsides and gardens, but in the southern California climate never flowered and grew seed heads.

Some members of the Crow Family show a remarkable "place memory" for these hidden stores. Eurasian thick-billed nut-crackers relocate their caches of pine seeds even when they are covered by snow: They fly to the spot and dig directly down to them. A Russian scientist, in a series of experiments, discovered that these birds, which recover up to 70 per cent of their stored foods, visually remember the exact places where they bury them. Victor Cahalane reported that in the Rocky Mountains a Clark's nutcracker dug directly down through eight inches of snow to recover a seed cone of a Douglas fir that it had apparently stored there.

In our garden we have watched tufted titmice take sunflower seeds from our bird feeders and store them in crevices of bark and also tuck them into the grassy sod of our lawn, but we have never seen them return to dig up food they stored in the ground. In North Carolina, one February day we watched a tufted titmouse pick up a sunflower seed from our feeder and fly directly with it to a blooming camellia bush where it tucked the seed deep inside one of the compact red flowers. Ten minutes later, either the same bird or another, returned, picked up the seed, and flew away with it.

REQUIREMENTS OF GARDEN BIRDS

The daily requirements of birds are about the same as your own. They need food, shelter, and water. Give them the proper food and you may attract *some* birds to your yard, but give them food in the right relation to shelter, and more will come. Provide them with bathing and drinking water, besides food and shelter, and soon, if you don't live in the middle of a city, your yard will be so enlivened by birds that it will look like an aviary.

Shelter to a bird does not mean a roof over its head. Shelter means a bush or tree into which the bird can fly to safety. The tree or bush may also offer a place to build a nest in summer, or it may provide some kind of seasonal food or protection from the cold winds and snowstorms of winter. Supply these requirements in your yard and you have built for this bird, and for others, both *a dining room and a bedroom.*

Birds are certain to come to you then; for, quite simply, the secret of attracting them is in knowing what their needs are, and giving them what they require. Once you try this, you'll be surprised how quickly they will move in on you.

Many years ago, in the yard of my home in the country, I started to attract birds. I have done so ever since. Even after my work compelled me to move to the suburbs of New York City, hundreds of birds came to my home grounds because I provided for them. Besides helping protect my trees, shrubs, flowers, and garden crops from insects, I have found, as you will, that attracting birds is a lot of fun. It is healthful because you are much out-of-doors with your bird-attracting program, and it is fascinating and deeply satisfying. Anyone, whether young or elderly, can attract birds, and you can enjoy them from your porch and yard, or, if you prefer, in the comfort of your house while sitting at the windows.

MUST YOU BE ABLE TO IDENTIFY BIRDS BEFORE ATTRACTING THEM?

One of the nice things about bird-attracting is its informality. The birds don't care whether you recognize them or not. You have invited them to your yard with food, shelter, and water and they will completely forgive your ignorance of whether they are robins, woodpeckers, or sparrows. Unlike the guests you invite to your house for dinner, the birds don't need a formal introduction. Perhaps your purpose in attracting them may be solely to learn their names, by watching them and comparing them so as to sort out the different kinds. You can go ahead confidently with your bird-encouragement program before you are able to recognize even an English sparrow, but it will add a lot to your fun if you know a few of the many kinds that will undoubtedly visit you. Identifying birds will get to be a very exciting game, and it can be sharply competitive if you get your family interested in seeing who can learn a new bird each day.

GETTING ACQUAINTED WITH BIRDS

Getting acquainted with birds is pretty much like getting acquainted in your new neighborhood. You must learn what the Joneses look like before you can tell them from the Finneys or the Johnsons.

If you have lived in the heart of any large city in our northeastern states, you have seen the little brown "English" sparrow, introduced into this country more than a hundred years ago, and the dark-feathered European starling, a more recent arrival. These two are common birds that you will find in city back yards, in city streets, in shade trees, and perched on buildings almost everywhere. If you haven't noticed birds before, it will help you if you know the looks and actions of these two. Like the Joneses and the Finneys, the first two families that you meet in your new neighborhood, you'll soon know them well enough to distinguish them from your other neighbors. English sparrows and starlings are easy to identify, and knowing them will help you to recognize the differences between them and the native birds that are going to visit you. If you buy one of those books written especially to help you identify birds, this will be an inexpensive and worth-while investment. I particularly recommend Roger Tory Peterson's excellent field guides or Richard Pough's Audubon Bird Guides. There are other bird identification books that may also be helpful to you as a beginner (see Recommended References).

When you have reached the point where you begin to notice birds and distinguish between them, you will probably fall under a spell as old as mankind—the *charm* of birds. You will make the exciting discovery that birds are, in many ways, like people—shy and timid, because of man's persecution—yet easily won over by your kindness and consideration.

You will discover, above all, that birds are *individuals*, as different in their characters as you and I, which may account for the fascination they hold for civilized men and women everywhere.

A PEANUT BUTTER MIXTURE FOR BIRDS

In June 1963, while living in Chapel Hill, North Carolina, I made one of the most rewarding discoveries of my years of experiments in attracting birds. I had tried mixing peanut butter with corn meal because peanut butter alone sometimes sticks in the throats of small birds and causes their deaths. I remembered the experience reported in 1961 by the late Charles K. Nichols, research associate, Department of Ornithology, American Museum of Natural History, New York City. Nichols, an experienced bird-attractor, learned of the dangers of offering plain peanut butter to birds when he autopsied the bodies of a number of small, well-fed wild birds that had collapsed and had died at his feeders in New Jersey. He examined at least six of the birds and found the esophagus of each so crammed with the sticky peanut butter that he believed that it had caused them to choke to death. He recommended thereafter that this problem could be overcome by mixing the viscous peanut butter with other food ingredients which would enable birds to eat it without danger of choking.

Some people I knew, with many years of experience in attracting birds and with whom I discussed this problem, had never known of a bird to die from choking on peanut butter. Some doubted it, and one skeptic suggested to me that the birds that died at Nichols' feeders may have succumbed from other causes. Of course this is possible, but to be sure that there is no potential risk for small birds that eat peanut butter, it is better, as Nichols suggested, to offer it to birds *only in a mixture.*

I soon discovered at Chapel Hill that corn meal (ground corn, so much liked by birds) added to peanut butter still made an adhesive mess, but if I added some shortening and some flour, this would prevent the peanut butter from sticking to my hands. It also made a doughy mix of manageable consistency. When I offered the mixture to birds, the results were astonishing.

Within a few months during that summer of 1963 and in the following fall and winter, thirty-five species of North Carolina birds came to my yard to feed avidly on the mixture. I called it Marvel-Meal because of its marvelous attraction for birds and for its basic corn meal so relished by them. The mixture also retained its soft consistency and ease of handling when I pressed it into the bark of trees in my yard or in cracks or compartments of my bird feeders. I also called the mixture the Bluebird Special because of its extraordinary attractiveness to bluebirds.

Marvel-Meal also had some advantages over other foods that attracted birds. I soon found that both the insect-eating and seed-eating kinds of birds seemed to have an insatiable appetite for it; therefore I needed this one food only to attract most kinds of garden birds. However, I continued to offer bird-seed mixtures as supplemental foods. This helped provide a broad nutritional diet so necessary for birds (see, The Well-Balanced Diet, pages 36–37 in Chapter 2).

I also found that the Marvel-Meal was far more attractive to birds than the suet I had been putting out for years for woodpeckers and other insect-eating birds. Another advantage was that the peanut butter mixture, besides protecting birds from choking, was cheaper than pure, or straight, peanut butter. And it can be offered to birds both in winter and summer with the assurance that it will attract more birds than either the suet or the seed-mixtures.

The following mixture that I prepared periodically and stored in my refrigerator will make about 2 pounds of the doughy mix which has the consistency of putty after it is thoroughly hand-mixed as one would mix a pie dough.

1 cup peanut butter   1 cup Dexo or other shortening
4 cups corn meal   1 cup white flour
(either white or yellow)

BIRDS SEEN EATING MARVEL-MEAL

USUALLY INSECT- AND FRUIT-EATERS	MOSTLY SEED-EATERS	BOTH INSECT- AND SEED-EATERS OR WITH SOME FRUIT
Bluebird, eastern	Cardinal, northern	Blackbird, red-winged (CA.)
Bushtit (AZ.)	Finch, house	Chickadee, black-capped
Catbird, gray	Junco, dark-eyed (slate-colored)	Chickadee, Carolina
Mockingbird, northern	Junco, dark eyed (AZ., CA., OR.)	Chickadee, chestnut-backed (CA.)
Oriole, (Baltimore) northern (MS.)	Junco, gray-headed (AZ.)	Creeper, brown
Oriole, (Bullock's) northern (CA.)	Siskin, pine	Crow, American (N.J.)
Ovenbird, on ground (MS.)	Sparrow, chipping	Flicker, common (yellow-shafted)
Robin, American	Sparrow, house	Jay, blue
Starling, European	Sparrow, field	Jay, scrub (AZ., CA.)
Tanager, scarlet	Sparrow, fox (CA.)	Jay, Steller's (CA.)
Tanager, summer	Sparrow, golden-crowned (CA.)	Kinglet, golden-crowned
Thrush, wood	Sparrow, song (CA.)	Kinglet, ruby-crowned
Veery	Sparrow, white-crowned (CA.)	Nuthatch, brown-headed
Warbler, pine	Sparrow, white-throated	Nuthatch, white-breasted
Warbler, yellow-rumped myrtle	Thrasher, brown	Titmouse, bridled (AZ.)
Wren, Carolina	Towhee, brown (CA.)	Titmouse, plain (AZ., CA.)
	Towhee, rufous-sided	Titmouse, tufted
		Sapsucker, yellow-bellied
Total of 51 species		Woodpecker, downy
		Woodpecker, hairy
		Woodpecker, red-bellied

Mammals seen eating Marvel-Meal at bird feeders in Chapel Hill include gray squirrels, flying squirrels, chipmunks, opossums, and raccoons.

I will venture a guess that every species of bird in the United States or Canada that will come to feeders for seeds, fruit, or suet, if each samples Marvel-Meal, will come for it as avidly as the thirty-five species in my North Carolina yard. I hope every reader will try it, observe the birds that eat it, then send me these birds' names % Harper & Row, Publishers, 10 East 53rd Street, New York, N.Y. 10022. This will help me extend the list of birds that eat Marvel-Meal for the next edition of *Songbirds in Your Garden*.

Desirable as Marvel-Meal is to birds, its costs may make it prohibitive to many bird-attractors. In 1963, I made the mixture for about 20 cents a pound, but I am sure that it would cost more today. It is eaten so rapidly by birds that readers may wish a cheaper peanut butter mixture. I have prepared one, a harder mixture which birds eat less rapidly, have field-tested it, and know that many birds, including many or most of those that eat Marvel-Meal, are strongly attracted to it: for example, most woodpeckers that come to feeders, jays, crows, chickadees, titmice, and nuthatches. It is:

1 cup peanut butter
2 cups melted suet
4 cups finely cracked corn
2 cups of corn meal (white or yellow)

First chop or grind beef suet into small pieces, put it into a pot, and melt it over a slow fire. When the suet has melted, stir in the 1 cup of peanut butter; remove from the stove, then stir in the other ingredients.

At Chapel Hill, after preparing the mixture and before the suet had time to solidify, I poured or ladled it into small, round cardboard containers. I had already perforated two opposite sides of each container about halfway up from the bottom with a small hole. Then I had drawn a piece of white cord through each hole with a large knot at the end of the cord on the inside so that the cord could not pull out of the container. This gave me two loose ends or tying pieces with which I could fasten each container to the trunk of a tree or to a limb where the birds could cling to the bark and feed or perch on the edge of the cup to get at the contents.

The containers were about the size of those holding a half-pint of ice cream. These were of convenient size for handling and placing in the garden; however, larger cardboard containers (tin cans with sharp edges could be dangerous to the pecking birds) might be used with the bottom taken out before placement so that birds can feed from either open end.

After the mixture hardened, I put the filled containers in the refrigerator to cool and for storage. I had discovered that this hard mixture slows consumption of the food by such rapid-eating birds as starlings, and it lasts much longer than the soft, puttylike mixture I call Marvel-Meal. However, I still prefer Marvel-Meal and recommend it as a superior attractant to birds.

Another doughy, pastelike mixture that birds like can be prepared of 2 cups of bacon drippings (save in a tin can or other container) and 2 cups of corn meal with flour added to bind the ingredients together. One winter day at Chapel Hill, Mrs. Matt L. Thompson was delighted when a ruby-crowned kinglet and then a pine warbler alighted on her hands as she was putting this mixture in one of her suspended feeding sticks (see illustration, page 24, Chapter 2) in her garden. By experimenting with this and with other mixtures, you will discover the one that seems highly attractive to many kinds of birds and will be one that you feel you can afford to offer in quantity.

Do Birds Taste Their Food?

Since the first edition of *Songbirds in Your Garden*, many people have asked me if birds like or dislike the taste of some foods, just as we do. I still do not know, as the sense of taste is probably the most difficult of all to test because it is subjective, and birds can not talk to tell us whether they like the taste of certain foods or simply bolt them because they are hungry.

A striking feature of a bird's mouth is its small number of taste buds, ovoid clusters of chemical sensory receptors that are mostly in the soft area at the base of a bird's tongue, although parrots with a fleshy tongue have them on the tongue itself. Each of us has about 9,000 taste buds; a pigeon has 27 to 59; a day-old chicken has 8, a three-month-old cockerel, 24; some parrots have about 400.

According to one scientist, many experiments with pigeons

and chickens suggest that both have an apparently well-developed sense of taste, and these birds markedly rejected a surprising variety of substances. He concluded from these tests and from others that these birds are able to detect at least some substances that taste salty, sour, and bitter; in general, however, he thought that taste plays only a small part when a bird selects its food.

Verne E. Davison, a biologist of the Soil Conservation Service in the southeastern United States, came to different conclusions about the tasting ability of birds. For four years he made backyard feeding experiments with forty-three species of wild, free-ranging North American songbirds, giving them a wide choice of natural foods. He concluded (see *Attracting Birds from the Prairies to the Atlantic*, T. Y. Crowell Co., 1967) that the songbirds in his garden selected their foods mainly on the basis of taste and that color, shape, and texture of the foods were not significant to birds in their choices, under the conditions of his experiments. Size was a factor in a bird's choice when the seed or fruit was too large for it to swallow.

Dr. Austin L. Rand, chief curator of zoology, Field Museum of Natural History, Chicago, experimented with the taste and learning of young curve-billed thrashers which he raised and fed by hand. He first offered them the white of hard-boiled eggs cut into small squares which the thrashers liked. Then he soaked some of the squares in formalin which, to Rand, was very distasteful. The birds ate some of the squares but then, for a week afterward, refused to eat them. Rand wrote: "They had quickly learned to avoid the ill-tasting food."

From Rand's experiment one might conclude that the proof of the pudding for some birds is indeed in the eating. However, if the birds in our gardens eat a food avidly, with an apparent liking for it, the debate as to whether birds do or do not taste their food may seem to many of us an academic one.

HAND-FEEDING, OR HAND-TAMING

I remember years ago two men in West Virginia, father and son, both fine naturalists, who went to, what we might consider today, extraordinary lengths to get birds to come to their hands to feed. They were the first to attract birds in their part of the country. The birds there were so shy that the naturalists felt it necessary to start feeding them by positioning their first feeder about 150 feet from the house, next to a shrub border where the birds usually remained under cover.

After the birds started eating from the feeder, the men moved it each day closer to the house until the birds had followed it to a window overlooking their yard. There the naturalists nailed a feeding board to the windowsill so that they could watch the birds close up from inside the house. This, they said, was about the limit to which most people go in attracting birds, but they wanted an even closer association with them. And so they clothed a stick with a sleeve of an old coat and attached a glove at the end and nailed the artificial arm and hand to the windowsill feeder. Withholding food from the feeder, they filled the artificial hand with black walnut kernels. This was a bird food that the West Virginia naturalists found to be "without a peer," favored by most of their wintering birds over all other foods.

Soon birds came to the walnut kernels in the gloved hand—a tufted titmouse first, then chickadees and a Carolina wren. Now they tried their next experiment. They took away the stick and dummy gloved hand. One of the naturalists opened the window and put out his own gloved hand filled with walnut kernels. Quickly the same birds came, along with some downy woodpeckers, to take food from his hand.

Then the naturalists decided to go one step further with their taming of the birds. They built a dummy, or scarecrow, man and stood him alongside the main feeder in the yard, which they had emptied of food. They dressed him in a long dark coat, put a crushed felt hat on his head, a corncob pipe in his mouth, and a glove on his hand lying on the feeder. In the hollow of the crushed felt hat, in the bowl of the pipe, and in the dummy's gloved hand, they poured the irresistible walnut kernels.

Although nervous at first about this manlike figure, the birds finally perched on its hat, then on the corncob pipe and on the gloved hand, and picked up the walnuts without hesitation. A few days later, after the birds were coming fearlessly to the dummy, one of the naturalists took the dummy away and stood by the feeder. He had put walnut kernels in the top of the crushed hat he now wore and into the bowl of the corncob pipe, clenched in his teeth. One of his hands, which he rested on the feeder, he had filled with walnut kernels. Quickly and confidently the birds came to him and fed—

tufted titmice, white-breasted nuthatches, juncos, tree sparrows, and downy woodpeckers. Even white-throated sparrows and cardinals alighted on his hand and fed. And within touching distance came song sparrows, hairy and red-bellied woodpeckers, towhees, and even the usually shy Bachman's sparrow.

When the man moved, he moved very slowly which did not seem to bother the birds. And all the while they fed, he spoke to them softly to get them accustomed to the sound of a human voice.

Now some of the chickadees came all the way to the kitchen door to be hand-fed. If the naturalists were slow to come outside with a handful of walnut kernels, the chickadees clung to the screens on windows and doors and hammered on them with their bills to attract their attention. If the birds did not see either of the men through the first-floor windows, they flew up to the second story and hammered on the window screens there.

One day, when a stranger on horseback came riding along the muddy public road, past the farmhouse, one of the naturalists' conditioned chickadees dropped to the rider's hat. It remained there a moment, then flew up to a telephone wire overhead. Feeling the touch of the small bird, the rider stopped, looked about in surprise, then started on. Again the chickadee flew to the man's hat, apparently hoping that it held food. The stranger whirled about on his horse, jerked off his hat, and looked at it closely. Then he looked all about him. Nearby sat a tiny bird but it seemed to offer no explanation, and so he rode on, shaking his head over the mystery.

After the elder naturalist died, his son left the farm, and the house was without an occupant for almost a year. With no one there to feed the birds, the naturalist had wondered and worried about how they would get along without their accustomed winter food. One spring day, on his return, he walked up the trail toward home. As he crossed a hill, in sight of the house, and walked through his old orchard, he heard a familiar *dee-dee*! When he drew a walnut kernel from his pocket, a chickadee alighted on his hand.

Today it is not difficult to get a wild bird to come to the hands for food. Perhaps it is easier than in the days of the West Virginia naturalists because so many people are feeding birds and hand-taming them. There is always the chance that a bird that comes quickly to your hands to feed—a black-capped chickadee especially—may already have been hand-tamed by someone else, although of this we can never be sure because of the general boldness of these small birds.

We followed the methods used by the West Virginia naturalists but did not use a dummy to condition birds to a human presence at the feeders. In the years we were in our suburban Long Island home, we virtually lived in our garden sanctuary, with its shrub border and an oak-beech woodland that edged a corner of our yard. In summer and often on mild days in winter, we sat reading, writing, or simply observing on chairs or on a chaise longue on the lawn near an open feeding tray set atop a post, with the birds feeding unconcernedly in it.

During our first winter there, early one cold morning, when I approached our empty center-of-the-lawn feeder, a chickadee flew to the pail of bird seed I carried and alighted on the rim. When I set the pail down on the snow, I scooped up a few sunflower seeds in my palm and rested the back of my hand on the empty open feeder. While I stood absolutely still, the chickadee made four quick flying trips to my hand, each time carrying away a sunflower seed to a limb of a nearby tree. There, while it held the seed firmly under its feet, it pounded the black-and-white-striped hull open with its bill and swallowed the exposed inner kernel. This was the first of a succession of chickadees and a few nuthatches that came regularly to our hands for food. All one winter, a very tame female downy woodpecker, at the slamming of our backdoor and our appearance in the garden, descended in little backward hitches down the trunk of an oak in our yard. There she clung to the bark about six feet above the ground and waited for us to approach. Then she leaned around the trunk to take delicate bites from a piece of suet held either in my wife's hand or mine, while we leaned motionless against the tree.

There are a few simple rules for your first trials at hand-feeding. Do not try until you have had birds accustomed to coming to your feeders. If you have tried in mild weather without success, try early in the morning on a cold, storm-threatening day or in the morning after a snow- or ice storm when birds are extremely hungry. Be sure your feeders are empty before you try it.

If a bird flies to your palm to pick up a seed or crushed

walnut kernel, do not stare into its eyes as this may frighten it (some authorities skilled in hand-taming say you must not swallow as this may alarm the bird, but in my own intense preoccupation with a bird on my hand, I don't think I have ever done so). Keep motionless, and above all, do not make a quick movement with your hands which birds seem to know can catch them. And never, never try to catch a bird that has learned to feed from your hands and trusts you. If you should, you may frighten it so badly that it may never come to you again.

Roy Ivor, a Canadian naturalist, had an experience that showed what a bad fright may do to an already tamed wild bird. In his large outdoor aviary, where his birds lived semi-wild, a pair of catbirds had grown so tame from Ivor's every-day presence that they flew to meet him and perched on his hands. One morning, he discovered that a rat had gotten in his aviary and had killed some of his birds. To confine the catbirds while he got rid of the rat, Ivor had to net them and then, when taking them from the net, catch them in his hands. The catbirds were so frightened that it was two years before they would come to Ivor and perch on his hands again.

Although Ernest Harold Baynes never caught any of the birds that came so readily to him in New Hampshire, he could easily have done so with a chickadee that once ate so many walnut kernels while perched on his hand that it could eat no more. As it sat comfortably on his one hand, Baynes slowly cupped his free hand around the trusting bird until he could see only the top of its head. Possibly the chickadee became drowsy from too much food, from the warmth of Baynes's hands, or from reduced light because it closed its eyes, tucked its head into its back feathers, and went to sleep.

Mabel T. Tilton of Vineyard Haven, Massachusetts, got a seemingly fearless red-breasted nuthatch to come to her to feed in winter. While on her hand, it sometimes picked at her finger nails and seemed to enjoy warming its cold feet in her hand. It was never in haste to leave. Once, when she put her thumb over its short tail, it was not disturbed but merely turned away from her and looked all about from the security of her hand.

You should not be discouraged if you do not have such remarkable experiences with birds in the beginning such as those of Mabel Tilton and Ernest Baynes. Usually one must work a long time with individual birds to gain such trust. And after you have hand-tamed a bird or birds, always carry a few walnut kernels or sunflower seeds in your pockets while out of doors for their visits to your hands for food.

CALLING THE BIRDS TO DINNER

Al Martin, who had remarkable success with hand-taming birds in Maine (see his *Hand-taming Wild Birds*, Bond Wheelwright Co., Freeport, Maine) believed in calling them to his feeders. When some pine grosbeaks he was hand-taming perched on his hands, he talked to them in the same tone he used to call birds at feeding time, but more softly—"Come and get it, come and get it." He found that by talking to his birds he got them to associate tones of his voice and certain words with food. This is an old training trick of falconers some of whom whistle a repeated phrase to their birds while the birds are feeding. Thereafter, the falcon, while flying free, can be called in by the same whistle, loudly repeated, or by calls.

We never practiced calling our birds. In winter, they came without any bidding, at their main feeding times in early morning and in late afternoon. Often they also came for a short period to feed in midmorning and in midafternoon, and on cold, stormy days, they flew in a steady procession to and from the feeders. Quite possibly their visits were according to their periods of hunger or from associating the slamming of our backdoor with our visits to the feeders to fill them.

Dr. Frank M. Chapman, former head of the Bird Department of the American Museum of Natural History, at his feeding station in Florida, experimented with calling birds by whistling to them while they fed. It was several weeks before he got a response. Then one day, when only a catbird was in sight, Chapman whistled. Within less than a minute, cardinals, painted buntings, and many other of his birds came flocking to his feeder.

Edith Werner, who operated a tearoom years ago near Sebring, Florida, had remarkable success in training Florida scrub jays to come to her when she whistled a bright little tune. Within minutes they flew from all directions and alighted on her arms and shoulders and ate bread from her hands. These jays, which live in scattered tracts of sand, pines, saw palmettos, and shrub oaks, became so tame about the houses of winter visitors to Florida that they not only took peanuts from people's hands but from their lips.

Some years ago, when I was editor of *Audubon Magazine*, the Reverend Benjamin Franklin Root sent me a photograph from California of a scrub jay on his hand eating a peanut. It even came into his car to feed when he called it.

INVITING THE BIRDS INTO YOUR HOUSE

Besides Ernest Harold Baynes (see Chapter 1, "Some Beginnings"), others have frequently invited wild birds into their homes to feed. Al Martin, who found that redpolls came to his feeders in Maine about four years out of ten, found them shy at first, but they soon became very tame. After the first arrival of a flock one winter, he had one feeding from his hands within a week. When a bitter cold spell came, he dressed warmly and sprinkled bird seed on his doorsill and kitchen floor. Then he opened the door and invited the redpolls to dinner. About forty came inside and were everywhere and made such a racket with their calls that in Martin's words, they sounded "like a million birds" instead of forty.

Edwin C. Brown of Minneapolis had an especially fearless white-breasted nuthatch at his window feeder one winter that came to his hands for walnut kernels. Brown opened a window and the nuthatch came into his bedroom to eat from a lump of suet Brown had set out for it on his dresser. In the yard, the bird flew down from a tree to eat food from the top of Brown's head, and it scrambled down the trunk of a tree to eat from his hand held against the tree, palm up.

But of all the remarkable stories about wild birds in America accepting human company, I know of none that exceeds the experience of E. R. Davis of Leominster, Massachusetts. In October 1925, he saw a pine siskin at his window feeding shelf, and within a few days, 150 were feeding there on mixed bird seeds and sunflower seeds, along with some American goldfinches. That winter the siskins became very tame and within a short time regarded him as a friend. Whenever he stepped outside the door, down came the siskins from the trees to alight on his head, shoulders, and arms, looking for food. They had learned that he carried seeds concealed in a small box or in a dish to lure them to him.

When he invited them inside through a small sliding door

in one of his kitchen windows, they came right into his home. Soon they perched on his head and shoulders or hopped about his desk where he was writing, looking for the handful of seeds they knew he would give them. On bitterly cold nights, some of them even spent the night in the kitchen, sleeping perched on a clothesline Davis had stretched across the room just below the ceiling.

In his upstairs bedroom, Davis had three windows which he left open at night regardless of the severity of the weather. Soon the siskins discovered his sleeping place and early each morning visited him, as Davis said, "to see that I did not over-sleep." If he was asleep, one of the birds would arouse him by alighting on his face or side of his head and pulling at his hair to awaken him.

Davis decided to test the intelligence of these small birds by offering them a problem. One night, before he went to sleep, he placed a box of sunflower seeds on the windowsill near the head of his bed, with a glass cover over the seeds to prevent the siskins from getting them. Next morning, one of the birds came through the open window. It alighted by the box and looked through the glass cover but could not get at the seeds. Then it flew to Davis's pillow and pulled his hair to awaken him, but Davis pretended to be asleep. Again the bird flew to the windowsill, tried to get the seeds, and failing, returned again to Davis. This time it not only pulled his hair and pinched his ear but even tweaked his nose with its bill. Three times it tried to get the seeds and each time returned to Davis who finally opened his eyes and reached for the box. Immediately the siskin flew to Davis's hand, waited until he opened the cover, then hopped into the box to enjoy its well-earned breakfast.

In another test of the problem-solving ability of the siskins, Davis arranged a feeding box, out of sight of the birds, behind a bedroom wall. Then he rigged a button on the front of the wall with a small platform just below the button on which the siskins could perch. If a siskin should press the button, a small quantity of seeds would pass down a chute to the bird's feet.

For awhile, the siskins could not understand why Davis had put out a container which held no food. Then one dis-covered the button and pecked it sharply. Down came some seeds to the bird's feet. It ate them, then tapped the button again. Soon several of the flock had learned the trick by watching and responding to the behavior of the first one. Apparently this was an example, by the first siskin, of what students of behavior call trial and error learning. Usually it is the bolder, perhaps more investigative or more ingenious bird (or birds) that first discovers the answer to a new problem of how to get food, and the habit may be quickly picked up by others.

SOME WILD BIRDS THAT HAVE FED FROM PEOPLE'S HANDS

Bluebird*	Nuthatch, white-breasted
Bunting, indigo*	Redpoll, common
Catbird, gray*	Redpoll, hoary
Chickadee, black-capped	Robin, American*
Chickadee, boreal	Siskin, pine
Chickadee, Carolina	Sparrow, chipping*
Chickadee, chestnut-backed	Sparrow, house
Cowbird, brown-headed	Sparrow, rufous-crowned
Crossbill, red	Sparrow, tree
Crossbill, white-winged	Sparrow, white-crowned
Finch, purple	Sparrow, white-throated
Flicker, common (yellow-shafted)	Tanager, summer*
	Thrasher, brown (corn bread)
Goldfinch, American	Thrush, wood*
Grosbeak, evening	Titmouse, tufted
Grosbeak, pine	Towhee, rufous-sided (bread)
Hummingbird, black-chinned	Vireo, red-eyed*
Hummingbird, ruby-throated	Vireo, solitary*
Jay, blue	Warbler, pine
Jay, gray	Waxwing, Bohemian (berries)
Jay, scrub	Waxwing, cedar**
Junco, dark-eyed (slate-colored)	Woodpecker, downy
	Woodpecker, hairy
Kinglet, ruby-crowned	Woodpecker, red-bellied
Mockingbird	Wren, Carolina
Nuthatch, red-breasted	Wren, house

* Usually take food in summer from one's hands—suet, bread, caterpillars, earthworms, mealworms, raisins, currants, etc.—to feed young.
** Rather than for food, usually come to one's hands for nesting materials.
In June 1959, Mr. and Mrs. Carl A. Kennedy of Valencia, Pa., watched a pair of cedar waxwings start building a nest in a tree in their garden. To help them, Mrs. Kennedy cut pieces of pink and white cord about four inches long and walked into the garden with the cords on one hand. Soon one of the waxwings flew to her hand, picked up a cord, and flew with it to work it into the nest. After several trips, instead of alighting on her hand for cord, it perched on Mrs. Kennedy's head, reached down and tried to pluck some of her hair for its nest. John K. Terres once saw a tufted titmouse pluck hairs from the back of a live woodchuck sitting just outside its burrow, and another from the back of a gray squirrel stretched out on a tree branch, then carry the hairs to the nest.

Since the first edition (1953) of *Songbirds in Your Garden*, the American Ornithologists' Union, our authority for the names of North American birds, has changed the common names of some of our garden birds and of many others. To conform to this new usage, I have listed below both the old, preferred English name and the preferred new one for those birds mentioned in this book for which changes have been made.

In 1973, a committee of the American Ornithologists' Union published a revised list of some North American bird names, both common and scientific. These changes were not made capriciously, or arbitrarily, but were based on scientific studies which have shown, for example, that the so-called yellow-shafted flicker of the eastern United States and the red-shafted and gilded flickers of the western United States, which hybridize extensively where their ranges overlap, are not three distinct species, but one. The name common flicker has now been given to all three birds. Similarly, the Baltimore oriole of the eastern United States and the Bullock's oriole of the West, which hybridize freely where their ranges meet, are considered to be one species with the now common English name of northern oriole. Catbird is now "gray" catbird specifically for its gray color; American goldfinch and American robin now distinguish these two from the European goldfinch and European robin, and so on.

Because one finds in the older bird books and articles only the older names, I have listed below the old and the comparable new names and the family to which each bird belongs to properly identify each. Name changes follow those of the *Check-list of North American Birds* (American Ornithologists' Union, sixth edition, 1983).

OLD NAME	PREFERRED NEW NAME	FAMILY	SOME LOCAL OR GENERAL NAMES OLD AND LESS USED
Catbird	Catbird, gray	Mockingbird	Black mockingbird, black-capped thrush
Flicker, yellow-shafted	Flicker, common	Woodpecker	High hole, yellow-hammer, wicker (from its calls), golden-winged woodpecker
Flicker, red-shafted	Flicker, common	Woodpecker	Red-hammer, yicker (from its calls)
Flicker, gilded	Flicker, common	Woodpecker	Wa-cup, or wake-up (from its calls)
Goldfinch, common	Finch, American	Finch	Lettuce-bird (eats leaves or seeds of), salad bird, thistle-bird (eats seeds of thistle), wild canary, yellow bird
Grackle, purple, or bronzed	Grackle, common	Troupial (blackbirds and orioles)	Crow, blackbird, maize thief
Hawk, sparrow	Kestrel, American	Falcon	Grasshopper hawk, killy hawk, windhover
Jay, Florida	Jay, scrub	Crow (jays, crows, ravens, magpies, nutcrackers)	"Bullfinch," scrub jay (from habitat in Florida scrub), smoky jay (from color)
Jay, California	Jay, scrub	Crow	Long-tailed jay, Nicasio jay, Santa Cruz jay, Texas jay, Woodhouse's jay, Xantus' jay
Junco, Oregon	Junco, dark-eyed	Finch	Mountain junco, pink-sided junco
Junco, slate-colored	Junco, dark-eyed	Finch (buntings, cardinal, grosbeaks, finches, sparrows, towhees, longspurs)	Black chipping bird, black snowbird, Carolina junco, snowbird, common snowbird, white-bill
Junco, white-winged	Junco, dark-eyed	Finch	Snowbird
Oriole, Baltimore	Oriole, northern	Troupial (blackbirds and orioles)	Fire bird, golden robin, hang-nest
Oriole, Bullock's	Oriole, northern	Troupial	Fire-bird, hang-nest
Robin	Robin, American	Thrush	Common robin, robin redbreast

THE PHONETICS* OF SONGS OF SOME
AMERICAN BIRDS

Nothing has given me more pleasure than listening to the songs and calls of birds in my garden and then trying to reproduce the sounds using words and phrases of human speech. It is a good way for each of us to memorize the rhythm and pitch of the song phrases so that we can, by using words, recall the song. We imitate the sound of a ticking clock by saying *tick-tock*, and the bark of a dog by *bow-wow*, and we can imitate the sounds a bird makes in the same way.

Each of us should use our own words and phrases, but I must confess that I have borrowed many of mine from the phonetics of some of our older naturalists and ornithologists. I have found that most of them fit the birds' songs very closely.

Dr. Frank M. Chapman, dean of early American ornithologists, in 1900, following Thoreau's 19th century words, thought the red-winged blackbird of our marshes, fields, and gardens, sang a liquid *Kong-quer-ree!* which, to me, in my North Carolina yard, sang *O-ka-lee!* John Burroughs thought the eastern bluebird called continuously, *Purity, purity;* in upstate New York and elsewhere, I heard it sing *Her-er-bert!* or *Sher-er-bert*, which I think gives the soft, quavering quality of its voice.

Approving the use of words for birds' songs, British scientist Dr. W. H. Thorpe, a distinguished authority on birds' songs, in a British ornithological journal with an associate wrote:

Many of us remember bird songs by means of little

---

* According to the *American Heritage Dictionary*, "representing the sounds of speech with a set of distinct symbols, each denoting a single sound."

rhythmic strings of words, or a sentence, or perhaps by nonsense syllables. These are most effective in reminding us of what the bird says if we invent them ourselves. We have in mind such sentences as "Take two cows, Taffy" for the [British] wood pigeon . . . "I go to Guayaquil" for the tropical-American slate-colored grosbeak* . . . or "Who are you?" for the pauraque** . . .

Of course, in fact, what the bird sings has phonetically little or no resemblance to these mnemonics of ours. The reason why they serve us so well is to remind us of particular bird songs chiefly because the rhythm is appropriate, and because the vowels that we include in such phrases reflect approximately the same changes in fundamental pitch as are found in the bird's song. . . .

Dr. Arthur A. Allen, whom I knew many years ago at the Cornell Laboratory of Ornithology, thought the indigo bunting sang *Sweet, sweet, where, where, here, see it, see it,* an almost perfect rendition to my ears. In my North Carolina garden, I heard it sing one short song; *Sweet-syrup, syrup, syrup, sweet!* Another, from a hedge outside my cottage door, sang a different song; *Sip, sip, Ray—see-you-first!,* and repeated it over and over for fifteen minutes, then silence.

There are probably more but similar renderings of the cardinal's loud, rich whistle than of the song of any other woods and garden bird. In 1900 Dr. Frank M. Chapman wrote that the song begins with long-drawn notes, *whee-you! whee-you!,* followed by a rapid *hurry, hurry, hurry, quick, quick, quick, quick.*

In North Carolina I heard a song, *Cheer! more wheat, more wheat, more wheat!* In my mother's garden in southern New

---

* *Pitylus grossus,* of Central and South America, related to North American cardinal, grosbeaks, etc.

** *Nyctidromus albicollis,* the common pauraque, from Texas south into Mexico, Central and South America, is related to the whip-poor-will, poor-wills and nightjars.

Jersey, one lovely March morning a cardinal sang, *Too-few! too-few! few! few! few! few!*

Thoreau fancied that the brown thrasher, singing its rich phrases, each twice over, from garden thickets, orchards, and country hedges, had advice for the Massachusetts farmer planting his corn—*drop it, drop it, cover it up, cover it up.* One of the most elaborate versions came in 1929 when a Mrs. H. P. Cook wrote to Dr. Chapman that a singing brown thrasher seemed to her like someone in a telephone conversation—*Hello, hello, yes, yes, Who is this? Well, well, well, I should say, I should say! How's that? I don't know! What did you say? What did you say?* and so on.

A. C. Bent, in one of his Life Histories of North American Birds bulletins, thought that all of these interpretations suggested the song—a succession of phrases of two to four syllables, each with a pause after it—loud, rich, and musical. A call note I often heard from a thrasher nesting in my North Carolina dooryard was a sharp *smack!* of alarm, sometimes followed by a whistled, melodic *pee-yore! pee-yore!*

Other bird songs in my garden are much simpler—the sweet, soft whistled *Spring com-ing!* or *fee-e-bee* of the black-capped chickadee, and its sputtering sharp call, *chicka-dee-dee-dee;* the tufted titmouse's *Pee-to! pee-to!* or *Pee-ter! pee-ter! pee-ter!;* the rufous-sided towhee's song, *Drink your tea-e-e-e* and from my garden hedge, *Sweet bird! s-i-n-g-g!*, and its questioning call, *To-whee? Chewink!* or *Joree?*, which have given the bird some of its common names.

The American robin, one of the most familiar of all of our garden birds, has had rendered many interpretations of its song, but none better than that of Mabel Osgood Wright who, in her book *Birdcraft*, noted its song at dawn as *Cheerily, cheerily, cheer up, cheer up!*, which I think could hardly be improved on.

E. H. Forbush in New England wrote that robins' songs vary considerably, and one of them, to him, was "an imitation of the well-known phrase, *'kill 'em, cure 'em, give 'em physic!'* "

The red-eyed vireo, from the trees surrounding our garden in Connecticut, sings tirelessly in summer from morning to night (more than 22,000 songs in a day reported by a Canadian ornithologist). He has been called Preacher Bird by many old-time birders because his repetitious, emphatic phrases, with pauses between, are sermonlike, described as a conversational monologue—*You see it—you know it—do you hear me? Do you believe it?*

If you keep these words in mind, advised one authority, you will recognize the bird the first time you hear it sing.

The bobwhite quail, that often came into my North Carolina garden, is not a so-called "songbird," but its songs and calls have great charm. The males whistle *Bob-WHITE!* or *bob-bob-WHITE!* and *Wheat-RIPE!* or, according to Forbush, *Buck-wheat-RIPE!*

The assembly call of the covey, or flock, is a plaintive *ka-loi-kee, ka-loi-kee!*, which, to Dr. Chapman, was *Where are you? Where are you?*

Margaret Millar, in her book, *The Birds and the Beasts Were There*, thought that the California quail in her garden bid her to *Sit-right-down, sit-right-down!* Ernest McGaffey, in 1922, described the call of the Gambel's quail as *Payt-eight-o, payt-eight-o, payt-eight-o*, the rhythm suggesting the calls of its close cousin, the California quail.

One of the most amusing interpretations of a bird's song came to me from Alexander Sprunt, Jr., at the time Superintendent of Southern Sanctuaries for the National Audubon Society. One day in Florida we were driving along a street in Okeechobee. I heard a white-eyed vireo sing its emphatic song, described by Aretas Saunders not only as different from the songs of other vireos, but from all other birds. Alex drawled, "he says, *'Take me to the rai-l-l-r-o-a-d, QUICK!'* "

From a thicket by a small stream near my garden in North Carolina, I heard one sing *That's for real! chick!* Another seemed to say *Mister T! Take me there, quick!*

Thoreau wrote that the song of the song sparrow, whose singing in our gardens has endeared it to so many, has been rendered by old-country people as *Maids! maids! maids! hang up your teakettle—ettle-ettle!*, and *If, if, if-you-please-sir!*

I like Margaret Millar's version as she heard it in her California garden—*Press, press, press, Presbyterians* (sometimes with one less press).

These are a few of my notes and those of others on the phonetics of birds' songs and calls. It might be fun in your own listening to see if the phonetics I have chosen are close to yours. Better, I suggest that you start keeping a record of your own phonetic renditions and apply them each time a bird sings. It will not only help in identifying the singer, but will make you much more attentive to birds' songs in general.

If you cannot identify the songs, and therefore the singer, of any birds—and many people cannot—the best and quickest way to learn them is to ask for help. Go into your garden with someone from your local bird club or Audubon Society who can hold up a hand at a song and say, "Listen, a *catbird!*" "There, a *cardinal!*", "*That* is a *towhee!*" or "Over there a *mockingbird!*," and so on. Get to know their voices like you know those of your intimate friends over the telephone. Then you will not need to see the hidden singer in a tree or shrub in your garden to know *who* is out there.

Listening to recordings of birds' songs offers the advantage, in the absence of the live, singing birds, of hearing songs over and over, to learn them by repetition, and to enjoy them and the information given about each by the narrator. A good source is the Cornell Laboratory of Ornithology, Ithaca, New York, which lists available recordings in its descriptive catalogues of the Crow's Nest Book Shop.

The Borror Laboratory of Bioacoustics, Columbus, Ohio, supplies recordings to people interested in research on birds' songs.

Recommended References

American Ornithologists' Union. *Check-list of North American Birds.* Sixth Edition. American Ornithologists' Union, 1983. (P.O. Box 368, Lawrence, Kan. 66044)

Armstrong, E. A. *Bird Display and Behaviour.* Dover, New York, 1975.

Austin, O. L., Jr. *Birds of the World.* Western Publishing, Racine, Wis., 1961.

Bent, A. C. *Life Histories of North American Birds.* Dover, New York, 1962–1964.

Berger, A. J. *Bird Study.* John Wiley & Sons, New York, 1971.

———. *Hawaiian Bird Life.* University Press of Hawaii, Honolulu, 1972.

Bull, J., E. Bull, G. Gold, and P. D. Pratt. *Birds of North America, Eastern Region.* Macmillan, New York, 1985.

Bull, J. (editor). *A Guide to Birds of the World.* Simon & Schuster, New York, 1981.

Brush, A. H., and G. A. Clark, Jr. (editors). *Perspectives in Ornithology.* Cambridge University Press, New York, 1983.

Burton, R. *Bird Behavior.* Knopf, New York, 1985.

Campbell, B. and E. Lack (editors). *A Dictionary of Birds.* Buteo Books, Vermillion, S.D., 1985.

Collias, N. E. and E. C. Collias. *Nest Building and Bird Behavior.* Princeton University Press, Princeton, N.J., 1984.

Cooper, J. E. and J. T. Eley. *First Aid and Care of Wild Birds.* Buteo Books, Vermillion, S.D., 1979.

Cornell Laboratory of Ornithology. *A Field Guide to Bird Songs of Eastern and Central North America* (recordings). Ithaca, N.Y., 1986.

Cornell Laboratory of Ornithology. *A Field Guide to Western Birds' Songs* (recordings). Ithaca, N.Y., 1986.

———. *Watching Birds with Roger Tory Peterson* (video-cassette). Metromedia Producers (New York) and Houghton Mifflin (Boston), Ithaca, N.Y., 1986.

———. *Seminars in Ornithology.* Dept. CN, Ithaca, N.Y., 1986.

Craighead, J. J. and F. C. Craighead, Jr. *Hawks, Owls, and Wildlife.* Dover, New York, 1970.

Dennis, J. V. *A Complete Guide to Bird Feeding.* Knopf, New York, 1975.

Dorst, J. *The Migration of Birds*. Houghton Mifflin, Boston, 1963.

Farrand, J., Jr. (editor). *The Audubon Society Master Guide to Birding*. Knopf, New York, 1983.

Fisher, J. and J. Flegg. *Watching Birds*. Buteo Books, Vermillion, S.D., 1974.

Gilliard, E. T. *Living Birds of the World*. Doubleday, New York, 1958.

Godfrey, W. E. *The Birds of Canada*. National Museum of Canada, Montreal, 1966.

Griffin, D. R. *Bird Migration*. Dover, New York, 1974.

Harrison, C. *A Field Guide to Birds' Nests, Eggs, and Nestlings of North America*. Buteo Books, Vermillion, S.D., 1976.

Harrison, H. H. *A Field Guide to Birds' Nests East of the Mississippi River*. Houghton Mifflin, Boston, 1975.

————. *A Field Guide to Western Birds' Nests*. Houghton Mifflin, Boston, 1979.

Hartshorne, C. *Born to Sing: An Interpretation and World Survey of Bird Songs*. Indiana University Press, Bloomington, 1973.

Hickey, J. J. *A Guide to Bird Watching*. Dover, New York, 1975.

Hochbaum, H. A. *Travels and Traditions of Waterfowl*. University of Minnesota Press, Minneapolis, 1967.

Howard, L. *Birds as Individuals*. Collins, London, 1952.

Jellis, R. *Bird Sounds and Their Meaning*. Cornell University Press, Ithaca, N.Y., 1984.

Johnsgard, P. A. *Hummingbirds of North America*. Smithsonian Institution Press, Washington, D.C., 1983.

Kress, S. *The Audubon Society Handbook for Birders*. Charles Scribner's Sons, New York, 1981.

Laycock, G. *The Birdwatcher's Bible*. Doubleday, New York, 1985.

Lentz, J. E. and J. Young. *Birdwatching: A Guide for Beginners*. Capra Press, Santa Barbara, Calif. 1986.

Lorenz, K. *King Solomon's Ring*. New American Library, New York, 1952.

Martin, A. C., H. S. Zim, and A. L. Nelson. *American Wildlife and Plants*. Dover, New York, 1951.

McClure, E. *Bird Banding*. The Boxwood Press, Pacific Grove, Calif., 1985.

McElroy, T. P., Jr. *The Habitat Guide to Birding*. Knopf, New York, 1974.

Mead, C. *Bird Migration*. Buteo Books, Vermillion, S.D., 1983.

National Geographic Society. *A Field Guide to Birds of North America*. National Geographic Society, Washington, D.C., 1983.

———. *A Guide to Bird Sounds*. National Geographic Society, Washington, D.C., 1983.

Nice, M. M. *Studies in the Life History of the Song Sparrow*. 2 vols. Dover, New York, 1964.

Palmer, R. S. (editor). *Handbook of North American Birds*. 3 vols. in multi-volume series. Yale University Press, New Haven, Conn., Vol. 1, 1962; Vols. 2 and 3, 1976.

Pasquier, R. *Watching Birds: An Introduction to Ornithology*. Houghton Mifflin, Boston, 1985.

Peterson, R. T. *Birds Over America*. Dodd Mead, New York, 1948.

———. *A Field Guide to Birds East of the Rockies*. Houghton Mifflin, Boston, 1980.

———. *A Field Guide to Western Birds*. Houghton Mifflin, Boston, 1961.

———. *A Field Guide to Birds of Texas and Adjacent States*. Houghton Mifflin, Boston, 1973.

Pettingill, O. S., Jr. *Ornithology in Laboratory and Field*. Academic Press, New York, 1985.

Piatt, J. *Adventures in Birding: Confessions of a Lister*. Knopf, New York, 1973.

Pough, R. H. *Audubon Land Bird Guide*. Doubleday, New York, 1949.

———. *Audubon Water Bird Guide*. Doubleday, New York, 1957.

Robbins, C. S., B. Bruun, and H. S. Zim. *Birds of North America: A Guide to Field Identification*. Buteo Books, Vermillion, S.D., 1983.

Simpson, G. G., C. S. Pittendreigh and L. H. Tiffany. *Life: An Introduction to Biology*. Harcourt Brace Jovanovich, San Diego, Calif., 1957.

Skutch, A. F. *The Life of the Hummingbird*. Crown, New York, 1973.

———. *Parent Birds and Their Young*. University of Texas Press, Austin, 1976.

Smith, R. L. *Ecology and Field Biology*. Harper & Row, New York, 1974.

Sparks, J. *Bird Behavior*. Grosset & Dunlap, New York, 1970.

Stefferud, A. and A. L. Nelson. *Birds in Our Lives*. U.S. Government Printing Office, Washington, D.C., 1966.

Stokes, D. and L. Stokes. *A Guide to Bird Behavior*. Vols. 1 and 2. Stokes Nature Guides, Carlisle, Mne. 1979; 1983.

Stresemann, E. and E. Mayr. *Ornithology: From Aristotle to the Present*. Harvard University Press, Cambridge, Mass., 1975.

Temple, S. A. *Bird Conservation* (annual volume). University of Wisconsin Press, Madison, 1986.

Terres, J. K. *The Audubon Society Encyclopedia of North American Birds*. Knopf, New York, 1980.

———. *The Walking Adventures of a Naturalist*. Algonquin Books of Chapel Hill, N.C., 1985.

Thorpe, W. H. *Learning and Instinct in Animals*. Methuen, London, 1956.

Tinbergen, N. *The Herring Gull's World: A Study of the Social Behavior of Birds*. Collins, London, 1953.

———. *The Study of Instinct*. Oxford University Press, New York, 1951.

Van Tyne, J. and A. J. Berger. *Fundamentals of Ornithology*. John Wiley & Sons, New York, 1976.

Wallace, G. and H. D. Mahan. *An Introduction to Ornithology*. Macmillan, New York, 1975.

Welty, J. C. *The Life of Birds*. W. B. Saunders, Philadelphia, 1975.

Wetmore, A., et al. *Song and Garden Birds of North America*. National Geographic Society, Washington, D.C., 1964.

Wyman, D. *Wyman's Gardening Encyclopedia*. Macmillan, New York, 1987.

Note: Building a basic reference library of bird books may require a long time, depending on one's resources and needs. Most books in the previous list may be ordered through one's local book store; however, in time, some may go out of print. The following are some sellers of both new and out-of-print books. Send for their catalogues.

Buteo Books
P.O. Box 481
Vermillion, S.D. 57069

Flora and Fauna Books
P.O. Box 3004
Seattle, WA. 98114-3004

Russell L. Ciochon
(Natural history books)
2510 Hill Court
Berkeley, CA. 94708

Donald E. Hahn
(Natural history books)
P.O. Box 1004
Cottonwood, AZ. 86326

Crow's Nest Book Shop
Laboratory of Ornithology
Cornell University
Sapsucker Woods
Ithaca, N.Y. 14850

Ibis Books
349 Exchange Street
Millis, MA. 02054

Peterson Book Company
P.O. Box 966
Davenport, IA. 52805

Bohdan Zaremba
3 Livermore Place
Cambridge, MA. 02141

Gary Wayne
P.O. Box 18, Route 3
Fort Payne, AL. 35967

The following are some magazines that publish articles entirely about birds, many of them about bird-attracting. They also carry advertising by dealers in bird-attracting supplies and bird-watching equipment, and by places to see birds (bird travel tours), reviews of bird books, and so on. Write to their subscription departments for information about each.

American Birds
950 Third Ave.
New York, N.Y. 10022
A popular and technical publication about bird distribution.

Living Bird Quarterly
Laboratory of Ornithology
Cornell University
Sapsucker Woods
Ithaca, N.Y. 14850

Birder's World
P.O. Box 1347
Elmhurst, IL. 60126

Nature Society News
Purple Martin Junction
Griggsville, IL. 62340

Bird Watcher's Digest
P.O. Box 110
Marietta, OH. 45750

TECHNICAL ORNITHOLOGICAL JOURNALS

The Auk: A Quarterly Journal of Ornithology
Ornithological Societies of North America
P.O. Box 21618
Columbus, OH. 43221
Official publication of the American Ornithologists' Union.

The Condor: Journal of the Cooper Ornithological Society
Ornithological Societies of North America
(See address under *The Auk*)

Journal of Field Ornithology: A Journal of Ornithological Investigation
(Formerly Bird-Banding)
Northeastern Bird-Banding Association
c/o Allen Press
P.O. Box 368
Lawrence, KS. 66044

The Wilson Bulletin
Ornithological Societies of North America
(See address under *The Auk*)
Official publication of the Wilson Ornithological Society.

Index

Allen, Arthur A., 88
American kestrel, *See* kestrel, American
American Wildlife and Plants, 154 (fn.)
anting, 97–98
ants, to avoid, 131
ants, used by birds, 97–98
apple trees, value of birds to, 20–21
arrowwood, 144, 149, 153
Aspergillus fumigatus, 36, 265
Audubon bird call, 169 (illus.)

baby birds, *See* birds, young
barberry, Japanese, 145, 148, 151, 152
bath, dust, 87–88
bath, sun, 87, 88, 108
bath, water, *See* birdbaths
Baynes, Ernest Harold, 3–5, 28–29, 278, 280
Beal, F. E. L., 154
beech, blue, 162
birch, gray, 143, 148, 152, 153
bird call, Audubon, 169–170, 169 (illus.)
bird calling, 165–173, 168 (illus.), 169 (illus.)
Bird Village, Meriden, N. H., 3–5

bird-attracting:
  enjoyments of, 5–6, 268–269
  experiments with, 61, 65–66.
    See also populations, bird
  feeding for, 7–37
  nest boxes for, 78–79
  plants for, 135–164, 211–213 (list)
  sounds for, 165–173, 279.
    See also names of individual birds, e.g., bluebird
birdbaths, 87–97, 89 (illus.)
  dealers in, 241
  drip, 91–93, 92 (illus.)
  heating, 93–97, 94 (illus.)
  in various seasons, 209, 210
  western songbirds that will use, 241–242 (list)
  on window shelf feeder, 30
  in winter, 30–31, 93–97, 209
birdhouses, *See* nest boxes
Bird-Lore, 87
birds:
  attachment to eggs and young, 102
  fed from people's hands, 274 (list)
  food for, *See* food
  food preferences of, 233–240
  fungus infection of, 36, 265
  getting acquainted with, 268–269

shelter (*continued*)
  defined, 267
  near feeders, 10
  for game birds, 173–174
  plants for, 154-155, 209-210
  for roosting, 76–78
shrikes:
  food preferences of, 233, 234
  protection from, 158, 204–205
shrubs, 148-150 (list), 158-160.
    See also plants
siskin, pine:
  food preferences of, 212, 233–240
    passim, 271
  taming of, 280–282
sketching birds, 17
snow, 9
    See also winter
solitaire, plants favored by, 212
Soule, Caroline G., 118–119
Southeast Region:
  plant literature on, 220–221
  plants attractive to birds in, 218–
    221 (list)
sparrows:
  black-throated (desert), food
    preferences of 234, 240
  chipping, food preferences of,
    234–240 *passim*, 271
  nesting records, 257
  English (house), 11, 269
    as competitors of purple
      martins, 67
    excluding from bluebird houses,
      264
    food preferences of, 235–238
      passim, 271
    nesting materials, 79–80
    nesting records, 257
    use of cliff swallow nests, 66
  field, food preferences of, 233–237
    passim, 271
  fox, food preferences of, 233–
    237 *passim*
  plants favored by, 212
  house, *See* sparrow, English
  song, food preferences of, 234–
    238 *passim*
  nesting records, 257
  nesting shelf for, 50
  plants favored by, 212
  tree, food preferences of, 29, 233–
    238 *passim*

sparrows (*continued*)
  plants favored by, 212
  vesper, food preferences of, 235
  white-crowned, food preferences
    of, 234–238 *passim*
  white-throated, food preferences
    of, 233–238 *passim*, 271
  plants favored by, 213
spring, 208, 209–210
squeaking, *See* bird-calling
squirrels, flying, 193
squirrels, protection from, 10, 25,
    187–191
Stanwell-Fletcher, Theodora, 170
starling:
  anting of, 97-98
  as competitor of bluebirds, 61
  as competitor of flickers, 46–47
  as competitor of purple martins,
    67
  food preferences of, 233–240,
    passim, 271
  identification, 269
  nest boxes for, 49 (table)
  nesting records, 258
  plants favored by, 213
Stoner, Emerson A., 80, 131–132
strawberry tree, 162
suet, 20–22, 25, 33, 233 (list)
sugar water, 118–122, 132–133
summer, 31–33, 208, 210
sunflower seeds, 15, 24, 26–27, 234–
    235 (list)
sunshine, 87, 88, 108
swallows:
  barn, 64–65
    nesting material used by, 85-86
    nesting records, 258
    nesting shelf for, 50
  cliff, 64–65, 66 (illus.)
    experiment with 64–66
    nesting records, 258
  tree, 61–64
    nest boxes for, 49, 62–63
    nesting records, 259
    plants favored by, 213
  violet-green, 64
    nest boxes for, 49
    nesting records, 259

table scraps as food for birds, 25-26
taming of birds, 7-8, 274–282

woodpeckers (*continued*)
  pileated, food preferences of, 233, 237
    plants favored by, 213
  red-bellied, food preferences of, 233, 235, 237, 271
    storage of food by, 266
  red-headed, nest boxes for, 49
    storage of food by, 266
  sapsucker, yellow-bellied, food preferences of, 233, 238, 239
    See also flickers
wrens:
  Bewick's, 56, 58
    food preferences of, 233, 234, 238
    nest boxes for, 49, 59
    nesting records, 263
  cactus:
    food preferences of, 233, 234, 238

wrens (*continued*)
    plants favored by, 213
  Carolina, 56, 58–59
    food preferences of, 233–240 *passim*, 271
    nest boxes for, 49, 59
    nesting records, 263
    plants favored by, 213
  house, 56–58
    food preferences of, 233–234
    nest boxes for, 49, 59
    nesting materials, 79, 81–82
    nesting places of, 56–59, 264
    nesting records, 263
  winter, food preferences of, 233, 234

Yellow-shafted flicker, 283, 284
yew:
  dwarf Japanese, 145
  Japanese, 146, 153
  Thayer's, 143
young birds, *See* birds, young

ABOUT THE AUTHOR

JOHN K. TERRES, former editor of *Audubon Magazine*, is the author or editor of fifty books of natural history. He also has had a distinguished career as a field naturalist, which gave him unusual skills for writing a book about attracting birds. For ten years before World War II, he was a field biologist for the Soil Conservation Service. During that time he worked in field ornithology, while associated with university and government botanists and horticulturalists and specializing in studies of the feeding, nesting habits, and ecological needs of wild birds on the farm. In his work as a service biologist, Mr. Terres planned and supervised the planting of thousands of native and exotic trees, shrubs, and vines on farms that combined erosion control with wildlife habitat improvement and wildlife conservation. Besides his field work, Mr. Terres, for more than twenty years, gave informal talks on bird-attracting, illustrated with his own color slides, before garden clubs, bird clubs, service clubs, farm groups, parent-teacher associations, and high schools and elementary schools. He gave up lecturing in the 1960s to write several books, among them, *Flashing Wings: The Drama of Bird Flight*, and *From Laurel Hill to Siler's Bog: The Walking Adventures of a Naturalist*, which won for him the John Burroughs Medal for distinguished nature writing. Over a period of fifteen years, with occasional interruptions for field work with birds, Mr. Terres has given most of his time to writing a one-million-word encyclopedia of North American birds, a single volume he considers his most important work.